A CHILD'S GEOGRAPHY
OF THE WORLD

Just suppose you could go way, way off in the sky, sit on a corner of nothing at all and look down at the World through a spy glass

A CHILD'S GEOGRAPHY
OF THE WORLD

BY

V. M. HILLYER

LATE HEAD MASTER OF CALVERT SCHOOL

*Author of "Child Training," "A Child's
History of the World," etc.*

Revised by

EDWARD G. HUEY

Assistant Head Master of Calvert School

With Many Maps and Illustrations by

MARY SHERWOOD WRIGHT JONES

APPLETON-CENTURY-CROFTS, INC.

NEW YORK

TO

The Nine-Year-Old
who said,

"I wish there were a hundred more 'Lands' in the World for you to tell us about"

TATTLE TALES

If you are under fifteen years, eight months and three
days old

DON'T READ THIS

THIS book is for the child who:
thinks heaven is in the sky and
hell is under the ground;
has never heard of London or Paris and
thinks a Dane is a kind of dog.

It is to give a traveler's view of the World—but
not a commercial traveler's view.

It is to show the child what is beyond the horizon,
from "Kalamazoo to Timbuktu."

It is to show him not only "the Seven Wonders
of the World" but the seventy times Seven
Wonders of the World.

When-I-was-a-boy in New England we had
for Thanksgiving six kinds of pie: apple, peach,
cranberry, custard, mince, and pumpkin, but I
was allowed to have only two kinds and I never
could make a satisfactory choice. I have had the
same difficulty in selecting geographical places
and subjects to tell about. There are too many
"most important" places in the World to be in-
cluded in this first survey, and there will inevi-
tably be those readers who will wonder why
certain countries and certain places have been

omitted, especially the place where the reader may live.

To me, as a child, geography was a bugbear of repellent names—Climate and Commerce, Manufactures and Industries, and *products,* PRODUCTS, PRODUCTS. It seemed that the chief products of every place in the World were corn, wheat, barley, rye; or rye, barley, wheat, corn; or barley, corn, rye, wheat. In my geography modern Greece had but a paragraph—because, I suppose, it did not produce wheat, corn, barley, rye. Geography was a "stomach" geography; the "head" and "heart" were left out.

I loved the geography pictures and maps but hated the text. Except for an occasional descriptive or narrative paragraph the text was wholly unreadable—a confused jumble of headings and sub-headings and sub-sub-headings: HOME WORK, *NOTES,* MAP STUDIES, *Suggestions to Teachers,* HELPS, *Directions, Questions,* REVIEWS, PROBLEMS, *Exercises, Recitations,* LESSONS, PICTURE STUDIES, etc., etc., etc.

The World was an orange when I went to school, and there were only three things I can remember that I ever learned "for sure"—that the Dutch children wore wooden shoes, the Eskimos lived in snow houses, and the Chinese ate with chopsticks.

We had a question and answer catechism which we learned as we did the multiplication tables. The teacher read from her book:

Q. "What is the condition of the people of the United States?" and a thirteen-year-old boy in the next seat answered glibly: *A.* "They are poor and ignorant and live in miserable huts." At which astounding statement the teacher unemotionally remarked, "No, that's the answer to the next question, 'What is the condition of the Eskimos?'"

When my turn came to teach geography to beginners nine years of age, I found the available textbooks either too commercial and industrial, on the one hand, or too puerile and inconsequential, on the other. Statistics and abstractions were entirely beyond the ken of the child of nine, and random stories of children in other countries had little value as geography.

As I had been a traveler for many years, had visited most of the countries of the Globe, and in actual mileage had been five times the distance around the World, I thought I would write a geography myself. Vain conceit! A class would listen with considerable attention to my extemporaneous travel talks, so I had a stenographer take down these talks verbatim. But when I read these notes of the same talk to another class, then it was that I discovered a book may be good —until it is written. So I've had to try, try again and again, for children's reactions can never be forecast. Neither can one tell without trial what children will or will not understand. Preconceived notions of what words they should or should not know are worthless: "Stupendous and appalling" presented no difficulties whatever but much simpler words were misunderstood.

I had been reading to a class from an excellent travel book for children. The author said, "We arrived, tired and hungry, and found quarters in the nearest hotel." The children understood "found quarters" to mean that the travelers had picked up 25-cent pieces in the hotel! Then again I had been describing the "Bridge of Sighs," in Venice, and picturing the condemned prisoners who crossed it. Casually I asked if any one could tell me why it was called the Bridge of Sighs. One boy said, "Because it is of big *size.*" A little girl, scorning his ignorance, said, "Because it has *sides.*" A boy from the country, with a far-fetched imagination, suggested it might be because they used "scythes"; and a fourth child said, "Because it belonged to a man named 'Cy.'"

The study of maps is interesting to almost all children. A map is like a puzzle picture—but new names are hard. And yet geography without either name or place is not geography at all. It is only fairyland. The study of maps and names is therefore absolutely essential and large wall maps most desirable.

Geography lends itself admirably to research on the part of the child. A large scrap-book arranged by countries may easily be filled with current pictorial news, clippings from magazines and Sunday newspapers, and from the circulars of travel bureaus. There is a wealth of such scrap-book material almost constantly being published—pictures of temples in India, pagodas in China, wild animal hunts in Africa, parks in Paris—from which the child can compile his own Geographic Magazine. Furthermore, the collection of stamps offers a most attractive field, particularly for the boy just reaching the age when such collections are as absorbing as an adult hobby.

Of course, the best way to learn geography is by travel but not like that of the business man who landed in Rome with one hour to see the city. Jumping into a taxi and referring to a slip of paper, he said: "There are only two things I want to see here—St. Peter's and the Colosseum. Drive to them as fast as you can and back to the station." He was accordingly driven to St. Peter's. Sticking his head out of the window he said to the driver, "Well, which is this?"

In the little town where I was born, there lived an old, old man whose chief claim to distinction was the fact that he had never in his whole life been ten miles away from home. Nowadays travel is so easy that every child may look forward to traveling some day. This book is to give him some inkling of what there is to see, so that his travel may not be as meaningless as that of the simple sailor who goes round the world and returns with nothing but a parrot and a string of glass beads.

"ALL ABOARD!"

When-I-was-a-boy, my nurse used to take me to the railroad station to see the trains. A man in a blue cap and blue suit with brass buttons would call, "All aboard for Baltimore, Philadelphia, New York, and points north and east!" and wave his arm for the train to start. My nurse said he was a conductor.

So when I went home I used to put on a cap and play conductor shouting, "All aboard for Baltimore, Philadelphia, New York, and points north and east!" over and over, again and again, until I was told, "For pity sake, stop it!"

But some day I hoped, when I grew up, to be a real conductor in a blue cap and a blue suit with brass buttons. And now that I *am* grown up, I am still playing conductor, for in this book I am going to take you to Baltimore, Philadelphia, New York, and points north, east, south and west—round the World!

xix

A CHILD'S GEOGRAPHY
OF THE WORLD

1

The World Through a Spy-Glass

You have never seen your own face.

This may surprise you and you may say it isn't so—but it *is* so.

You may see the end of your nose.

You may even see your lips if you pout out—so.

If you stick out your tongue you may see the tip of it.

But you can't go over there, outside of yourself, and look at your own face.

Of course you know what your face looks like, because you have seen it in a mirror; but that's not yourself—it's only a picture of yourself.

And in the same way no one of us can see our own World—all of it—this World on which we live.

You can see a little bit of the World just around you—and if you go up into a high building you can see still more—and if you go up to the top of a high mountain you can see still, still more—and if you go up in an airplane you can see still, still, still more.

But to see the Whole World you would have to go much higher than that, higher than any one has ever been able to go or could go. You would have to go far, far above the clouds; way, way off in the sky where the stars are—and no one can do that, even in an airplane.

Now you cannot see the World in a mirror as you can see your face. So how do we know what the World looks like?

A fish in the sea might tell her little fish, "The World is all water—just a *huge* tub; I've been everywhere and I know." Of course, she wouldn't know anything different.

A camel in the desert might tell her little camels, "The World is all sand—just a *huge* sand pile; I've been everywhere and I know."

A polar bear on an iceberg might tell her little polar bears, "The World is all snow and ice— just a *huge* refrigerator; I've been everywhere and I know."

A bear in the woods might tell her little bear cubs, "The World is all woods—just a *huge* forest; I've been everywhere and I know."

In the same way, once upon a time, people used to tell their little children, "The World is just a big island like a huge mud pie with some water, some sand, some ice, and some trees on it, and with a cover we call the sky over us all; we've been everywhere and we know."

When some inquisitive child asked, "What does the flat World like a mud pie rest on?" they really truly said, "It rests on the backs of four elephants."

But when the inquisitive child asked, "And

what do the elephants stand on?" they really truly said, "On a big turtle."

Then when the inquisitive child asked, "What does the turtle stand on?" no one could say—for no one could even guess farther than that—so the turtle was left standing——on nothing.

That's the old story that parents long ago used to tell their children as to what the World was like. But just suppose you could go way, way off above the clouds; way, way off in the sky, sit on a corner of nothing at all, dangle your feet over the edge and look down at the World far, far below. What do you suppose it would really look like? I know—and yet I have never been there.

The World from way off in the sky and through a spy-glass would look just like a full moon—round and white; not round like a plate, but round like a huge snowball. Not exactly white, either, but bright—for the sun shines on this big ball, the World, and makes it light just as the headlight on an automobile shines on the road at night and makes the road light. Of course, the sun can shine on only one side of this big ball at a time; the other side of the World is dark, but the World keeps turning round and round in the sunlight.

If you looked at the World through a telescope—you know what a telescope is: one of those long spy-glasses that make things seem closer and bigger—as men look at the moon, you would see on one side of the World two big

patches that look like queerly shaped shadows
and on the other side of the World twice as many

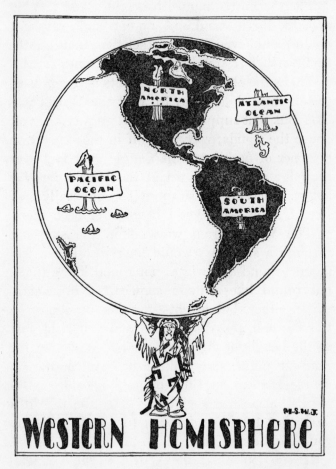

big patches, four queerly shaped shadows. These
patches which look like shadows are really land
and are called by a long name: con-ti-nents.
These continents have names, and if their names

were printed across them in letters a thousand
miles high—which they are not—so that the man

with a spy-glass could read them, he would read
on one side of the World

NORTH AMERICA
SOUTH AMERICA

and if he waited until the World turned round, until the other side showed in the sunlight, as I've seen the World do in "the movies," he would read on this continent EUROPE and on that continent ASIA and on the other continent AFRICA, and the smallest one would have the longest name, AUSTRALIA. At the very bottom would be ANTARCTICA.

We call one side of a piece of money "the head," because there is usually the head of some one on that side, and the other side we call "the tail," as that is opposite from the head. It would be easy to tell which side of the World was which if we could call one side heads and the other tails. But there are no heads or tails on the World—only these queer shadows—so we use two big words instead of "heads" and "tails" to tell which side of the World is which. We call one side the "Western Hemisphere" and the other side we call the "Eastern Hemisphere." Whew! Why don't they call it something easy?—well, let's call it "Half-a-Ball," for that is what Hemisphere means. The Western Half-Ball has two continents and the Eastern Half-Ball has four continents.

The tip top and the very bottom of the World are called the Poles, although there are no poles. Around the top and bottom Pole it would be all white—snow and ice—for the Poles are so cold there is snow and ice there all the time.

The part of the World that isn't patches of

shadow or snow is water. The water all around
the continents is the ocean, and though of course
there are no walls nor fences dividing it into
different parts, its different parts are called by
different names.

Do you know your right hand from your left?
Of course you do if you're over six years old.
But do you know the west side from the east
side? If you are over nine years old you should.
The east is where the sun rises, the west is where
it sets. And if your right hand is east, your left
hand is west, your face is north and your back
is south.

The Atlantic Ocean is on the east side of
North and South America. The Pacific Ocean
is on the west. The ocean entirely in the Eastern
Hemisphere is called "Indian." No, it is not
named for our Indians. At the top of the World
is the Arctic Ocean. At the bottom, all around
Antarctica, is the Antarctic Ocean. The Arctic
and Antarctic Oceans are mostly ice, for it is so
cold there the water freezes and stays frozen. If
we wanted to put names on the oceans so that a
man off in the sky could read them, we would
have to stick huge signs in the water, as we can't
paint letters on the ocean.

There is no reason why I should show you the
World turned this way with North America on
top. I might just as well show it upside down or
sideways, for there is no upside nor downside on
the World. I suppose the reason the north side is

always shown on top is because the people who made maps and geographies all lived in the north part of the World and they wanted their part of the World on top.

So this is our World. You may wonder, "Are there any other Worlds besides ours?" Some have guessed that there may be—that some of those sparks in the sky that look like stars at night may be other Worlds like ours with people living on them. But no one knows, for the strongest telescope is not strong enough for us to see what is on those far off sparks, so we can only guess about them.

2

The World Is Round, for I've Been Round It

Dɪᴅ you ever run away from home?

I did—once upon a time—when I was younger than you are.

I wanted to see the World.

My Mother had told me the World was a huge ball and that if I kept on, straight ahead, following my nose, I would go round the ball and come back to where I started.

So early one morning, without telling any one, I set out to go around the World.

But I didn't get very far before night came on, and a big kind policeman brought me back home.

When I was grown up and had no home, I started out once again to go around the World. This time I got on a train headed toward the setting sun. Night came on, but no big, kind policeman brought me back home; so I kept on and on, day after day, week after week, month after month—sometimes on trains, sometimes on boats, sometimes in automobiles, sometimes on

the backs of animals—but always toward the side
of the World where the sun sets, the side which
the people call "the west."

I passed broad fields and thick forests, small
towns and big cities—I went over bridges, round
hills, and through holes in mountains—I reached
a great ocean and sailed
across it on a big ship
to another continent—I
came to strange lands
where people dressed in
strange clothes, lived in
strange houses,
and spoke
strange lan-
guages; I saw
strange animals,
trees, and flow-
ers; I crossed
another great
ocean and at
last, after many,
many months,
always going in the same direction, I came back
here to the exact spot from which I had started.
So I knew the World was round, for I had been
round it—but it was not round and smooth like
a tennis ball, but humpety and bumpety, and so
huge that it didn't seem like a ball at all.

It took me nearly half a year to go round the
World—that seems like a long time, but then it

was a long way—over twenty-five times a thousand miles. But others have been around the World in much faster time. The airship *Graf Zeppelin* flew around the World in three weeks. Two flyers took less than nine days to circle the globe in their airplane and return to their starting point, New York. An American Air Force plane flew around the World without stopping in less than four days.

If a man could start out when the sun rose in the morning and keep up with it all day long, go over the side of the World when the sun set, and keep up with it on the other side of the World, he would be back again where he started the next morning. He then would have gone round the World in one day. But to do that he would have to travel over 1,000 miles an hour to keep up with the sun for each of the twenty-four hours in a day and night.

All around the outside of the World—as you probably know—is an ocean of air that covers everything on the World as the ocean of water covers everything in the sea. What you probably don't know is that this ocean of air is wrapped only round the World—it does not fill the sky. Men and animals live in this ocean of air as fish live in the ocean of water, and if a huge giant picked you out of the air you would die just as quickly as a fish does when taken out of the sea. The air is thick near the ground but gets thin and thinner the higher up you go off the ground.

That's why airplanes can go up but a few miles high—there is not enough air to hold up the plane, for the plane must have air to rest on and for its propeller to push against, just as a boat in the water must have water to rest on and water for its propeller to push against. Or if it's a jet plane, it must have air to feed its jet motors. An airplane could not rise beyond the ocean of air and sail off into the sky where there is no air any more than a steamship on the sea could rise out of the water and sail off up into the air.

There is only one thing that men can send up high enough to travel above the ocean of air. That is a rocket, which doesn't depend on air for its motor or to hold it up. Someday rocket ships will probably carry men on trips to the Moon or even to the planet Mars. How would you like to go exploring in a rocket ship beyond the World's atmosphere out through empty, airless space? How would you like to be the first Man in the Moon? You wouldn't find any living thing on the Moon, for the Moon is a dead, lifeless ball without any air on it at all. But if your rocket got to Mars you would almost certainly find some living plants—and perhaps, who knows?—even some living animals.

Some mountains are so high that their tops almost stick out of the ocean of air; at least, there is so little air covering their tops that people can't go all the way to the top unless they take along canned air to breathe.

You can't see air—you may think you can, but what you see is smoke or clouds, not air. When air is moving, we call it wind. Then you can feel it when it blows your hat off, you can hear it when it bangs the shutters and whistles round the house; but no one has ever seen air itself.

The World wasn't always as it is now. It was once a ball of fire—a huge burning ball. That was millions of years ago, and of course long before there were any people or animals or plants on the World. But the fiery ball got cooler and cooler until it was no longer burning but a hot ball of rock. There were then no oceans, no water on the World, for water won't stay on anything very hot—it won't stay on a hot stove —it turns to steam when there is fire under it; so there were only clouds of steam, an ocean of steam, around the World. But the World kept getting cooler and cooler until at last the steam turned to water and fell on the World—rain, rain, rain, until there perhaps was one big ocean covering the whole World.

But the World still kept on cooling and cooling, and as it cooled it shrank and shriveled and wrinkled and crinkled and puckered like the outside of a prune. You know a prune was once smooth and round when it was a plum. These little wrinkles and crinkles rose up out of the ocean and were the continents and mountains, so you see how big the wrinkles and crinkles really are. The earth is still wrinkling a bit even now, and when it does so it shivers and shakes and we say there has been an earthquake. But the

The World was once a ball of fire

Then it rained on the World and the oceans formed

Then the World wrinkled and crinkled like the outside of a prune

And the continents and mountains arose out of the ocean

earthquakes nowadays are as nothing to what may have been the tremendous shudder when the continents rose out of the first single ocean. The thunderous roar of that quake may have reached the stars with a stupendous and appalling boom of a bursting, cracking, rending, groaning World, as if the last day had come. Don't you know what stupendous and appalling boom means? Why, it means "stupendous and appalling boom." But that's all guess—for the continents may have risen out of the sea as softly, slowly, silently as a blade of grass grows out of the ground. No one knows. We only know the continents did rise out of the water—we can find seashells on the tops of high mountains, and we know they could only have been made under the water when the mountain was under the water.

3

The Inside of the World

WHEN I was a very little boy I was very inquisitive. At least, that's what my nurse called me.

One day when I was walking with her along the city pavements, I asked:

"Jane, what's under the pavement?"

"Oh, just dirt," she replied.

"And what is under the dirt?"

"Oh, more dirt," she replied.

"Well, what's under that?" I asked. I wasn't satisfied.

"Oh, nothing—I don't know—why are you always so inquisitive?" she asked.

I knew there must be something underneath that, and I just wanted to know what it was—I was just inquisitive.

I had heard that the place bad boys went when they died was down under the ground somewhere —a big cave, perhaps—and I wanted to know if that were so.

And then I had heard that all the way through on the other side of the World Chinamen lived, head down, and walked upside down like flies on the ceiling. I wanted to find out if that were so too.

So I made up my mind I'd dig down through the World; down, down, down, till I came through on the other side, and then I'd know. I was a very little boy, you see. With a tin shovel I started a hole in the back yard behind the grapevines, where no one would know what I was doing. I wanted to keep it a secret until I had dug all the way through. Day after day I worked, digging up first soft ground —that was easy—then I got down to solid ground; that was hard. I had a hole which I could stand in up to my waist.

With a tin shovel I started to dig down through the World

Then one evening my father asked, "What's that hole in the back yard?"

My secret was out. He didn't laugh when I told him—at least, out loud—but he asked me if I knew how far I'd have to dig.

"Could you dig *down* as deep as the Washington Monument goes *up?*" he asked.

I thought perhaps I could, but I was a little doubtful, for the Washington Monument seemed terribly high.

"Men have dug wells many times as deep as

the Washington Monument," my father told me, "but never all the way nor nearly all the way through the World. You would have to dig many thousands of times deeper than the Washington Monument to get down even to the center of the World. It's eight thousand miles straight through the earth and most all the way is rock—just rock, and more rock, that's all."

Then I gave it up.

"How do you know it's eight thousand miles if no one has ever been through the World?" asked the inquisitive child. I don't know what my father answered. I was too young to understand. I wonder if you are too young, if I tell you how we know it's eight thousand miles; for without ever having been through the World, we do know how far it is.

This is how we know. It's a funny thing, but every ball, whether it is a little ball or a medium-sized ball or a great big ball, is always just a little more than three times as big round as it is through. I have often wondered why this was so—why a ball shouldn't be exactly three times or four times or five times as big round as through, but it isn't. You can try it yourself it you don't believe it. Take an apple or an orange and measure it around and then cut it and measure it through.

Now we know the World is a ball, a huge ball, and yet as it is a ball it must, like all other balls, be a little more than three times as big around as it is through. It is twenty-five thousand miles round the World, because men have actually measured that. So we know that the distance through must be about eight thousand miles, as twenty-five is a little more than three times eight. That is not geography; it's arithmetic. If you want to use big words for "around" and "through," as they do in geographies, you must say "circumference" for "around" and "diameter" for "through"—which mean the same thing: the circumference of the World is twenty-five thousand and the diameter is eight thousand.

The outside of the World is a crust of rock like the skin of a baked potato over the hot inside. Some of the crust that you go through first is in layers, like layers in a jelly-cake, one layer after another, only these rock layers look as if they were made of sand and shells, or coal or little stones, and that's what they *are* made of. If you could cut the World in half as if it were an apple, it might look something like the picture on the next page. We call it a "Cross Section."

Between some of the layers of rock there is coal like jelly in a jelly-cake and in other places there are gold and silver and diamonds and rubies, and in some of the rock there are pools of oil. That's why men dig wells down through these layers of rock to get oil, and that's why men dig mines to get coal and gold.

And still farther down the rock is not in

layers—it is just solid rock; and still farther
down it gets hotter and hotter where the world

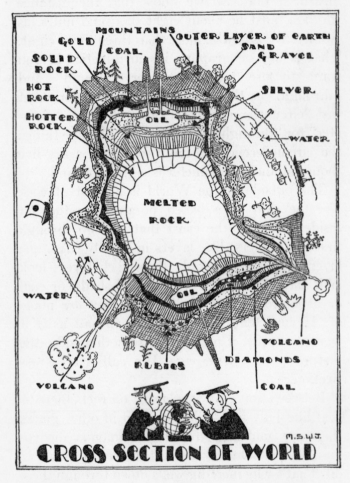

CROSS SECTION OF WORLD

has not cooled off even yet, until the rock is no
longer solid, but melted.

Whenever you see a chimney you know there

is a furnace beneath it, and when smoke and fire come out of its top you know there is a fire in the furnace. Well, there are many places on the World where fire and smoke come out of the ground as if through a chimney from a fiery furnace. These places are called volcanoes.

Why was the World made of rock instead of brass or glass or china? Why is the World shaped like a ball and not like a box, a roller, or an old shoe?

4

The Endless Parade

Dɪᴅ you ever see a parade—a very long one?
I once saw a parade of soldiers that took all
day to pass by. Tramp, tramp—tramp, tramp—
tramp, tramp, hour after hour, all day long. I
never had seen so many men in my whole life.
There must have been a hundred thousand of
them. It didn't seem possible that there were so
many people in the World. But if all the people
there are in the World should pass by in one long
parade, it would take not one day but a lifetime for them to pass by, for there are over two
billion people in the world.

A hundred new people—babies—are born
every minute of the day and of the night; many
are born while you are reading this, and with
every tick of the clock some one has died. But
more people are born than die each day, so that
the World is getting fuller and fuller of people
all the time.

The people on the World are all about the
same size and shape. Only in fairy-tales are people as small as your thumb or as tall as a church-
steeple. None have wings instead of arms or
wheels instead of legs. They all have one head,

one nose, one mouth; they all have two ears, two
eyes, two arms, and two legs. And yet in all
these two billion people there are no two alike,
there is not a single person exactly like any other
one. Even twins are not exactly alike.

The chief difference in people is their color.
Most of the two billion are white, but a great
many are black and a larger number are half-
way between white and black—they are sort of
yellow-brown. These three colors of people we
call "races." "It's a good day for the race,"
my father used to say. I thought he was talking
of a horse-race or a boat-race, but when I asked,
"What race?" he would smile and say, "It's a
good day for the white race, the black race, all the
races."

Each race used to live by itself in its own part
of the World, but many have wandered away
to other parts. Most of the people in our part of
the World are white, but there are also many
black and a few yellow-brown.

Suppose you had been born black.

Suppose you'd been born yellow or red.

Suppose you had been born in

      Africa or

      Asia or

      Australia.

Suppose you had been born with another father
      and mother.

Suppose you had been born in another world
      instead of this World.

Suppose you hadn't been born at all—where would you be now?

The endless parade of all the people on the World

There are only six continents where people live, but on each of these there are several countries. *A* country doesn't mean *the* country. *A*

country means cities, towns, villages *and* country
under one ruler. There are eighty countries on
the World. Some countries are small with only a
few thousand people in the whole country, and
some countries are large with many millions of
people. Our country, the United States, has over
one hundred and fifty million people, but there
are several countries with more. China, which is
on the other side of the World, has the most
people. It has three times as many people as the
United States; and India, another country on
the other side of the World, has the next largest
number of people. Both these countries are in
Asia—the largest continent with the shortest
name and the most people.

Each country has a ruler, just as every family
has a father or every football team has a captain.
Some countries have a king for a ruler and some
have a president, and most countries have other
people to rule with the king and the president.

A king is a king because his father was a king,
and his son will be king for the same reason. A
president is president because he was chosen by
the people in the country, just as the captain of a
football team is chosen by his team. Choosing we
call "voting." A king is king for his whole life,
but a president is president for only a few years.

The country of a king is called a kingdom. If
one man rules over several countries, he is called
an emperor and the countries an empire. A country with a president is called a republic. Our

country is a republic. The king or the president
and the others who rule with him are called the
government. The government makes the rules,
but it also does two things that no one else is
allowed to do. The government makes the money
of the country and the postage-stamps. The
money of one country is not good in another
country and neither are the postage-stamps. And
neither is the language of one country good in
another—usually.

The people on the World speak many different languages. Even in the same country many
different languages are spoken. There are over
3,000 different languages in all—3,000, just
think of that! You probably speak only one of
these, and couldn't talk to any one nor understand any one who spoke any other language than
your own. In the United States almost every one
speaks English, which, strange to say, is the language of another country—England. But on a
continent like Europe you could hardly go a
day's journey without hearing a different language on the street, in the shops, at the hotel.

I happened to be born in the United States,
and as I heard everybody around me speaking
English I learned to speak English too. But I
might have been born in Asia, a yellow boy, and
learned to speak Chinese, or I might have been
born in Africa, a black boy, and learned to speak a
language I don't even know the name of. I know
a man who speaks a dozen different languages,

and I know *of* a man who speaks 100! You can understand how wonderful this is when it usually takes years to learn to speak *one* other language besides your own. Letters of most of these languages are like ours, like the letters on this page—they are called Roman, because a people called Romans first used them long ago. But letters of Chinese and Japanese and some other faraway languages are different—they look like this:

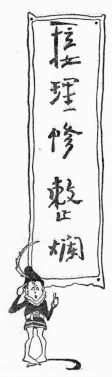

5

The 13 Club

A MAN may pay millions of dollars to have a hospital, a library, or a museum named after him, and another who has paid nothing, done nothing, deserved nothing, and asked nothing has two of the biggest things in the World—the two continents North and South America—named after him, and people will go on forever calling them America after him—an unimportant, almost unknown man named Amerigo.

Do you know the song that begins, "My Country, 'Tis of Thee"? What do you mean by "My Country"? It is a part, the smaller part, of North America.

Have you a buffalo nickel in your pocket—a 5-cent piece? If not, perhaps you can borrow one just to look at. On the head side is the picture of an Indian with feathers in his hair. Why do you suppose our country has the picture of an Indian instead of a white man on the nickel? On the tail side is the picture of a buffalo. Why do you suppose our country has a picture of a buffalo on the nickel instead of a horse or a cow?

Well, long before there were any white men here at all, or any horses or cows, there were a

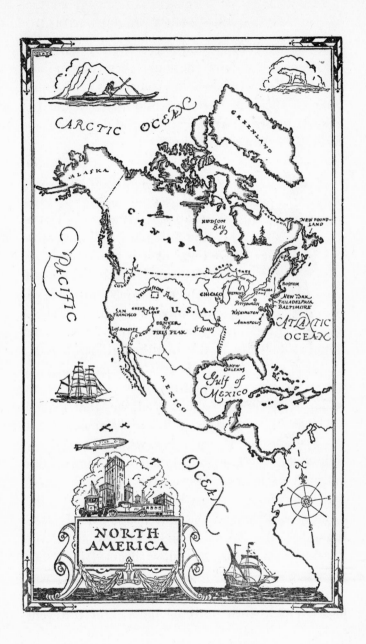

NORTH
AMERICA

great many Indians and a great many buffaloes in this country. Now there are very few Indians and very few buffaloes in America, so these pictures on the nickel are to remind us that the Indian is the first American man and the buffalo is the first American animal.

So the old fellow dressed in a flag we call U.ncle S.am

If you will look at the printing on the nickel you will see it says "United States of America." That's the full name of our country, but it is too long for us to say United States of America every time, so we usually say just United States or just America or use just the initials U. S. A.

Have you ever seen a picture of a tall man with a suit of clothes that looked as if it had been made out of a flag, with red and white striped breeches, a long-tailed coat, and a tall hat with stars on it? There never was such a man really, but he is supposed to be the picture of the United States. As the initials of the United States are U. S., some one said they stand for Uncle Sam, so the old fellow dressed in a flag we call Uncle Sam.

The map of the U. S. looks as if it were made like a patch-work quilt of patches of different

sizes and shapes. These patches are the States
that are United—that means, joined to one another. As a matter of fact, of course, there are no
lines between the States. The lines on the map
are marked on the ground by stone posts set so
far apart that you may cross from one State to
another without even knowing when you are in a
different State. Each State has towns and cities
and country. I live in a city and the city is in
the State of Maryland. You may live in a city
or a town or in the country in another State.
But every one in the U. S. must live in some
State unless—I'll tell you later the few places
he may live without being in any State.

Some of the States have straight sides and
some have one, two or more crooked sides. Some
are big and some are little. The biggest State
is Texas, at the bottom, near the center—only we
don't say bottom, we say south. The smallest
State is Rhode Island, which is not an island at
all. It is near the upper right-hand corner—only
we don't say upper right-hand corner, we say
northeast. Texas would make more than 200
Rhode Islands. That is, you could put more than
200 Rhode Islands in Texas.

Not so long ago there was no United States.
There were only thirteen little States along the
shore of the Atlantic Ocean. These States were
so small they thought they ought to form a club.
There is an old story about a man who wanted
to break a bundle of sticks. He tried and he tried

but he couldn't break the bundle. Then some one
told him to take the bundle apart and break each
stick separately; so he did, and broke them
easily. The States thought that they, in the same
way, might be broken easily if separate, so they
tied themselves together like a bundle of sticks
in order that they might not be "broken" by
an enemy. And so the 13 States formed a 13 club
and called themselves the United States. They
took as their motto "In Union is Strength,"
which means "In one bundle we are strong."

Now thirteen is generally considered an un-
lucky number, but these 13 States were not afraid
of bad luck. In fact, as the new country had to
have a flag, they made a flag with 13 stripes—
seven red stripes and six white—and they put a
white star for each State in a blue corner of the
flag. Other parts of North America thought
they'd like to join the club too, and more and
more pieces kept on joining until there were
forty-eight States, and these States that were
united stretched from the Atlantic Ocean on
one side to the Pacific Ocean on the other—that
is, from where the sun rises from the ocean on one
side to where it sets over the ocean on the other.
Each time a piece joined the U. S. another star
was put in the corner of the flag, but the number
of stripes was not changed, for there would have
been too many; so now there are forty-eight stars
—that means forty-eight States united into one
country. That's why there are on our coins the

words *"e pluribus unum,"* which means "one from many."

Not all of America joined the club, however. The country north of the U. S. called Canada and the country south of the U. S. called Mexico did not join. And yet the people in Canada are Americans, and the people in Mexico are Americans too, but both Canada and Mexico have different rulers from what we have, for they are different countries.

Though there are very few Indians left in the U. S., we still use some of their names in naming our States. See if you can pick out some of the States on the map that have Indian names. Maryland and Virginia, of course, are *not*—for they are girls' names. States beginning with "New"—like New York, New Jersey, New Hampshire—of course are *not* Indian. They are named after old places in another country. But Minnesota, which means "sky blue water"; Ohio, which means "beautiful river" or "great"; and many others *are* Indian.

6

A City Built in a Swamp

A CAP which you wear on your head means "head."

A *cap*-tain also means "head"—he's the head of a company of soldiers.

A *cap*-ital means "head" too—it's the head city of a country or of a State.

When I was a boy I lived in the *capital* of the United States, but I did not live in the *Capitol* of the United States. That may sound funny, but it's true, for there are two kinds of capit^o_als. The capit-Al is a city, the Capit-Ol is a building, and of course I didn't live in the Capit-Ol building. Not even the President lives there.

When our country was started men tried to find a suitable place for the capital. Eight places were tried out and at last a swamp was chosen as the proper place to build the city, because it was then near the center of our country. So a city was built there and called Washington after George Washington, because he was the First President of the United States. Even when-I-was-a-boy there was a part of Washington which every one called "Swamp Puddle" or "Swam-

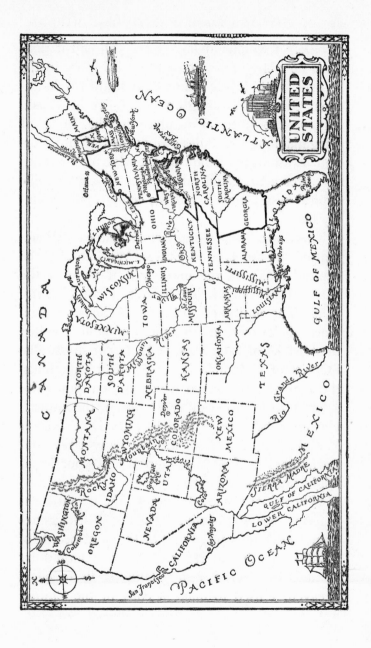

poodle." I wonder if boys there still call it that. It is now one of the most beautiful cities in the World, with lovely parks and beautiful buildings. George Washington didn't live in Washington. He lived at a place in the State of Virginia about ten miles away called Mount Vernon. Washington is now on the edge of our country, over a thousand miles from the center. The capital hasn't moved, but the center of the country has.

There are twenty-eight cities named "Washington" in the United States. Washington, the capital, looks on the map as if it were in the State of Maryland, but it isn't. It isn't in any State. The capital of all the States had to have a place all its own; so this piece of land is called the District of Columbia, or D. C. for short. The District of Columbia is named after Columbus, the man who discovered America. So if you write a letter to any one in Washington, the capital, you must be very careful to put "D. C." after Washington, for there are so many cities and towns named after Washington that your letter might not go to the right one.

When-I-was-a-boy I thought the Capitol was the most beautiful building in the World. Since then I have seen nearly all of the most beautiful buildings in the World, and I have changed my mind. I have even seen a building fit to be in Heaven. I used to make a copy of the Capitol as nearly as I could in my sand-pile. I would fill

a shoe-box with wet sand, then turn it carefully
upside down so as to empty it out without breaking, and I made the dome on top in the same way
with a tea-cup.

I thought all capitols of other countries must
have domes too. I didn't learn until later that
not capitols but churches were the first buildings
to have domes, and that many capitols have no
domes. As a boy I used to climb to the top of
the dome—for there was
no elevator—to see the
view of the city, and to
look down on the inside at
the floor far below where
people walking seemed like
ants crawling.

On one side of the Cap-
itol is a large room called
the Senate, and on the
other side is a still larger
room called the House of

I thought it the most beautiful building in the World

Representatives. In both the Senate and the
House of Representatives men sit at desks like
boys in school. These men are the ones who make
our laws, which are rules that everybody in the
United States must obey. The men in the Senate
are called Senators. The men in the House are
called Representatives. When I say "men," I
mean women too, for some of the Senators and
Representatives are women.

Each State chooses two Senators to go to the

Capitol in Washington. No matter whether the State is big like Texas or whether it is little like Rhode Island, it sends only two Senators. And each State also sends to the Capitol in Washington other men or women called Representatives, but the number of Representatives each State sends depends on the number of people in the State; New York has the most people, so it sends the most Representatives. Several States have so few people that they send only one Representative. The Senate and the House of Representatives together are called "Congress," and when Congress is holding a meeting a flag is flying over the Capitol.

Look in the front of this book or any other book and you will see printed there "Copyright." Just across a park from the Capitol is a large building with a golden dome on top. This building is the Library of Congress. Every one in the United States who prints a book sends two copies of it to this library, and the library sends him a "copy right," which means that no one else has the "right" to copy it or print it without his permission. In the Library of Congress there are more books than in any other building in the country.

Look on your camera or phonograph, or any other machine in your home, and see if you can find the word "Patented." Any one in the country who invents anything new and useful—

whether it is a fountain-pen, an airplane, or a mouse-trap—sends one—a model, it is called —to another building in Washington called the Patent Office and asks for a patent. If the thing is really new and no one has ever made anything of the kind before, the Patent Office gives him the sole right to make and sell it, and no one else is allowed to make or sell it. That is called a patent. Some of the models are very curious. One model that some one had invented was a steam-engine that walked with iron legs. When-I-was-a-boy I invented a "snapback" handkerchief. I would blow my nose, then let go the handkerchief, and a rubber pulled it back into my pocket. But I didn't get a patent.

Parades! Soldiers! Bands of music! Flying flags! Some of the greatest parades have passed down a very wide street in Washington called Pennsylvania Avenue, or usually just *"The* Avenue." It might be called "Parade Avenue." It stretches from the Capitol to another building about a mile away that looks like a big bank. This other building is called the Treasury. There is a picture of it on the $10 bill. In the Treasury is kept money of the United States. We write United States with two letters, U. S., and we write the sign for "dollars" with the same two letters, written one on top of the other, with the bottom of the "U" cut off—thus, $.

Paper money and postage-stamps are printed in another building.

"You see that man over there turning the handle of that printing-press?" says the guide who shows you around. "He makes a million dollars a day!"

"Whew! He must be the richest man in the World."

"Oh, no. He only *gets* $5 a day."

The money made out of silver, and gold, and copper is made in another city—not in Washington—at a place called the Mint.

When-I-was-a-boy I had an old bookcase which I called my museum. In it I had a starfish, some shells, a bird's nest, a "gold" rock, and so forth. In Washington there is a large museum called the National Museum in which there is a huge collection of all sorts of curious and remarkable things from all over the World.

You might live there some day

There are many white houses in the country, but next door to the Treasury is a White House that is different from any other, for in this house the President lives. There is a picture of it on the $20 bill. From the back porch of *The* White House the latest President of the United States can look across his back yard and see a monument to the First President—Washington. The Washington Monument is the highest piece

of stone work in the World. It's like a giant
finger, five hundred and fifty-five feet high. It
seemed a mile high, but it is really only about a
tenth of a mile high—not even as high as a low
mountain. No man has ever been able to build as
high as God. Though there is an elevator, I used
to run up the stairs, two steps at a time, to the
top of the monument—
just for fun—to see how
quickly I could do it, and
whether I could beat the
elevator. Boys are like
that. They will run a race
with anything. I could
beat the elevator down by
jumping half a dozen steps
at a time, but not up. My
heart did the beating go-
ing up.

It seemed a mile high

There is a long pool of water at the foot of
the Washington Monument in which you can
see the monument as in a mirror. At the other
end of this pool is a marble building with columns all around the four sides. It was built in
honor of Abraham Lincoln, the sixteenth President after Washington. It is probably the most
thrilling memorial ever built to a human being.
There is a picture of Lincoln on the $5 bill and
on the other side a picture of his Memorial. Lincoln was born in a tiny house made of logs, so
small that the whole house could be put in one

room of your home. No boy was ever poorer, or
had less money or less chance, and yet he became
President of the United States. While he was
President two parts of the United States fought
a terrible war with each other and almost became un-United, but Lincoln kept the States
together. That's why this beautiful building was
built in his honor. The only thing in the building
is a statue of Lincoln sitting in a chair. He looks
down on the crowds of people who visit him,
as if his spirit were inside that figure of
stone.

7

Mary's Land, Virginia's State, and Penn's Woods

DID you ever trade a top for some marbles or an apple for an orange? Long before there was any Washington or any United States there used to be trader Indians living on the shores of the river that flows by Washington. These Indians paddled their canoes up and down the river and traded with other Indians, swapping things they had for things they wanted—beads for furs, bows for arrows, corn for potatoes. In the Indian language the name for Traders was Potomac, so we call the river after these trader Indians, the Potomac River. The Potomac separates two States with girls' names: Maryland and Virgina. They are named after two queens. The Potomac Indians paddled their canoes down the river till they came to a much broader piece of water. This piece of water was so big it seemed to them like the ocean, and they called it "the Mother of Waters," which in their own language was "Chesapeake." You can see it on the map. Chesapeake Bay is not the ocean, but it is the biggest bay in the United States.

Did you ever eat snails or terrapin or frogs'

legs? Some people like them. The Indians found
oysters growing in the Chesapeake Bay. At first
no one thought of eating oysters—they didn't
look good to eat. But one day an Indian who
was very hungry broke an oyster-shell open and
ate the oyster inside. It tasted good and it didn't
hurt him, so others began to eat oysters, and now
almost every one likes oysters, either raw or
cooked. Oysters grow in other parts of the World
too, but many people say that those in the Chesapeake Bay are the largest and best, but they are
not supposed to be good unless they are eaten
during the eight months that have an R in their
names. They are good in MaRch but not in June.

Near "the Mother of Waters" are two cities.
One is named Annapolis. The other is named Baltimore. Annapolis means Anna's City, and it
too was named after a queen. That makes three
places—Anna's City, Mary's Land, and Virginia's State—named after queens. Annapolis is
the capital of the State of Maryland, just as
Washington is the capital of all the States. At
Annapolis the United States has a school for
teaching boys to be sailors and fit to fight the sea
battles of the United States if the country should
ever have any. This school is called the Naval
Academy. Some of the best boys chosen from
each State in the United States go to Annapolis.
They study all about boats and fighting and
about geography; they visit other countries and
learn to command ships.

Baltimore is the largest city in Maryland. It was named after an English lord. The first railroad in our country started in Baltimore, and as it ran from Baltimore to the State of Ohio, it was called the Baltimore & Ohio, or the B. & O. for short. Baltimore is famous for the Johns Hopkins University and Hospital. Boys come from all over the World to study at the "Hopkins," and people come from all over the World to be treated at the "Hopkins Hospital."

A man named Penn once owned the State just north of Maryland. It was then all woods, so it was called Pennsylvania, which means Penn's Woods. But ages before Penn's Woods other woods were there—huge forests of trees and giant plants growing high and thick and fast. More ages passed and these forests died and became buried and mashed down under the ground and turned into black rock. More ages passed and men dug up this black rock, and by accident they found that unlike other rock this rock would burn. Of course it would burn, because, as we know now, it was really only hardened wood—which we call coal.

There are two kinds of coal. One is called hard and the other is called soft. Soft coal doesn't mean soft like a cushion; it means it crumbles easily. Hard coal is the best; soft coal is dirtier and smokier, but is a great deal cheaper. Why is it that the best things almost always cost the most? In the eastern part of Pennsylvania the coal that comes out of the ground is *hard;* in the western part it is *soft.*

Hundreds of thousands of men, called miners, work underneath the ground, where it is like night all day long, digging out the coal to run steam-engines and to heat our houses. They have been digging away for years and years, so that there are huge hollow places underneath parts of Pennsylvania.

Coal is in layers underneath the ground and between layers of rock like the chocolate in a chocolate layer-cake. But there are also iron mines in Pennsylvania, and iron is not in layers; it is all mixed through the rock under the ground and is called ore. To get the iron out of the ore, men build huge fires under the ore and the iron melts and runs out, like water, into troughs which they make in the ground to catch it. When the iron cools, the blocks of iron are called "pigs" —perhaps because they are about the size of pigs —or perhaps because a pig goes into a trough.

To get iron out of iron ore you must have heat, and to have heat you must have something to make heat with, like coal. Some places have iron ore but no coal, and some places have coal but no iron. It is as if some boys who wanted to play baseball had a ball but no bat, and some other boys had a bat but no ball. But Pittsburgh, in the western part of Pennsylvania, had both iron and coal near-by. That is like boys who have both a bat and a ball.

From the ore they make iron, and from the iron they make steel, and from the steel they make rails for railroad tracks and beams for tall buildings and bridges to cross rivers.

A name that is in the Bible is the name of a city, Philadelphia. It means the City of Brotherly Love. This name was chosen to give to the largest city in Pennsylvania, in fact, the third largest city in all the United States, but I don't know whether it suits or not. Philadelphia was the capital of the United States before there was any Washington, D. C., but now it isn't even the capital of its own

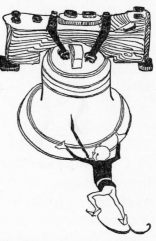

The Liberty Bell is cracked

State. Here in an old building, called Independence Hall, is the bell that rang out the news when the United States was first made a country. It is now cracked, so will not ring any more, but is more treasured than any bell in the United States that *can* ring.

The biggest bathtub in the World is not far from Philadelphia. It is an ocean bath called Atlantic City, on the coast of New Jersey. People from all over the World go there to take salt baths and sun baths and to be amused. There

is a boardwalk miles long and as wide as a street
close by the ocean, and along its side is every
kind of thing to amuse you and your "stum-
mick." If you want to see a board "walk," go to
Atlantic City.

If you want to see a board "walk," go
to Atlantic City

8

The Empire State

SEVERAL countries together are called an "Empire." So New York State is often called the Empire State, because it has as many people, who do as much business and make as much money, as several countries put together.

Down at the corner of New York State is New York City, the second largest city in the World, with more shops, more hotels, more people, and more money than any other city on this side of the World, and with more tall buildings than on any side of the World. It was named after a city across the ocean called York, but *New* York is now hundreds of times bigger than old York. It is the city of millionaires and millions who are not. People from all over the world come to New York hoping to be millionaires too. Some used to think the streets were paved with gold, and were disappointed when they found them just asphalt.

The main part of New York City is on an island which the Indians called Manhattan. White men bought it from the Indians and paid them about $24 for the whole island—not in money, for the Indians didn't know what money was, but in beads and ornaments worth $24. A piece of ground only large enough to stand on would now cost many times more than what the whole island once cost. That may seem a big price for a small piece of ground, but a plot of ground is not like a sheet of paper, without thickness. The owner owns everything above and below the ground— down to the center of the earth and up to the sky. That is why men in New York build buildings

up to the sky—"sky-scrapers" we call them—for a fifty-story building takes up no more land than a one-story building.

To me there is nothing in the World made by the hand of man more wonderful than New York's giant buildings. They are marvelous, magnificent, awe-inspiring, stupendous, amazing, overpowering, thrilling, Brobdingnagian. Have you read "Gulliver's Travels"? Brobdingnag was the land of the giants. They stand unmoved by thunder and lightning, by wind, storm, or tempest, and they look down on their creators—mites of men who, with their hands of only five fingers, have built them. New York's motto is "Excelsior," which means "Higher," and that is the motto of its builders. There is a saying, "Great oaks from little acorns grow," and one of the greatest of these buildings—sixty stories high—was built from the nickels and dimes made by Woolworth's Five and Ten Cent Stores. The most marvelous building of all is called the Empire State Building. It is one hundred and two stories high, taller than any other building in New York City, or in America, or in the whole World.

One group of high buildings in New York might be called the capitol of the World. After World War II most of the countries of the World wanted to find some way of keeping a third World War from happening. These countries each sent men to meet together as our States send men to Congress. At their meetings they discuss matters that are of interest to all the countries of the World. When any country quarrels with another these people try to have them settle their quarrel without fighting. This congress is called the United Nations. The United Nations decided that New York City would be the best place to have its meetings and carry on its business. So there it built its offices. When the buildings were dedicated, or solemnly set apart for United Nations use, the speeches were broadcast in twenty-six different languages.

At a meeting of the United Nations each speaker speaks in his own language, yet he can be understood by all the other people there, for everyone wears earphones and hears a translation of the speech in the language he understands. Of course the people who do the translation must know two languages, for they have to listen in one language and speak into a microphone in another language. What they speak into the microphones is what is heard in the earphones. Millions of other people watch the United Nations meetings on television.

On a little island in New York Harbor is a huge bronze statue called the Goddess of Liberty holding aloft a torch-light. Her hand is over sixteen feet long. What a hand to shake! One finger

STATUE OF LIBERTY

Her nose is four and one-half feet long. What a nose for smelling!

is eight feet long. What a finger for a ring! Her nose is four and one-half feet long. What a nose for smelling! Her mouth is a yard wide. What a mouth for talking! You can climb up on the inside into the Goddess's head and arm, and a dozen people can stand inside her torch. Ships pass by her, and their passengers crowding the deck greet her with a thrill of "My Country, 'Tis of Thee, Sweet Land of Liberty," and wave her farewell as they leave for afar, perhaps never to return.

On one side of Manhattan Island is the Hudson River and on the other side is the East River. A bridge was built across the East River by stretching ropes made of steel from one side of the river to the other and hanging the floor of the bridge from these steel ropes. This is called a suspension bridge. It is called the Brooklyn Bridge because at the other end of it on Long Island is another big city called Brooklyn. Brooklyn is now a part of New York City. Such bridges had been built over small streams before, but this was the first big, long bridge built in this way. It is suspended in the air so high above the water that even the greatest ships easily pass beneath it.

At first people were afraid to cross the Brooklyn Bridge, for, said they, "A bridge hung on ropes, even if made of steel, will fall." It swayed and shook as trucks and cars rumbled over it, and it still does —but still hangs. Several other bridges have been built over the East River and the Hudson River to New York City. Also, tunnels have been dug *under* the Hudson. The tunnels are called "Tubes" because they are like big tubes under the river.

At first people were afraid to cross the Brooklyn Bridge

Two of the most famous streets in the World run the length of Manhattan Island and still farther north. One is named Broadway and the other Fifth Avenue. Broadway was at first only a short street, but it seemed very broad, so they called it that. Broadway, however, is now so long that it might better be called "Longway." One part of it is lighted so brightly at night by thousands of electric lights and flashing electric signs that it is often called "The Great White Way." Fifth Avenue is a famous street of once fashionable homes, and many of the finest and most expensive shops are there, so that Fifth Avenue has come to mean Fashion Avenue. The streets of New York are so crowded that most of the people travel from their homes to their work by trains that run in tunnels underground. These underground tunnels are called Subways.

In spite of the fact that land in New York City is worth more than any other land in the World, there are two big parks where city people may have a little country. Central Park is fifty blocks long and several blocks wide, and Bronx Park has a wonderful Zoo where there are strange and curious animals which hunters have brought alive from the jungles, mountains, deserts, and wildernesses of far-off lands.

A man from across the ocean once landed in New York and spent the day seeing the sights. Just before dinner he said he would like to drive out and see Niagara Falls, which he had heard were the most wonderful falls in the World. When he was told that it would take all night on a fast train to get to Niagara, he couldn't understand.

"But isn't Niagara in New York?" he asked.

"Yes," was the reply, "but not in New York

City. Niagara is all the way across the State of
New York."

On the west edge of New York State are two
great lakes with Indian names—Lake Erie and
Lake Ontario. Lake Erie on the map looks lower
than Lake Ontario, but it really is much higher.
So the water from Lake Erie falls over a high
and broad cliff to reach Lake Ontario. This
waterfall is called Niagara, and though there are
other falls in the World higher and other falls
broader, Niagara is the most beautiful and most
famous, and people go from all over the World
to see it. The roar of the water as it thunders over
the edge can be heard for miles, and when the sun
is shining there is always a rainbow in the spray
that rises from the bottom of the falls. Thousands
of people view the falls each day, and of each
thousand—

> 358 say "Isn't it wonderful!"
> 247 say "Isn't it grand!"
> 136 say "Isn't it beautiful!"
> 93 say "Isn't it lovely!"
> 45 say "Isn't it pretty!"
> 24 say "Ah!"
> And the rest say "Oh!"

A part of Niagara is caught in a huge bucket
as it falls, and the falling water turns giant
wheels in the bottom of the bucket. The wheels
make electricity, which is carried on wires to turn
the wheels of mills, to run the trolley-cars, and to

light the houses and streets in the city of Buffalo near-by, and other places farther away.

For some reason or other, every now and then some man tries to jump the falls in a barrel, and at least one man has done it and lived. But boats on Lake Erie that wanted to go to Lake Ontario couldn't jump the falls. So men

PART OF
NIAGARA FALLS

The roar of the water can
be heard for miles

dug a river around Niagara Falls from Lake Erie to Lake Ontario and put water steps in it so that boats could go downhill to Lake Ontario or uphill to Lake Erie. This man-made river is called the Welland Canal.

It may seem strange for a boat to step downhill, but it not only can step downhill, it can step up too. A water step down a hill is called a "lock," and a lock is like a huge bathtub set in the canal. Perhaps you have floated toy boats in your bathtub. If you have, you know that as you fill the tub the boat rises as the water rises, and as you let the water run out of the tub the boat lowers as the water lowers.

Now a canal lock works the same way with large boats as the bathtub with small boats. If a boat wants to go downhill it sails into the lock.

The water in the lock is then let out and the boat lowers as the water lowers. When the boat is at the bottom, doors at the end of the lock are opened and the boat sails out on the lower canal. If a boat wants to go uphill it sails into the bottom of the lock through the open doors, the doors are then closed, and the water is turned on. As it fills the lock the boat rises with it, for water will lift anything that will float, no matter whether it be the smallest chip or the biggest ship. Water, just plain water, has more power to lift and lower the largest steamship than even giant machinery would have. It lifts the largest battle-ship as easily and softly as it would the lightest feather floating on the surface—as easily as you might lift a snowflake on your hand.

Boats that wanted to go to New York City— and almost all boats did want to go to New York —once had to go down through the Welland Canal and locks to Lake Ontario, then all the way out the St. Lawrence River, which runs from Lake Ontario to the Atlantic Ocean, then sail down the coast to New York. To avoid this long detour, this long way round, men dug a canal all the way across New York State from Buffalo on Lake Erie to the Hudson River, so that big boats can now cut across from Lake Erie to New York City. This is called the Barge Canal. It's one of the longest canals in the World.

9

Yankee Land

A PAIR of shoes, a hat, or an automobile we should not call "New" if they were a year old, but there is a corner of our country which is 300 years old and yet we call it "New." About 300 years ago people from England, across the ocean, came to the northeast corner of the United States and made their homes there. So the six States north of New York, where they settled, we call *New England.* The Indians tried to call the white people "English," but the best they could say was "Yenghees" or "Yankees," just as a child in trying to say "brother" might say "buddy"—so the people of New England we still call "Yankees." We could put all six States of New England in any one of several States out West; but though the New England States are small in size, they are big in many other things.

The largest and most important city of New England is Boston, named after a town in old England. Many people call Boston "the Hub," by which they mean to say that the rest of the World turns round Boston, for the hub of a wheel you know is the center, around which the rest of the wheel turns. Of course, the World

really turns around the North and South Poles
and these Poles are the real hubs of the World;
so people are only joking when they say the
World turns round Boston.

Rocks and cold weather are bad for farming.
New England in winter is very cold and it also is
very rocky, so rocky that men make their fences
of stones gathered off the fields. The cold and the
rocks make it very hard to grow things there,
but there are many, many waterfalls in New
England, and waterfalls can be used to turn the
wheels of factories to make things, so what people chiefly do in New England is to *make* things
for the rest of the United States—thousands of
different kinds of things—not big things such as
railroad tracks and bridges that they make in
Pittsburgh, but small things for a person's use,
such as needles and pins, watches and clocks,
boots and shoes. If the wheels of the factories are
turned by waterfalls they are called mills. Nowadays, most of the waterfalls are used to make
electricity, and the electricity is used to run the
machinery, but the factories are still called
"mills."

When-I-was-a-boy my idea of perfect happiness was to go barefoot. In some countries rich
and poor alike go barefoot all the time, but in
America almost every one wears shoes all the
time. One of the chief things they make in these
New England mills is shoes. In New England
they make enough shoes for every pair of feet in

the United States. Shoes wear out, so we can understand why the mills should keep on, year after year, making so many shoes. But in one of the States—the one with the Indian name, Connecticut—they make pins—enough for every man, woman and child in the United States to use 100 every year. What becomes of so many pins, do you suppose? They don't wear out like shoes, and yet they disappear—billions of pins every year.

And clocks and thread and boots and shoes and needles and pins

And clocks and watches—they make millions of them too, though one clock or one watch should last a person a lifetime—little watches for the wrist and little clocks for mantelpieces and big clocks for clock towers.

And spools of thread—enough thread is made in one mill in a single day to wind round the World—that is, over twenty-five thousand miles of thread in one mill in one day!

Where do you spend your vacation? Do you go to the seashore, to the mountains, or "down on a farm"? New England is the vacation land of many people from other parts of the country, because there are so many lakes, waterfalls, and beautiful spots for camps, streams for fishing, and in the Maine woods places for hunting deer and moose. In New Hampshire there are mountains called the White Mountains, and one of these White Mountains, named after our First President, is Mount Washington. It is the highest mountain in this part of the country, and just because it is so high many people like to climb it. Some people are like that. In Vermont, which means "green mountain," there are the Green Mountains, not as high as the White Mountains, but very lovely. All along the New England coast are places where people go to spend the summer, because this part of the country is so cool while the rest of the country is so hot.

But the thing that New England is proudest of is its schools and colleges. In their mills they make *Things,* in their schools and colleges they make *Men.* Two of the most noted colleges in the country are in New England—Yale is in Connecticut and Harvard is in Massachusetts. Harvard is the oldest college in the United States.

Sticking out from Massachusetts like a long, bent finger, as if beckoning to people across the water to come to Massachusetts, is a piece of land called Cape Cod. It was named in honor of the codfish, because codfish are so plentiful in those waters, and they are caught and dried in great quantities and shipped everywhere.

The finger of Cape Cod has beckoned to people

of other lands than England. People who speak strange languages have come to New England to work in factories and mills, so that now almost one quarter of the people in New England are not from England; they are not Yankees.

10

Five Big Puddles

DID you ever wonder what an ant must think of us giants who tread on his ant-hills, or what he must think of a puddle of water?

There are five big puddles of water along the northern edge of the United States—at least they look like puddles on the map—as if a gigantic giant had left his wet umbrella standing and the water had trickled out over the land. We call these puddles "The Great Lakes," for they are the biggest lakes on this side of the World, though a giant with legs a mile long would think them only puddles to wade across. Two of the lakes—the smallest two—I have already told you about. They are Lake Erie and Lake Ontario. Two of the others also have Indian names, Lake Michigan, which means "Great Lake," and Lake Huron. The Greatest Lake of all the Great Lakes is called Superior, which means simply Greater Lake, as we say a boy who is a better football player or who makes better marks is "superior" to some other boy. Lake Michigan is the only one of the Great Lakes that belongs entirely to the United States, as it is entirely inside of the United States. Half of the other four lakes belong to the country north of the United States—the country called Canada—because these other lakes are along the border between the two countries. The United States owns its side of each of these lakes and out to the middle; Canada owns its side and out to the middle.

Lake Superior is not only bigger, it is higher than the other lakes. It empties its water into Lake Huron through a little river called St. Mary's, and in this river are falls. These falls in the St. Mary's River are called St. Mary's Jump, because the water jumps, jumps down. These falls are not nearly as high as Niagara Falls, but they are too high for boats to go over the jump, so men had to build canals with locks around the falls to lower boats down and raise them up from one lake to the other. As there are so many boats that want to go down and up, one canal was not enough to take care of all the boats that wanted to go round the falls, so men have built five canals round St. Mary's Jump. St. Mary's Jump in French is Sault Ste. Marie, and as this is so difficult to say, people simply call the falls Soo, the river Soo, and the canals Soo too.

Some of the boats on the Great Lakes are as big and fine as those on the ocean; and they have to be, for the Great Lakes are like small oceans. When you are out, far out, you cannot see land, and at times there are high waves and storms,

just as at sea. The chief difference is that the
water in the lakes is fresh, not salt.

"Business before pleasure."

A great many people take trips on these big
lake boats just as they do on the ocean—for
pleasure; but the chief reason for the great number of ships that go from one end of the lakes to
the other is not pleasure but business. The business is carrying things, which we call freight. It
is much cheaper to send things by ship than by
train, for one big ship can carry much more than
many trains, and ships do not have to have land
and tracks to run on, as trains do. When we send
freight by train we also call that "shipping,"
which seems strange. Every one would ship by
ship instead of by train if he could, because it
is so much cheaper, but of course you have to be
near the water to ship by ship.

Fortunately, eight out of our forty-eight
States are on the Great Lakes, although some of
the States have only a small "frontage" on a lake.
Michigan has the most frontage, by far. It fronts
on four of the Great Lakes, all except Lake Ontario.

You remember that the Potomac Indians
were great traders, paddling their canoes up and
down the river, and swapping things they had for
things they wanted. The Indians of the Great
Lakes used to do the same thing. Nowadays the
white man's huge ships—thousands of times bigger than the Indians' canoes made out of a single

log—do the trading. They carry huge loads of freight from one end of the Great Lakes to the other, unloading at different places along the way the things that people want, and loading up with other freight to go back.

Most of the ships start at the far end of Lake Superior at a place called Duluth. Trains loaded with wheat come to Duluth from the wheat-lands west of that city, and other trains loaded with iron ore from mines near-by. Then huge machines on the shores of the lakes, with giant hands of iron, lift whole cars of wheat and ore and dump them into the ships waiting to be filled, as you would lift a toy car of your toy train and empty its load with two fingers. Other ships collect copper ore and also iron from that part of Michigan which is on Lake Superior. They then carry their loads through the Soo Canal and unload at a place called Detroit, between Lake Huron and Lake Erie, or carry their iron ore to Cleveland and Buffalo on Lake Erie. Most of the ships do not go past Niagara Falls. They load up again with things that have been made in New England, or in the east of the United States, or with coal from Pennsylvania, and go back to Duluth.

But when winter comes, all this trading up and down the lakes has to stop, for this part of the country is very cold and ice forms and stops the ships.

A baby is born every second, but in Detroit an

automobile is born every minute. Most of the automobiles in the World are made in Detroit. Into one end of a Detroit factory go iron and

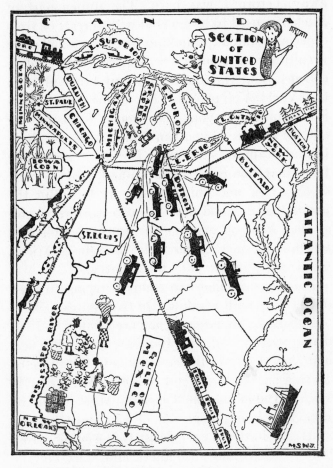

wood, leather, etc., and out at the other end comes an automobile. Every hour of the day hundreds of automobiles are finished and run out of the factories, to be shipped over the whole World.

I am sitting in a chair that was made from a tree that grew in Michigan, a thousand miles away, before I was born. The upper part of Michigan used to be covered with forests of trees especially suited for making furniture—and more furniture was made there, especially at a place called Grand Rapids, than at any other place in the World. You probably have some Grand Rapids furniture in your own home. Look on the bottom and see if you can find a label "Made in Grand Rapids." So much furniture was made there that men have cut down and used up most of the trees, and only stumps are left. But the people had learned how to make furniture, and so they kept on making furniture, though now much of the lumber has to be brought to Michigan from other parts of the country.

Side by side, like two children trying to peek out of one small window, are two States looking out on Lake Michigan. They are Illinois and Indiana, written "Ill. and Ind." for short. The second largest city in the country is in the State of Illinois on the lower end of Lake Michigan. It has an Indian name—Chicago. More trains of cars come into and go out of Chicago than any other city in the World. Most trains going across the United States stop there and start there—freight trains carrying things and passenger trains carrying people.

There are a great many kinds of animals in

the World, and yet of all these animals there are only three kinds that people generally eat. These three are the cow, the sheep, the pig. It takes millions of these animals every year to feed all the people in the United States, and millions of these animals are raised in the States near-by and far from Chicago. These animals have to be fed, and the food that is best to make them fat is corn, so whole States grow corn, just to feed cows and sheep and pigs. The State of Iowa grows more corn than any other State, so it is called the Corn State. Some of the corn is shipped to Chicago, but most of it is shipped "on the hoof"—that is, it is fed to the animals and the animals are sent alive to Chicago to be killed. They are kept in big pens called stock-yards until they are killed. From Chicago they are sent in refrigerator cars or ships, everywhere, even to Europe. Chicago is the greatest butcher-shop in the World. The bacon I had for breakfast, the ham sandwich I had for luncheon, and the roast beef I had for dinner came from Chicago.

11

The Father of Waters

THE biggest *bay* in the United States I told you is called "the Mother of Waters." The biggest river in the United States is called "the Father of Waters." Although the river is called a "father," he is not a Mr. He is a "Miss." In the Indian language he is *Miss*—issippi, and is spelled in this jingly way:

M
i double s
i double s
i double p
i

which is very easy to learn.

If I asked you to draw a picture of a river, and

also of a tree without any leaves on it, you would probably draw the tree this way—a main stem, with big branches, and big branches with little branches, and little branches with tiny branches—like the picture to the left. And you would probably draw the picture of the river as just a wiggly line—now wouldn't you? As a matter of fact, the picture of a tree and the picture of a river should be drawn exactly the same way, for they each have a main stem with big branches, big branches with little branches, and little branches with tiny branches—although you may not see all the branches in the picture of a river on the map.

But there is this big difference between a tree and a river:

A tree *grows* from the bottom to the top of its branches.

A river *flows* from the top of its branches to the bottom. The sap runs up a tree, water runs down a river. If a river were just a single line and had no branches at all, it would be just as big at the finish as at the start. It's the river's branches that make it bigger and bigger. The biggest river in the United States, the Mississippi, starts almost at the top of our country, at a little lake called Itasca, in the State of Minnesota, and flows all the way to the bottom of our country, getting bigger and bigger all the time as its branches flow into it, until at last it reaches a corner of the ocean we call the Gulf of Mexico. The Mississippi River really cuts our country into two parts, but the two parts are not the same size. The part west of the Mississippi is about twice as big as the part east of the Mississippi.

The Mississippi River hardly gets a good running start on its long journey south to the Gulf of Mexico before it falls down, and where it falls men have built big mills, the wheels of which are turned by the falling water. These mills, however, are not like those in New England. They do not make things. They grind wheat to make flour to make bread, for more and better wheat grows near where the Mississippi starts and the States near-by than anywhere else in the whole World.

An acre seems to me, who lives in a city, a large piece of ground, a hundred acres seems immense, and a thousand acres seems enormous, but some farms in Minnesota where they raise wheat have as many as *ten thousand* acres of wheat in a single farm! The farmers would never get through planting or gathering the wheat if they did so by hand or even with a horse. So they plow with an engine and often with ten plows in a row, and they use machines for gathering the wheat and for separating the grains of the wheat from the straw, which has to be done before it can be ground into flour.

On opposite sides of the Mississippi near these falls two large cities of almost the same size have grown up. These two cities are connected by a bridge, and they are so nearly the same size they are called Twin Cities. One of them is named Minneapolis, which means "Water City," as Annapolis means "Anna's City"; and the other is named St. Paul. Notice that almost all names around the Great Lakes and the Mississippi are named either after saints or after Indians. That's because priests were among the first to come to this country to make the Indians Christians, and they named places either after the Indians or after the Christian saints.

The water city—Minneapolis—is the greatest flour-making place in the whole World. I have to say "in the whole World" so often, I'm going to use only the first letters from now on— i for "in," t for "the," w for "whole," W for "World"—thus: i.t.w.W. Minneapolis is the greatest flour-making place i.t.w.W. Minnesota and the States near it are the greatest wheat-raising States i.t.w.W.

As the Mississippi River flows south toward the Gulf of Mexico it passes other cities, but the biggest one is St. Louis, about half-way down. St. Louis—another saint—is near the two biggest branches of the Mississippi River—the Missouri, which comes in from the west, and the Ohio, which comes in from the east—both rivers named after States and both States named after the Indians. The Missouri is such a big branch that it is hard to tell whether it is a branch of the Mississippi or the Mississippi is a branch of it. Indeed, if you can find where the Missouri River begins you will see that from that point to the end of the Mississippi the river is much longer than the Mississippi itself—it is over 4,000 miles

—so the Missouri-Mississippi together is the longest river i.t.w.W.

The Mississippi gets bigger and bigger as it gets more and more branches, and in the spring when the snow melts and the rain rains so hard and flows down into the branches, the river swells and swells until it finally bursts over its banks and floods the country. So, down where this is likely to happen, men have built banks along the river on each side, to hold the water in. These banks are called levees; but sometimes the river grows too big and strong even for these levees to hold it in, and the river breaks through or over the top and floods the country. If there happen to be any farms or houses or towns with people in them, the water washes houses away and drowns people and animals, and destroys thousands upon thousands of farms and other property.

The Mississippi near its end passes the city called New Orleans and at last flows into the Gulf of Mexico. The end of a river where it flows into the sea is called its mouth. I never knew why, because a mouth is where water flows in, not where it flows out. At any rate, the Mississippi has several mouths instead of one mouth, for the water in the river brings along with it so much mud that it settles right in the way of the river's mouth and forms mud islands which the river has to go round, so the river blocks itself.

Where the Mississippi begins in the far north of the United States it is very cold in winter, but as the river flows farther and farther south it gets warmer and warmer and warmer. This warm country is nicknamed "Dixie." When the river is near its end at New Orleans, flowers bloom even at Christmas and it is warm all the year round. Where the river begins you see white people in the fields and on the shores, but when it gets down south in Dixie Land you see more and more colored people working in the fields. The chief thing they are doing is growing cotton, for "Dixie Land," as the song says, is way down south "in the land of cotton," and more cotton is grown here than anywhere else i.t.w.W. Strange to say, there was no cotton in America at first. A cotton plant was brought first to Maryland from the other side of the world and grown only for its pretty flowers.

Cotton grows on a low bush in little white balls, and inside each white ball are troublesome little seeds. The cotton is picked off the bush and then these seeds have to be picked out of the cotton before it can be made into cotton thread, and then into cotton cloth, and then into cotton clothes, sheets, towels—can you think of anything else made out of cotton? Things made of cotton were once very expensive, because it took such a long time to pick the seeds out of the cotton, but a school-teacher—a man—invented a way to pick the seeds out by a machine—an "engine" which the colored people called "a gin," for short, and now cotton goods can be made very cheaply. Indeed, it is now hard to understand how we ever got along without cotton, for this little plant that was once grown only for its flowers is used in more things and in more ways than anything that grows out of the ground. This is why it is often called "King Cotton."

12

The Fountain of Youth

BIRDS go south in the winter to get warm.
Some people in the cold Northern States do the
same. The farthest south they can go in the
United States is to the corner State, shaped like
a dog's paw, called Florida, which means the land
of flowers. On the automobiles that go to Florida
you can read the tags of every one of the forty-
eight States. People go to Florida in the winter
to sit in the sunshine, to bathe in the sea in January, to get rid of shivers, sneezes, and handkerchiefs. It is a winter playground, as New England is a summer playground. I know a man who
is supposed to live in Baltimore, but he spends
his winters in Florida and his summers in New
England, so he only lives in Baltimore a few
weeks in between.

The first white people who came to America
came to Florida, because they had been told
there was a fountain of youth there. The fountain of youth was supposed to be a spring which
was said to have magic powers. It was believed
if old people bathed in it or drank its water they
would become young again. But no one has ever
found a fountain of youth in Florida or any-

where else, though many old people after they have spent the winter in Florida say they *feel* young again.

But not everybody in Florida plays all winter long. Many have to work. They have to run the hotels for the people who do come to Florida to play. And a great many others are busy raising "fresh early vegetables" to ship to the cold Northern States, where they would have only canned or frozen vegetables during the winter otherwise. Just as there is a top time, a kite time, a football time, and a baseball time, there used to be certain times or seasons for certain fruits and vegetables; but in most of Florida it is so warm they seldom or never have frost or snow or ice, so they can raise fruits and vegetables the year round. Farmers ship the vegetables they raise out of season to other States, so that people in the North can now have fresh strawberries at Christmas, and asparagus too, and lettuce and radishes every month in the year.

The chief fruits from Florida are oranges and grapefruit, which will grow only where there is no frost. Grape-fruit grows in bunches like big, yellow grapes—that's why it is called "grape"-fruit. Grape-fruit was at first thought not fit to eat—too bitter and not sweet like an orange; but people have learned to like it. More grape-fruit grows in Florida than in any other place i.t.w.W.

Once there was no Florida at all—the United States had no "paw" sticking out into the sea. It grew a paw and this is the way it grew it. The sea was warm and shallow and in the sea there lived millions, billions, trillions of little animals, each like a tiny drop of jelly with a tiny stony speck in the center, or a tiny stony shell on the outside, and millions and billions and trillions of these little sea animals died. As they died, millions, billions, trillions of these stony specks and shells fell to the bottom of the sea like a snowfall of chalk dust, and this piled up until the water was filled up. This stony, bony, chalky pile is Florida. On this kind of ground of which Florida is made plants grow very well indeed. In fact, this soft, chalky ground is so good for growing things that people dig it up and send it to other States to be put on the ground to make vegetables grow better.

Long, long years ago, before there were any people on the World, our whole country was at the bottom of the sea, and a great deal of our country was made under the sea just as Florida was made, from bones and shells of sea animals. This kind of bone and shell rock—for it is rock —is called limestone, because if you burn it it makes lime. Limestone is really bone-stone; stone made of the bones of sea animals. Then the earth wrinkled and crinkled and rose out of the water and formed our country. We know it was once under the sea because in many places now, high above the sea, even on mountain tops, we find this limestone with shells and bones of fish and other sea animals still showing in it. Marble, the most beautiful of all stone, is a kind of limestone, for it also is made of bone. People build houses

MAMMOTH CAVE

and palaces of it and make statues and tombstones of marble or limestone.

Many of the people who go to Florida stop on their trip to see sights, and one of the greatest sights is in Virginia and Kentucky where the rock under the ground is all limestone. The "sights" are huge caves, and in Kentucky they are so large they are called Mammoth Caves. These caves have not been dug out by men but by water. Water, you know, melts sugar; but perhaps you didn't know that water melts rock too—not ordinary rock, but it melts limestone, and these caves are in limestone rock. The Mammoth Cave is like a huge cellar underground—a cave so large and high that you could put a whole city with its tall buildings in it. You could easily get lost and wander for miles. Men have been lost and unable to find their way out again and died and their skeletons have been found long years after.

Through the roof of the cave water drips drop by drop, and each drop leaves a bit of limestone, until in the course of time the dripping water makes icicles of rock that hang down from the roof of the cave. Drops of water from each icicle fall on to the floor of the cave, and the limestone gradually piles up and up like a stone post until at last the icicle above meets the post beneath. The trickling water also forms pools in the bottom of the cave, and in these pools of water live fish that are different from the fish in the water above ground. As it is pitch dark in the caves, these fish have no use for their eyes, so after long, long years they at last grew none. They are blind. Instead of seeing, they feel with the part of their heads where their eyes were.

13

The Covered Wagon

NOT so many years ago the Mississippi River was the far edge of the United States. Beyond the Mississippi it was wild, wilder, wilder-ness. Few people had ever been all the way across our country to the Pacific Ocean. There were wild Indians, wild animals, and high, high mountains in the way. Why did people want to go across the country anyway, and what sort of people were they? They were hunters who wanted to hunt wild animals, they were missionaries who wanted to make the Indians Christians, and they were people who were just inquisitive and who wanted to see what the wilderness was like.

Then one day a man told another, that another man had told him, that another man had told him, that still another man had told him that he had found gold in California, a land way off on the edge of the Pacific Ocean—plenty of gold; all you had to do was to dip it up in pans out of the rivers and pick it out of the sand and water.

Gold! Gold! It was almost as if some one had cried Fire! Fire! Thousands of people dropped their tools, stopped their farming, shut up their shops, loaded their beds and cooking things on wagons, put a cover over the wagon so that they could live under it as under a tent, took along a gun, and rushed for the Far West to hunt for gold. There were no roads, there were no bridges, there were no sign-boards to tell which was the right way—it was just wild, wilder, wilder-ness. For months and months they traveled. Many of them died of sickness, many were killed by the Indians, many were drowned in crossing rivers, many lost their way and died of starvation or of thirst —but many also, at last, reached California, found gold just where they heard it was to be found, and made

Loaded their beds and cooking things on wagons and started for the West

their fortunes. This was in the year 1849, so these people who went West were called "Forty-niners."

Since that time roads and railroads have been made all the way across the country; great cities have been built where once was only wilderness; and the wild Indians have been tamed. The United States has given the Indians large pieces of land to pay them for having taken other land away from them. These places given to the Indians are called "Reservations," because they are reserved for them, just as a seat in the theater that is reserved for a person is called a "reserved seat."

The first railroad to the Pacific coast took the middle route from Chicago to San Francisco. But you can now take a train from Chicago and cross to the Pacific by the north, middle, or south. It took months when the "Forty-niners" went across in their covered wagons, but now it takes less than one day by airplane.

People used to say, "Go West, Young Man, if you want to make a fortune," and many thousands did go West, not looking for gold, but for farm lands, which were given them free by the United States if they would raise crops. Some of these men who went to Oklahoma and Texas and other places, chiefly west of the Mississippi, found oil oozing out of the ground on their farms. This oil spoiled the land for farming and made the water unfit even for the horses and cows to drink. The land was ruined—no good—so many farmers gave up and moved away.

There are three kinds of oil in the World— vegetable, animal, and mineral. Did you ever play the game called Animal, Vegetable, and Mineral? It's a good game. The "Old Man" shouts, "Vegetable!" and you must name a vegetable, any vegetable—"potato," for instance— before he can count ten. Or he shouts, "Mineral!" or "Animal!" and you must name a mineral or an animal before he counts ten. In this game a mineral is anything that isn't animal or vegetable.

But no matter whether he says "Animal," "Vegetable," or "Mineral," you will always be right if you say, "Oil!" for it is one of the few things in the World that can be all three.

The oil from vegetables, like olive oil, and the oil from animals, like cod-liver oil, is good for food, but mineral oil from the rocks under the ground is not good for food. But some one found out that mineral oil could be burned to give light and heat, and then the automobile was invented, and from this mineral oil was made the gasoline to run automobiles. Many other things are now made from this kind of oil—medicine, colors for dyeing, and even perfumes.

People who thought their farms had been spoiled by oil found that the oil was worth a fortune, worth much more than what they could make out of chickens and pigs, or corn and wheat. Some wells had to be dug and the oil pumped up, but others sprouted up like fountains—these were called gushers.

This oil that comes out of the rock underneath the ground is called petroleum, which means rock oil. Some of the petroleum companies are nicknamed "Pete" for short, which is a pretty good name because Pete means "rock."

If you take a train by the middle route you cross Iowa, the Corn State, passing through endless fields of corn. You next cross Nebraska and gradually rise higher and higher as the ground slopes gently upward, until you reach the State called Colorado. Colorado means "color red." Colorado is at the foot of the highest mountains in America—they are called the Rocky Mountains. The capital of Colorado is Denver and Denver is just about half-way from Chicago to the Pacific Ocean.

Not so far from Denver you can climb to the top of a Rocky Mountain peak, if you want to and if you have a good heart. The first man who tried to climb this mountain was named Pike, but he gave it up, so ever since it has been called "Pike's Peak." When I was in school we used to try to say this "tongue-twister": "Speak Pike, Speak Pike, Speak Pike" over and over as fast as we could *without saying* "Pike's Peak." We couldn't do it—neither can you! Pike couldn't climb to the top of his mountain, but nowadays thousands of people climb to the top each year just as a "stunt" to see in how many hours they can do it. Pike's Peak is so high that there is snow on the top in the summer as well as in the winter, and it is so high in the air that there is very little air to breathe when you are at the top. A great many people cannot stand it at the top; they have to sit down. They gasp for breath as if they had been running, or like a fish out of water; their hearts beat fast and so hard they can hear it drumming in their ears, and they feel faint and weak. There are now an auto road and a railway up to the top, so that you don't have to climb Pike's Peak if you don't want to.

The railway track, however, is so steep that an ordinary railway car would slide down like a sled, so the track has small iron steps between the rails, and the car has a wheel that catches into the steps so that it cannot slip backward or run away down-hill—it walks up and down the steps.

14

Wonderland

"ALICE IN WONDERLAND" is a fairy-tale, but there is a real Wonderland out in the West. One of the wonders is a river. It is called the Colorado River, but it is not in the State of Colorado. It is in Arizona.

The river runs deep down in the bottom of the deepest ditch in the World, a ditch a mile deep in places. This ditch is called by the Spaniards a Canyon. You can stand on the edge of the Colorado Canyon and look almost a mile down to what seems a slender little thread of water—the Colorado River—running at the bottom, and yet this little stream has cut this ditch in which it runs —worn it down—all by itself. Here we can see, better than any place i.t.w.W., what the World looks like on the inside if we could dig down into it a mile deep, for here a little river has dug down a mile deep for us. I asked my guide how far it was across to the other side of the Canyon.

"Oh," he replied, "about ten or twelve shouts." That was a new distance to me, for I didn't even know how far one shout was. My arithmetic says twelve inches make a foot and three feet make a yard, but does not say how many feet make a "shout." You can look across to the other side of the Canyon and see the opposite wall almost a mile high—not a plain, blank wall like the wall of a building, but more like the walls of heaven —layers of rock, pile upon pile, colored yellow, red, green, orange, purple, mixed with sunshine and shadow. All of this rock was once under the sea, for it is limestone and sandstone. Each layer has been dyed a different color by minerals like iron and copper; if there was iron in the water, it turned the rock the color of iron rust—red; if copper, it turned the rock green.

GRAND CANYON

You can look almost a mile down

I once bought a souvenir pencil. In its end was a pinhole, and when you squinted into the hole with one eye, there you saw in all its vastness the Colorado Canyon. It seemed impossible, and yet there it was, stretching off in the distance, mile upon mile, in a picture the size of a pin head!

Some of the branches of the Colorado run in smaller canyons, and high up on the walls of these canyons are houses built in caves in the rock. Once upon a time, long, long ago, people whom we call "cliff-dwellers" built these homes there to be safe from their enemies.

A giant hop and skip north from the Grand

Canyon would bring one to the State of Utah, where there is a great lake, but this Great Lake is different from the five "Great Lakes." The water in the five Great Lakes is fresh, the water in this great lake is salt, so it is called Great Salt Lake, though it is really a little ocean. As in the case of the ocean, rivers run into the Great Salt Lake, but no rivers run out of it.

CLIFF
DWELLINGS

What makes it salt?

The same thing that makes the ocean salt.

What makes the ocean salt?

The ground through which rivers flow is salt. If you ever tasted the ground, you would know it, but, of course, I don't suppose you ever have, unless you have fallen and gotten some in your mouth or on your lips. Rivers, as they flow along, wash some of this salt out of the ground, carry it along, and dump it into the ocean. They carry so little salt at a time you would never know by tasting the river water that it was salt at all, but the rivers pour in this ever so little bit of salt all the time, all the time, and so the salt gradually does collect in the ocean and in Great Salt Lake, for there is no way for the salt to go out once it's in the ocean or the lake. The water gets out of the lake as it does out of the ocean—by rising into the air as vapor— evaporating, we call it—but the salt doesn't evaporate, it can't rise into the air, and so it has no way of getting out.

The Great Salt Lake is getting saltier and saltier all the time. It is already much saltier than the ocean. Salt water holds up a person or any- thing in it much better than fresh water, and the saltier the water the more it holds the person up. So in Great Salt Lake you couldn't drown whether you knew how to swim or not. You can stand in the water or sit in the water or lie down on the water as you would on a sofa. You can read the paper or eat your luncheon while sitting in the water, but you have to be very careful not to get any of the water in your eyes or in any small cut you may have on your hands or body, for the salt water is so strong it smarts. Some day the ocean will be as salty as Great Salt Lake, for the ocean too is slowly, very slowly, getting salt- ier and saltier all the time. Then, even if there were a shipwreck, people would not drown—they would bob about in the sea like corks.

Still farther north, a hop, skip, and a jump from the Colorado Canyon, in the corner of the State of Wyoming, is a place that looks on the map like a little State within the State. It is called Yellowstone Park. There are so many wonderful things in this part of the State—

freaks, funny things, and lovely things—that the
United States thought people would like to see
them, so they made a Park of this corner of the
State, with good roads and hotels, for people who
wish to see the sights. No hunting is allowed, so
wild animals and birds can live and raise families
without fear of being killed. There are bears in
Yellowstone Park, but as they are not allowed to
be hunted or shot, they become very tame and
people can even go close enough to photograph
them.

The World in that part of the country has not
yet cooled off altogether, and it is still very hot
not far down under the ground. If a person asked
me to have a glass of spring water, I should expect a nice cool drink; but if the spring were in
Yellowstone Park the water would probably
scald my throat, for there are hundreds of springs
in Yellowstone Park heated so hot by underground fires that they boil up and over like a pot
on the fire.

There is a big lake in Yellowstone Park called
Yellowstone Lake. You can stand on its edge
and catch a fish in the lake and, without taking
the fish off the hook, drop it into one of the hot
springs near shore and cook it. In other places the
water is blown up by the steam underneath into
fountains. These fountains are called "geysers,"
and some are quite big and some are quite beautiful. One called "Old Faithful" spouts regularly
about once every hour, throwing a beautiful

stream of water straight up into the air like a gigantic fire-hose. It does this so faithfully that it seems almost as if a person turned the water on and off, but it has been spouting this way ever since it has been known—never missing an hour, night or day, never forgetting, never running down, more faithful than any human being would or could be.

15

The 'Est, 'Est West

A LAND where they have the b-est, the bigg-est, the fin-est, the high-est, the loveli-est of everything—so they say—the b*est* oranges, the bigg*est* prunes, the fin*est* grapes, the tall*est* trees, the high*est* mountains, the loveli*est* weather—i.t. w.W. No, it's not Paradise. That's the 'est, 'est West.

California was named after an island in an old fairy-tale and in many ways the real California is a fairy-tale land. When gold was found in the rivers there, the story sounded like a fairy-tale, but it turned out to be a true tale. Many stories they tell nowadays about California still sound like fairy-tales to people in the East. Who would believe that there are trees in California so tall they seem to brush the sky—trees so big around that men have cut tunnels in them for automobiles to go through—trees so old that they were born before Christ was born! It's true, there are. They are called Giant Redwoods. How more wonderful than a fairy-tale it would be if those trees could tell us the true story of what has happened in their long lives!

Let us see how many 'ests we can count in California.

California is the long*est* State in the United States. If you could take up California and put it down on the Atlantic coast it would stretch from Florida to New York. That's one 'est.

California has the high*est* mountain in the United States. It is called Mount Whitney. That's two 'ests.

California has the lowest place in America. It's a valley, and the valley is more than two hundred feet lower than the ocean. It is so dry and so hot down in this hollow—this lowest spot —that nothing can live there, either animal or vegetable, except horned toads and lizards, both of which animals love heat—the more heat the better for them. Some people say they can even live in fire—but that's a fairy-tale. This low hot valley is called Death Valley. People usually keep away from it, but some men have strayed into it looking for gold and have lost their way, or some who wanted to get to the other side tried to cross it and before they could get out or reach the other side they have died of heat or thirst. That's why it is called Death Valley. That's longest, highest, lowest—three 'ests.

Besides Death Valley, California has another valley—but this is one of the loveli*est* valleys. It is called the Yosemite. It is a very deep trough, and streams of water fall over the edge into the trough from many high places. One of these falls turns to mist before it reaches the ground and looks like a huge veil of a bride, so it is called Bridal Veil Falls. Half a dozen of these water-falls in the Yosemite Valley are higher than Niagara, and two of them tumble headlong a quarter of a mile from the top to the bottom of the valley, the highest falls in America—loveliest valley, highest falls; that makes two more 'ests.

California has, beside these 'ests, the sweet*est* oranges, the sour*est* lemons, the bigg*est* grape-fruit, so they say, but they didn't *come* from California; they *went* there. There were no oranges and no lemons growing in America at all before white men came to this country. The first white people to settle in California came from the country of Spain on the other side of the Atlantic Ocean. In Spain oranges and lemons grew, and the people from Spain, called Spaniards, brought over orange and lemon plants and started them growing in California and also in Florida.

The Spaniards built houses like those back in Spain, with white stucco walls and red tile roofs and with the "back yards" in the center of the house. They gave their cities Spanish names—Los Angeles, which means The Angels; and they named many of their cities after saints—San Francisco after St. Francis, Santa Barbara after St. Barbara—for many of the Spaniards were priests, who built mission churches up and down the land.

The City of the Angels is now the largest city
on the Pacific coast. Near the City of the Angels
is Hollywood, the great*est* (another 'est) moving-picture place i.t.w.W. There are 365 days
in the year, as you know, but in Hollywood they
say the sun shines on 400 days a year—fairy-tale
land! At any rate, the weather is fine most of the
time for taking moving pictures. This is one reason why it is such a good place for making movies,
but another is that there are so many different

Hollywood is the greatest moving-picture place
in the wide World

kinds of natural scenery near-by. If they want
to make a picture of a ship scene or shipwreck,
there is the ocean. If they want to make a picture
of the desert with camels and Arabs, there is the
seashore. If they want to make a picture in the
hot countries, there are palms and flowers. If
they want to make pictures of winter scenes, all
they have to do is to go to the mountains near-by
and there is snow and ice all the year round.

The city of San Francisco on the coast north of Los Angeles is nearly as large as Los Angeles. It might have been larger, but not so many years ago a terrible earthquake shook down the city. The quake only lasted a few minutes, but in that few minutes it rocked the city, cracked open the ground, and knocked down buildings as if they were houses of children's blocks, and hundreds and hundreds of people were killed. But the worst thing the earthquake did was to upset stoves and lamps that started one of the worst fires ever known—fires that burned up most of the city. Were the people discouraged? Not at all. They collected their insurance money—and they built the city up again.

San Francisco has one of the finest harbors in the World. Its harbor is a long bay—fifty miles long. Ships enter the harbor from the Pacific Ocean through an opening called the Golden Gate. The city is built on many hills so steep that it is difficult for automobiles to climb them, but houses built on them have lovely views of the ocean, the bay, or the Golden Gate. Across the Golden Gate is a huge suspension bridge much bigger than the Brooklyn Bridge.

Ships enter and leave San Francisco for all the countries on and across the Pacific Ocean. Across the Pacific Ocean are China and Japan, and in days gone by so many Chinese came to the United States and landed in San Francisco that there is a part of the city called Chinatown, where there are Chinese houses and shops and theaters. Many Japanese too came to the United States from Japan, and bought farms where they raised fruits and vegetables.

16

The 'Est, 'Est West
(*continued*)

HERE is a riddle for you. What is it that has no legs and yet can jump as high as the Washington Monument? I'll tell you the answer in a minute.

What is it that can jump as high as the Washington Monument?

Between Oregon and Washington is a river named Columbia, after Columbus. In the Columbia River are large fish called salmon. Salmon live in the salt ocean, but when Mrs. Salmon wants to lay her eggs she goes way up the Columbia River, far above the falls to fresh water, looking for a quiet place to do so. How can she get by the falls? She jumps the falls. You may wonder how fish without legs can jump at all, and it is peculiar that they can, but they do. They bend their tails into a kind of spring, then flip!— up they go; for a salmon can jump as high as the Washington Monument.

"Are the falls as high as the Washington Monument?"

"No, they are all low."

"But you said a salmon could jump as high as the Washington Monument."

"A salmon *can,* for the Washington Monument can't jump at all!"

Millions of salmon together called "schools" swim up the river and fishermen catch them in nets, but they leave most of them so that they can lay eggs from which little salmon are born, and the little salmon swim down the river and out into the ocean, where they live and grow up until it comes time for them also to lay eggs, and then they in their turn swim up the river, jump up the falls, and are either caught or left to raise more families of little salmon. Salmon meat is pink; we call it salmon color. It is packed in cans. You have probably eaten salmon from the Columbia River yourself.

The oldest fruit in the World is the apple. It is the fruit that grew in the Garden of Eden, but people believe the apple that Eve gave Adam was a very poor one compared to the apples that grow in the State of Washington. People in Washington, D. C.—all the way across the country—buy apples that have been shipped from Washington State—3,000 miles away—for they are so much better than ordinary apples. They are "skookum." That's what the Indians of the

Northwest call something very nice—whether it is a girl or an apple.

There are great forests in Washington and Oregon. The forest trees are cut down to make lumber for building houses; and the paper I am writing on was made from trees that grew in Oregon. How do I know that? When I hold the paper up to the light, there is printed in white —we call it a watermark —the word "Oregon."

"Skookum"

At the northwest corner of America is a large country that belongs to the United States and yet it is not a State. It is called a Territory. It is Alaska. The highest mountain in North America is there. It is called Mount McKinley. Alaska is so cold, so far off, and so hard to get to, and yet the United States bought it and paid millions of dollars for it, not because it had the highest mountain, but chiefly because of the fish in its waters and the fur on its animals, and then one day gold was discovered there.

Gold is a magic word. Again, as in the days of the Forty-niners, thousands of people, when they heard of the gold, left everything and, with nothing but shovels to dig the gold and sieves to strain it out of the water, started off to that far-away place, hoping to make their fortunes be-

fore the new year. Many foolishly went off with
nothing to live on after they reached Alaska.
They didn't seem to know that where the gold
was to be found there was no food, nothing to
eat, and no stores where one
could buy food. Others, more
wise, carried cans of food with
them, and when the foolish
gold-diggers had found gold,
the wise ones sold them food
for their gold. For a can of
beans they often asked hundreds of times what it had cost,
and the foolish gold-diggers
had to pay it or starve, for
they couldn't eat gold and they
had to eat or die. So the wise
ones came back with the gold
which the foolish ones had dug,
and the foolish ones were lucky
to get back at all.

Totem Poles

In the parts of Alaska where
fish can be caught for food,
Indians live in small villages. In the center
of each village they put up a tall pole carved
and painted in the forms of birds and animals
with big ugly faces. These are called Totem
Poles. Each tribe or family has some bird or
animal such as an eagle or a bear for its mascot,
as you might call your club "the Lions" or "the
Owls," and the Totem Pole is the tribe's sign.

If you should suddenly see at night the whole northern sky hung with curtains of fire and ablaze with flashing flames shooting from the ground far up into the heavens, you might think, as I did the first time I saw it when a boy, that the World was coming to an end. It looked as if the World were on fire and were about to explode. This amazing sight is called the Aurora Borealis or Northern Light, and it may be seen often in Alaska and sometimes, though perhaps only once or twice in a lifetime, much farther south. It is a terrifying sight to those who have never seen or even heard of such a thing before, and yet the Aurora Borealis does no more harm than a beautiful sunset or a rainbow in the sky.

What causes the Aurora Borealis? That's a hard question to answer. Electricity has something to do with it and so have sun spots. Have you ever heard of sun spots? Sometimes a dark spot will appear on the sun and move slowly across it. You can't see sun spots because the sun is much too bright to be stared at. But men who look through telescopes with darkened glass to protect their eyes can see these spots and they can photograph them with special cameras. After a sun spot appears on the sun there is usually a very bright Aurora Borealis.

That's all I can tell you. A little girl once asked, "What is a thought made of?" That's a hard question to answer too.

17

Next-door Neighbors

THERE is a saying that "Good fences make good neighbors," but that depends on the neighbors. North of the United States is a country bigger than the United States called Canada. It stretches across America from sea to sea, from the Atlantic to the Pacific, and there would have to be a fence 3,000 miles long if there were a fence, but there is none—nothing but an imaginary line. An imaginary line is a line on the map but not on the ground. On this imaginary line the two countries set up a stone on which they said something like this, "Canada and the United States agree never to fight"; that's all—a gentlemen's agreement. It is called the "Peace Stone."

Boys often say "findings is keepings." The French people found Canada, but England thought she had a better right to it, so she fought for it and took it away from the French. That was a long time ago, but there are a great many French still in Canada, and in the city of Quebec more people speak French than English.

I once had a Newfoundland dog. He was woolly and big and ate as much as a man. New-

foundland dogs came from an island on the Atlantic side of Canada which an Englishman
found, and so he called it New-found-land. Newfoundland is now a part of Canada.

Just off the coast of Newfoundland is a shallow part of the sea called the Grand Banks. But
the Banks are under the water. It is a great fishing ground, but men go fishing there, not for
pleasure, but for business. Thousands of small
boats go off and stay off and do not return until
they have caught all the fish they can carry. It is
often very foggy on the Grand Banks, and sometimes big ocean steamships coming over from
across the Atlantic Ocean cannot see the small
fishing boats and run into them and sink them
with all on board.

Canada is big in size but small in number of
people. There are not as many people in all of
Canada as there are in the State of New York.
Most of the people in Canada live as close along
the edge of the United States as they can, because it gets very cold in winter farther north
than that. Close to the United States people do
pretty nearly the same things and raise the same
things as people south of the border in the
United States. For instance, Canada raises more
wheat than any other country in the World except the United States.

One of the biggest concerns in Canada is a railroad company called the Canadian Pacific. The
railroad runs all the way across Canada from the

Atlantic Ocean to Vancouver on the west coast of Canada. But it doesn't stop at the Oceans. It has big steamers that cross the Atlantic Ocean and it has big steamers that cross the Pacific Ocean. The Canadian Pacific owns all the hotels along the railroad, too. Along one part of the railroad there is very wonderful scenery—beautiful mountains and lakes. Lake Louise, in the Rocky Mountains, is so beautiful that many people go there on their vacations or on their wedding journeys.

No woman likes a wild animal such as a fox or wolf close to her, but as soon as the animals are dead she loves their skins close to her and will pay high prices to get them. There is a big bay in Canada, almost as big as the Gulf of Mexico; it is called Hudson Bay and named after the man who discovered it. He is the same man who discovered the Hudson River, but Hudson Bay and Hudson River have no other connection. Hudson Bay is filled with ice all winter long, and all around Hudson Bay the winters are so cold that men do not live there unless they have to. The chief reason some men do live there is to hunt animals. The animals in that cold country can't buy overcoats, so they grow overcoats on themselves—fur overcoats, which are the very best kind of overcoats. Hunters trap and kill wolves, foxes, and other animals, skin them of their overcoats, and sell them to ladies who can pay big prices for them. This company of people who

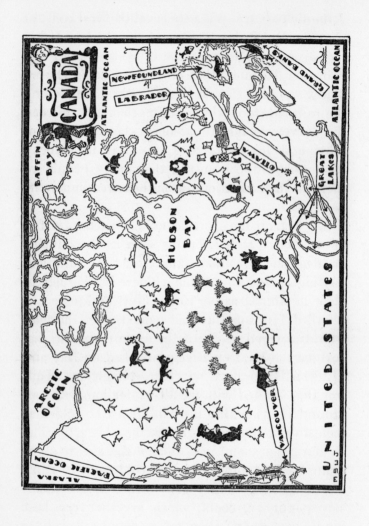

trap animals and sell furs is called the Hudson's Bay Company.

As we have States, Canada has provinces, but there are only ten provinces in Canada. The chief one is called Ontario, after Lake Ontario. Ontario, however, borders all the other Great Lakes too, except Michigan. In Ontario is the capital of Canada. It is called Ottawa. England sends a man across the ocean to Canada, called the Governor-General, but the people in Canada send men to Ottawa to make their own laws.

As you go north in Canada the country gets colder and colder, till at last it gets so cold that it is too cold even for trees to grow. The trees that grow farthest north hold their leaves and stay green the year round like the pine and spruce. They are called "evergreens." The wood of evergreens is soft. The trees that cannot grow as far north as evergreens drop their leaves in the winter, like the oak and maple. Their wood is usually hard. The hard-wood trees are used chiefly to make furniture, but the soft-wood trees are ground up to make paper.

The paper on which this book and almost every other book is printed and all the paper used for newspapers is made from wood. A great city newspaper will use up many acres of trees in a single day. It takes as many trees as grow in a space the size of a city block to feed a single paper a single day. So you see how fast trees are being cut down in Canada to keep the presses in the United States going. Day after day miles upon miles of trees are cut down, ground into pulp, made into paper, and shipped to us in large rolls, that we may have the news—only to be burned up the day after. As people are fed wheat, and animals corn, printing presses must be fed trees for their daily meal, year in and year out, without ceasing.

One of the first geography lessons I ever had was about Eskimos, who lived in snow houses and fished through a hole in the ice. One of the homes of the Eskimos is Labrador on the northeastern corner of Canada. The Eskimos are related to the Indians, and both are very distantly related to the Chinese, but I'll tell you more about them later.

18

The War-God's Country

TOMMY TINKER was eating a slice of bread
and butter. He was biting it very carefully round
the edges and between bites he looked at it
thoughtfully.

"What in the world are you doing!" asked his
father.

"I'm biting a map of North America," replied
Tommy. He placed it carefully on the table-
cloth. "There's Alaska on this corner, Labrador
on this corner, Florida on this corner, and Yucatan opposite it." Then he rolled out a little tail
of bread and placed it on the other corner. "And
there's Lower California."

"I ought to send you from the table for playing with your food," said his father; "but I
won't if you can tell me where the Gulf of California is."

"It's *not* in California," said Tommy. "You
didn't catch me that time. It's in Mexico and
so is Lower California too—both are in Mexico."

"Right," said his father. "When I was a boy
my teacher asked me where the Gulf of California and Lower California were and, though I

hadn't studied my lesson, I answered 'California,' for I felt sure that must be right."

"Did your teacher ever show you this one?" asked Tommy. He curved the finger and thumb of his left hand to form the letter "G." *"G* is for Gulf of Mexico," he said. "My finger is Florida, my thumb is Yucatan and here is Mexico. Do you see it?"

"They didn't teach me geography that way when I went to school," said his father.

"They don't now," said Tommy. "I made that up myself."

Perhaps you have heard people speak of some place as "God's Country." Well, the country just south of the United States is named "God's Country," but it is the War God's Country. It is called Mexico after the Indians' God of War, Mexitli.

When you cross the line from the United

States to Canada you hardly know you are in another country—the people are the same, they talk the same language. But when you cross the line from the United States to Mexico you *do* know you are in another country—the people are different and they talk a different language. Mexico used to belong to Spain across the Atlantic; it now belongs to itself.

I told you there was a Peace Stone on the Canada line and that Canada and the United States agreed long ago never to fight each other. There is no peace stone on the Mexican border line and there have been many fights between the United States and Mexico. Our States of Texas, New Mexico, and Arizona once belonged to Mexico. Between Texas and Mexico is a river called the Rio Grande, which means River Grand or Grand River. The Rio Grande runs through such a dry country, however, that part of the time there is no river, only a dry place where the river did run, so that people can walk right across from the United States to Mexico in certain places, or at certain times of the year.

When the white people came to America there were Indians living all over our country. The white people pushed the Indians farther and farther off to the corners and out-of-the-way places until now there are so few Indians in the United States that many boys and girls have never seen an Indian except in the circus or on the 5-cent piece. When the white people came to Mexico there were Indians living all over that country too, but in Mexico there still are more Indians now living than there are white people. Many of the white Spanish people have married Indians, so some Mexicans are Spanish, more are Indian, and still more are mixed Spanish and Indian.

The people in the United States speak English and do many things as the people in England do. The people who came to Mexico were white people from Spain. So they speak Spanish and do many things as the people in Spain do.

When the Spanish first came to Mexico they found the Indians there wearing silver necklaces and silver bracelets and silver ornaments, so they knew there must be silver in Mexico. The Spaniards were really looking for gold, but silver was next best, so they set to work to dig for silver and they are still doing so, and even now, more than 400 years after white people came to Mexico more silver is mined there than anywhere else i.t.w.W. except the United States. Silver mines are in the mountains, the same chain of mountains as the Rocky Mountains in the United States, only in Mexico they are called Sierra Madre.

Up in the Sierra Madre Mountains, in a bowl-shaped valley, is the capital of Mexico. It is called Mexico City, so you don't have to learn a new name. The farther north you go the colder it gets, but not always. The farther south you go the warmer it gets, but not always. But the higher

up you go in the mountains the colder it gets—
always. Mexico City is so far south you would
think it would be very hot, but it is not, because
it is so high up in the mountains. They have mild
weather in Mexico City all the year round.

Near Mexico City is an old volcano with the
peculiar name: Po-poca-tepetl. It sounds something like Po-poca-teakettle. Why didn't they

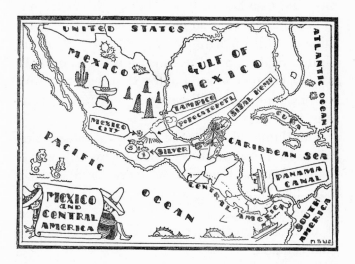

give it an easy name, you may wonder. They did,
for in the language of the Indians who named it,
Popocatepetl means "smoking mountain." Popocatepetl is so far south we should expect it to
be warm, but it is so high that its top is cold and
is covered with snow all the year round. Popocatepetl is no longer firing up, but clouds of sulphur smoke pour out of it all the time and sulphur collects in its mouth. Indian workmen climb

up the sides of Popocatepetl and climb down inside to get the sulphur, which is used in making matches and medicine and other things.

On the Gulf side of Mexico, along the shore, it is very warm indeed, very damp and unhealthful, so no one would live there if he didn't have to; but great lakes of oil were found down under the ground, along the shore near a city called Tampico, and men have dug wells through the ground to get the oil. It is so close to the sea that tank ships can fill up with the oil and carry it to the United States and other places in the World. It is much cheaper to send oil by ship than by train, for one tank ship will carry as much as a thousand tank cars.

The thumb-like piece of Mexico is called Yucatan. In Yucatan grows a plant with tall sword-shaped leaves. From these leaves a fiber that looks like long gray hair, called sisal, is obtained. It is used to make rope and twine. From the juice of another plant that grows in Yucatan, chewing-gum is made.

19

So Near and Yet so Far

N-A-M-E-R-I-C-A and S-A-M-E-R-I-C-A
are two names printed in large letters across my
map of North America and South America.
Namerica and Samerica sound like brothers:
Nam and Sam Erica. They look as if the Creator had pulled them just as far apart as He could
without pulling them quite in two. They are held
together by a little piece of land called Central
America, and the very thinnest part of Central
America—the part as thin as a leaf stem—is
called the Isthmus of Panama: spelled "isthmus,"
but sounded "ismus."

On one side of the Isthmus is the Atlantic and
on the other side the Pacific Ocean, so near to
each other and yet so far. Ships that wanted to
get from one ocean to the other couldn't get
across this little strip of land—they had to go
the long way round, all the way round the bottom of Samerica, thousands of miles out of the
way. There was no way at all round the top of
Namerica, for both land and ice were in the way
up there. It seemed a terribly long distance for
a ship to have to go just because it couldn't cross
this little strip of land. It was as if you were

motoring and the road came to a river and there was no bridge, and a sign said "Detour 10,000 miles." It was the longest detour i.t.w.W. Naturally, people tried to find a way not to make that detour. Some men suggested wheeling ships across the Isthmus. They said, "Let us lift a ship out of the water on a kind of huge elevator, then put it on a huge truck, push it across the Isthmus to the other ocean, then lower it into the water again by another huge elevator." But it seemed simpler to cut a canal across the Isthmus so that a ship might sail straight through from one ocean to the other. On the map this looked easy enough—just a snip with the scissors or a nick with a knife; but that little stem of land was over thirty miles across and there were mountains in the way too.

They have many earthquakes in Central America, and if one of these earthquakes had only cracked the Isthmus of Panama across and broken Namerica and Samerica apart it would have been very convenient; but earthquakes don't do helpful things like that—they make cracks where you don't want them.

Why did ships want to get from one ocean to the other, anyway? Why shouldn't those on one side stay on that side, and those on the other side stay on the other side? Well—your mother goes downtown shopping for things to wear and things to eat and furniture for the house; so ships go shopping—shipping, shopping—around the

World. Ships from the countries around the Atlantic Ocean go shopping to countries around the
Pacific Ocean for tea and China dishes and silk
stockings. And ships from countries around the
Pacific Ocean go shopping to the countries
around the Atlantic Ocean for things they want
and haven't got. That's one reason why ships
wanted to get from one ocean to the other, and
they didn't want to go the long way round, ten
thousand miles out of the way, if they could pos-
sibly help it. So at last a company of men from
France on the other side of the ocean, who knew
how to dig canals—for they had already dug a
long canal—started to dig a canal across the
Isthmus.

Now the Isthmus of Panama used to be the
most *un*healthful place i.t.w.W. The Indians and
black men who lived there didn't seem to mind
it, but with white men it was different. One out
of every three white men who went there died
of fever. The company of men from France set
to work and worked for several years on the
canal, but so many of their men died and so much
money was spent and so little canal was dug that
at last they gave it up, stopped digging.

Later the United States rented from the little
country of Panama a piece of land forever, a
piece of land ten miles wide like a belt right across
the Isthmus. This belt of land is called the Canal
Zone. But before the United States started to
dig the canal they said, "We must make the

Canal Zone a healthful and fit place for white people to work so that they won't die as soon as we send them down there." So they sent a famous doctor down to the Canal Zone to see if he could make the Zone a more healthful place for white men to live in.

This doctor found out that what made the Isthmus so unhealthful was—what do you suppose? —nothing but little mosquitos. These mosquitos were different, however, from those we have that merely leave an itchy spot where they bite. The mosquitos down there were of an entirely different kind. Some of them were town mosquitos and some were country mosquitos. The country mosquitos gave people malaria, which was bad enough, but the worst kind of mosquitos were the town mosquitos. They gave people a terrible disease called yellow fever—a disease that turned people yellow and killed almost every one who caught it. So the doctor said I'll find out how to get rid of the mosquitos and keep them from killing the people. Accordingly, he went after the mosquitos first, and this is the way he killed them. The town mosquitos he killed with sulphur smoke—sulphur from Popocatepetl— and the country mosquitos he killed with oil—oil from Mexico too. Then he cleaned up the marshes and other places where the mosquitos lived and raised their enormous families, so that they had no place to live, and in these ways he changed the Canal Zone from the most unhealthful place i.t.w.W. to one of the most healthful places i.t.w.W.

Then, and not until then, the United States went ahead and made the Canal. They didn't cut the land straight through, however, as the French had started to do, so that the Atlantic and Pacific could run together—that would have meant too much digging, even with dynamite, for dynamite blows up land, and the land has to be carried away after it is blown up. So the United States dug a ditch across the Isthmus on top of the land and used a river and a lake already there to keep this ditch filled with water. At each end of this ditch or canal they made locks to raise ships from the sea at one end, and to lower them to the sea at the other. So ships now go across from one ocean to the other, but most of the way they sail on fresh water, for neither ocean runs into the other. Namerica and Samerica are not cut apart —they are still joined and always will be, until the Creator does the separating.

20

Pirate Seas

I WAS once on a train leaving Baltimore when a man asked me where I was going. I told him I was going to Baltimore. He looked at me as if I must have made a mistake and exclaimed, "You are on the wrong train; this train is *leaving* Baltimore."

"I know that," I replied, "but I'm going to Baltimore the long way round, round the World to Baltimore. I'm going west to get east."

On the other side of the World from us are some islands called "The Indies." People had always gone to the Indies, far, far away, by traveling toward the east. Columbus thought he could go in just the opposite direction—toward the west—and reach the Indies that way. People said it was foolish to go west to get east, but Columbus believed the World was round, and if it were round he knew he could get to these islands by going west just as well as by going east. So he sailed, and he sailed, and he sailed, always toward the setting sun, and at last he did come to some islands. He thought these islands were the Indies, so he named them the "West Indies." As a matter of fact, we know, but he didn't know, that he hadn't gone half far enough to reach the Indies. He didn't know that even if he had gone on farther, Central America would have been in the way, anyway.

Living on these islands were men with red skins, painted faces, and feathers in their hair, and Columbus called them Indians. Other people called these Indians "Caribs," which means "brave," because they were brave, and the blue sea which surrounded these islands they called the Caribbean Sea—the sea of the Caribs.

Columbus was looking for a new *way* and he found it, but after Columbus other men came along looking for gold and silver and they found that. Some they found in Mexico and some they found in South America, and some they took away from the Indians who had already found it. They robbed them, that's all. This gold and silver —treasure—found and stolen, they loaded on ships and started back to Spain.

But many of those ships bearing treasure never reached Spain. Pirates—sea robbers—lay in wait to rob the land robbers. It was better sport to rob robbers than to rob the poor Indians. These pirates were bold and bad and cold and cruel. They wore blood-red sashes round their waists, blood-red handkerchiefs round their necks, and blood-red handkerchiefs round their heads. They hung huge rings in their ears and huge bracelets on their arms, and they were "armed to the teeth"—whatever that means. They hid behind these little islands in the Caribbean Sea, and when they saw a treasure ship coming from afar they hoisted a black flag to their ship's mast, a flag with a skull and two bones crossed on it, and sailed forth and captured the ship, its treasures, and its crew. They made the crew slaves, or if the pirates didn't want any more slaves, they made their captives "walk the plank" —that is, walk blindfolded out on a plank set over the ship's edge. They would reach the end and suddenly step off into the sea and be drowned. Then the pirate would load the treasure he had captured into a huge iron-bound chest, sail back to his little island, and bury the treasure chest in a hole in the sand. He would mark the spot on a map with an X so that he might find it when he wanted it, and so that no one else could find it.

These pirates are gone long years ago, and the ships that sail the blue Caribbean have now no fear of pirates any more, and few of these ships carry anything that pirates would want. But the sea is so blue and the weather so warm and the islands so lovely that many people make voyages to the Pirate Seas just for pleasure. I did once myself.

I left New York when it was snowing and in two days I was on an island called Bermuda, where it was warm and sunny. Easter lilies were growing in the fields, and new potatoes and onions. Farmers were raising them to send to

shivering New York so that Americans might
have warm-weather flowers and warm-weather
vegetables long before warm weather itself came.

Another two days' sailing south and I was on
another island called Nassau, the capital of a
group of islands called the Bahamas. In Nassau
sponges are gathered from the bottom of the
sea and sent back to U.S. for US to USe.
Would you believe that the sponges you use were
once alive? They were once like jelly with the
sponge inside. Men dive down into the sea and
tear the live sponges off the rocks where they
grow. Then they wash off the jelly-like part and
what is left is the sponge.

Another one of the Bahama Islands is the little
island on which Columbus first landed—the most
famous little island i.t.w.W. A monument marks
the spot where he stepped out of his little boat
after his long voyage across the ocean, kneeled
down in the sand, and thanked God for directing
him safely to the New World. He called the island after his Saviour, "Holy Saviour," which in
Spanish is San Salvador.

There are three large islands of the West Indies—tit-tat-to, three in a row. There is also another island a little smaller, and many, many
very small islands besides in the Caribbean
Sea.

The largest island of all the West Indies—
the first one of the tit-tat-to, three in a row islands—is Cuba. Columbus found the Indians in

Cuba carrying burning torches in their mouths. They breathed in the smoke and blew it out again in a most strange and amazing fashion, as if they were dragons. It seemed an extraordinary thing for people to do—to breathe in smoke of a burning weed, for that was what it was; yet they seemed to enjoy it. No one across the water had ever seen such a sight before—people breathing fire. But now people all over the World copy the red Indians of Cuba. The weed was called tobacco. Tobacco is now grown in many parts of the World, but the finest tobacco i.t.w.W. for cigars still grows in Cuba, and Havana, the capital of Cuba, ships "Havana" cigars everywhere.

People from Spain went to live in Cuba and Cuba belonged to Spain until not so many years ago, but now Cuba belongs to itself.

Almost all vegetables and fruits in the World have sugar in their juice; they are sweet. Some have a great deal, some have very little. But two vegetables have such sweet juice that they are raised for the sugar that can be made out of their juice. These vegetables are the beet and sugarcane. You know what a beet looks like. Sugarcane looks something like stalks of corn. Men press the juice out of the cane and boil it to make sugar. In Cuba they grow more sugar-cane than any other place i.t.w.W.

The Island of Haiti—the tat of the tit-tat-to islands—although it is not large, has two little countries on it. Both these countries are republics like the United States, with presidents and senators and representatives chosen by the people, but their presidents are colored and their senators and representatives are also colored. That may seem strange until I tell you that the people on the island are colored too.

When Columbus died he was buried on this island of Haiti. Many years after, men dug up what they thought were Columbus's bones and sent them back to Spain, where they are kept in a great cathedral. But many people say they were not Columbus's bones at all that they took back, but some one else's, and that Columbus's body still lies in Haiti.

Puerto Rico, the third of the tit-tat-to islands of the West Indies, belongs to the United States. In Puerto Rico they raise tobacco too, but there seems to be some difference in the land, for they can't seem to raise quite as good tobacco as the people in Cuba do.

Jamaica is a small island south of the tit-tat-to islands. It belongs to England. In Jamaica they grow many of the bananas that we eat. They are picked when they are still green, but by the time they have been shipped to the United States and are put in the fruit shops on sale they are yellow and ripe—sometimes. If you eat them before they are ripe, you may need a little Jamaica ginger, which is good for "tummy aches"—that comes from Jamaica too.

Tobacco and sugar, sponges and early vegetables, bananas and lilies!—pirates would have
turned up their noses in disgust if they had captured a ship laden with such a cargo!

21

North South America

SOUTH AMERICA looks like a carrot, a turnip, a top, a funnel, a leaf, a fig, a pear turned upside down, a paddle, a lamb chop, a leg of mutton, an ice-cream cone—but the only thing it really looks like is: South America. The stem is Panama; the hook at the bottom is called Cape Horn.

From the tip top to the tip toe of South America, from Panama to Cape Horn, stretches a long wall of high mountains called the Andes. It is the highest range of mountains in the Western Half Ball, and it is the longest range of mountains i.t.w.W.

Columbus, who discovered America, had only one country named after him. This country is in South America nearest Panama, nearest the stem by which South America seems to hang to Central America. It is called Colombia, spelled with two o's instead of an "o" and a "u."

When white men first came to the northern shore of South America they found a land next to Colombia where the Indians lived in houses built on stakes in the water. This reminded them of a city in Italy across the ocean, called Venice, where the houses are built in the water, so they named this new country Little Venice, which in the Spanish language is Venezuela. Off the shore of Venezuela is a peculiar island called Trinidad. On this island is a lake—but the lake has no water in it. Instead of water there is a kind of tar called asphalt. This asphalt is dug up and loaded on to ships and brought to the United States to make roadways.

The three little countries next door to Venezuela are called the three Guianas. They belong to three different countries in Europe. In fact, they are the only countries in South America that do belong to countries outside of South America. The first Guiana belongs to England, the second belongs to Holland, the third belongs to France.

In British Guiana far back in the wilds is a waterfall nearly five times as high as Niagara, yet so far away from everything that hardly any white men have ever seen it or even heard of it. It's name is Kaieteur. Just for fun ask your father if he knows what Kaieteur is.

The line around the middle of the World, if there were a line—which there isn't—is like the belt around a very fat man. It is called the Equator. The Spanish for Equator is Ecuador. Ecuador is also the name of a little country in South America that straddles the Equator. We should expect it to be very hot there, for the nearer the Equator one goes the hotter it usually gets; but most of Ecuador is high up in the Andes Mountains, so high up that it is quite cool all the year round. The capital of Ecuador is Quito, pronounced Key-toe. From Quito you can see two of the highest volcanoes in the World. They have

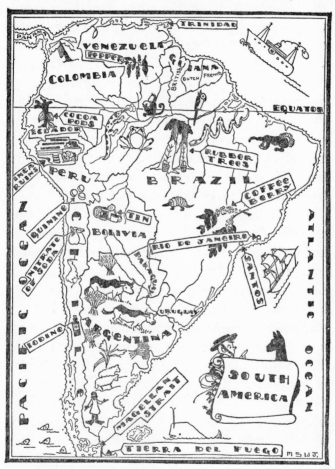

names that sound strange to us; both begin with "C." Chimborazo is the name of the higher, but it no longer smokes or sends forth fire. The other is Cotopaxi, not quite so high but still very much alive, for fires inside have not gone out.

It seems strange that from this far country in the mountains, from Ecuador, something comes which you eat or drink, perhaps every day—chocolate and cocoa. They are both made from beans which grow in a large pod—a pod as big as a melon. These pods grow, not on branches, but right on the trunk of the tree. This tree is called the ca-ca-o tree. Notice how cocoa and cacao are spelled: See-o see-o-a comes from the see-a see-a-o-tree. Cocoa does not come from the cocoanut-tree. The cocoanut-tree is an entirely different tree that bears cocoanuts but not cocoa.

The Indians of Ecuador are very wild and savage. They are called head-hunters. One family or tribe will fight another tribe whenever they want something they haven't got—wives, perhaps—or simply because they want to fight. When they kill a man they cut off his head and save it for a souvenir, as the American Indians used to cut off a man's scalp and save it as a souvenir or trophy. The Indian who has the greatest number of heads is considered the greatest fighter. They often fight, not with bows and arrows, but with huge blow-pipes—as long as a man—using clay balls or little darts which have been dipped in poison. With these blow-pipes they can kill men and animals. These savage Indians catch fish for food, not with a line or net, but by putting poison in the streams where the fish are. The poison kills the fish and they float on the top, but it doesn't spoil them for eating.

The Indians of Ecuador are the most savage Indians now known, but in the country just south of Ecuador, in the country called Peru, once lived the most civilized Indians ever known. They lived not in tents or wigwams or huts, but in palaces, and they were very intelligent and very rich. They were called Incas and their capital was named Cuzco. The Incas had great treasures of gold and silver, and when the Spaniards first came to South America looking for gold or silver they found it in Cuzco already mined. All they had to do was to take it away from the Incas. This was easy because the Spaniards had guns, and the Incas, who had no such thing, were no match for them in a fight. So the Spaniards won and simply helped themselves to the gold, and made the Incas work in the mines for more. However, the joke was on the Spaniards, for many of their ships sailing back to Spain with their stolen treasure were captured by the pirates.

Many of the Spaniards who stayed in Peru married Indian women, so now most of the people in Peru are a mixture of Spanish and Indian.

There is little left of Cuzco, except ruins of the old Inca palaces. The present capital of Peru is Lima, but Lima beans don't come from there. A medicine that is often given for fever does come from Peru, however. The Indians found that the bark of a certain tree when stewed in water made a kind of tea that was good for fever. When the white man came, he found it was good for fever too. So now the bark of this tree is gathered and sent to other countries to be used in making medicine to cure fevers. The medicine is called quinine.

The little llama carries big loads in the Andes

In the United States loads are usually carried on freight trains or trucks but in the Andes Mountains they are usually carried on the backs of a little animal called a llama. A llama is something like a small camel without a hump.

Have you ever heard of a man named Simon Bolivar? Probably not, but in South America every boy and girl knows him as you know George Washington. In fact, he is often called the George Washington of South America. Just as England once owned the thirteen colonies, Spain once owned a great part of South America. Then this man Bolivar, Simon Bolivar, who lived in Venezuela, thought, as a great many others did, that Spain was not treating his country right. Bolivar had been in the United States and had heard how the United States once belonged to England and how George Washington had led the revolution against England until the United States belonged to itself. So Bolivar went back to South America and started a revolution to make his country and other countries of South America independent of Spain. He had a very hard time of it, indeed. Again and again he had to flee for his life, but again and again he returned to South America and at last succeeded in making five countries of South America independent of Spain. After he died one of these countries that he had freed changed its name from High Peru to Bolivia, after him. Bolivia is one of the few countries in the World that do not touch the sea, from which there is no way to get to the sea by boat.

Much of the tin in the World comes from mines in Bolivia. Tin pans and tin cans are not made of pure tin—it would cost too much if they were. They are made of iron and simply plated with tin. Pans and cans made of iron would rust and so be unfit for food, but tin doesn't rust and that's why the pans and cans are covered with a thin coating of tin. When this thin tin wears off, the iron rusts easily enough, and that's why most tin cans you see on the ash pile are rusty; the tin has worn off.

Between Bolivia and Peru there is a very large lake. Its name sounds funny, like a person stuttering. It is Ti ti ca ca. It is the highest lake of its size i.t.w.W. I once built a rowboat in my cellar. When I had finished it I found it was so big I couldn't get it out of the house. So I had to take it apart, carry it outside, and put it together again. There are steamers on Lake Titicaca, but in order to get them there from where they were built they had to be taken to pieces and carried up the mountains to the lake, piece by piece, and there put together again.

22

Rubber and Coffee Land

MOUNTAINS make rivers. If a continent were flat—absolutely flat and level like a table—there would be no rivers. Rain falling would run off the continent like water poured on a table. The water running off the Andes Mountains makes the greatest river in the World—not the longest, but the biggest. The name of this river also begins with an "A." It is called the Amazon. On the map the Amazon looks like a vine with many branches. It gets so broad and wide as it goes on that you cannot see across it. The Amazon empties more water into the ocean than any other river i.t.w.W.

You may wonder why, with all the big rivers in the World pouring water into the ocean all the time, the ocean does not fill up and run over as a bathtub would fill up and run over if you left the water running into it all the time. It is because the water in the ocean is always turning into vapor, rising high into the air and making clouds. The clouds rise over the sea, then blow over the land, then turn to rain: the rain falls on the ground, a great part of it is taken up by trees and plants but the rest runs into the rivers, the rivers flow into the ocean and then the same thing goes on over and over again —rivers, ocean; ocean, clouds; clouds, land; land, rivers; rivers, ocean; ocean, clouds, and so on forever and ever. No water is ever lost in the World. It may be in a different place, but there is never any more nor any less water in the World than ever has or ever will be.

All the great rivers in South America flow into the Atlantic Ocean—none flows into the Pacific, because the Andes Mountains lie so close to the Pacific edge there is no room for great rivers on that side.

The Amazon runs through a country by the name of Brazil. Brazil is the biggest country in South America. It is bigger than the whole of our United States! People called the country Brazil after a tree growing there. The brazil-tree is used for making a colored dye. But it would have been more fitting if the country had been named "Rubber" or "Coffee," for more rubber-trees and coffee-trees grow in Brazil than do brazil-trees.

The land around the Amazon River is called "Selvas"—which means "woods." It is not only woods but jungles and swamps, and it is very wild, hot, damp, and unhealthful. It is so hot and damp that everything grows big and thick and fast—so big that water lilies grow leaves as big as the top of a dining-room table; so thick that a man can hardly make his way through; and as fast as *Jack the Giant Killer's* beanstalk.

There are many animals but few men in the Selvas, and the men are mostly Indians. There are many monkeys, the kind organ-grinders use. There are parrots, which sailors catch and teach to speak and bring back home. There are butter-flies and moths of great size and beautiful colors that a boy would love to have for his collection. There are huge snakes called boa-constrictors, that look like heavy vines hanging from branches to fool other animals which they catch, coil around, and hug to death, then swallow whole and go to sleep for a week or month while the meal is being digested. There are animals that hang from trees by their toes like a boy on a tra-peze, and even sleep upside down; lazy, sleepy animals that never seem to be awake, and move, when they do move, so slothfully they are called "sloths." There are animals like dragons, called "iguanas." There are huge bullfrogs whose croaking sounds like the roar of lions. And there are mosquitos, the country mosquitos that give you malaria. You may wonder why any one goes to the Selvas at all. They go a-hunting for ani-mals for museums and zoos, but the chief thing they go hunting for is the juice or sap of a tree that grows wild in the Selvas.

White people found the Amazon Indians playing with balls that bounced and bounded. They had seen nothing of the sort before. These balls, they found out, were made of the sap of a tree. That gave the white man the idea that this sap might be used to make balls for white children and white men to play with—babies' balls, tennis-balls, golf-balls. Then they found that lumps of it would rub out—so they called it rubber—and that they could make rubber erasers, automobile tires, rubber bands, and rubber boots of it. Soft rubber and hard rubber and pully rubber and springy rubber are all made from the sap of the rubber-tree by treating it in different ways as a cook makes taffy and gum-drops and caramels by cooking sugar in different ways.

Men go through the Selvas and wherever they find a rubber-tree they cut notches in the tree trunk and fasten a cup underneath to catch the tree's sap, which flows out from the notches like blood out of a cut finger. Then they go round again and empty the cups of rubber sap into a bucket and carry it to their camp. When they have collected enough sap they take a stick, pour some of the sap on it, and dry it over a fire. They do the same thing again and again until there is a big lump of rubber on the stick. These lumps of rubber they pile into canoes and carry down the Amazon River to larger boats that carry the rubber to the United States and to other countries.

But there is something that grows in Brazil that begins with a "C"—that almost every family in the United States has at breakfast each morning. Can you guess what it is? It's coffee. Coffee doesn't grow in Brazil wild as the rubber-tree does. In fact, coffee didn't grow in Brazil at all until some men brought coffee bushes from across the ocean and planted them in Brazil. They planted them on high ground near the shore, not in the Selvas. They found that the high ground and the weather were just exactly right for growing coffee, and now much more coffee grows in Brazil than in the place where coffee came from first, and indeed more than in any other place i.t.w.W.

Coffee grows on a small tree, and the coffee berries look something like cherries. Inside of each cherry-like berry are two seeds. These seeds are coffee, but before coffee can be made into a drink the coffee seeds must be toasted brown and then ground to powder.

One New Year's Day a long time ago a man was sailing along the coast of Brazil when he came to what seemed to be the mouth of a river. As it was the first day of January he named the place River of January, which in his language was Rio de Janeiro. It turned out to be no river; but the city that grew up at that place is still called Rio de Janeiro, and it is the capital of Brazil. In the harbor of Rio, as it is called for short, there is a huge rock which is called "The Loaf of Sugar," and as you see Rio from a ship the mountains back of the city look like a "Sleeping Giant," and that is what they are called.

More coffee is shipped from Rio than from any

other place i.t.w.W., except another place on the coast of Brazil just south of Rio. This other place is called Santos. The cup of coffee your father drinks in the morning probably comes from either Rio or Santos. If coffee and cocoa could talk, and tin cans and asphalt streets and rubber tires, as such things do in fairy-tales, what tales they could tell of their homes and travels!

Coffee from Brazil for Daddy's breakfast

23

Silver Land and Sliver Land

WE give babies names when they are born, but
sometimes when the babies grow up the names
do not fit them. "Charles" means "strong" and
"Ruth" means "beautiful," but when Charles
grows up he may not be strong, and Ruth may
not be beautiful. You never can tell. When white
people came to South America to the land south
of Brazil they saw Indians there wearing silver
bracelets and silver necklaces, and they supposed
there must be a great deal of silver in the land, so
they named the country "Silver Land," which in
their language is "Argentina." But Argentina
turned out to have very little silver, yet we still
call it Silver Land just the same.

Although Argentina has little silver, the people there have a great deal of money; in fact,
they have more money than any other country in
South America. They do not get the money out
of the ground, but they make it by selling wheat
and meat, so it would have been a more fitting
name if they had called Argentina "Wheat
Land" or "Meat Land" instead of "Silver
Land," but not nearly so pretty. In Argentina
there are enormous farms where they grow wheat

and corn, and enormous fields called pampas where they raise cattle and sheep. The men that look after these cattle and sheep we should call "cowboys," but there they are called "gauchos." Gauchos wear ponchos. A poncho is a kind of square blanket with a hole in the center through

Gauchos wear ponchos

which the gaucho sticks his head. He uses it as a coat by day and as a blanket by night. A gaucho always carries a big knife, which he uses as a sword, as a hatchet, or as a table knife.

Corn feeds the cattle. Cattle makes meat and meat makes money. From the skin of the cattle leather is made, and from the wool of sheep cloth is made, and from both money is made.

Argentina is so much like the United States in a great many ways that it is often called the United States of South America. Both countries are alike in this—that they have hot weather part of the time and cold weather part of the time. But there is this big difference: in Argentina they have winter when the United States is having summer, and summer when the United

States is having winter. In Argentina Christmas comes in hot weather and snow and ice in July and August. They have flowers and vegetables and vacations in January and February, and snow and ice and sledding and skating in July.

The capital of Argentina is often called the New York of South America, as it is the largest city of South America, as New York is the largest city of North America. Its name, however, is not New York but "Good Airs," or, in Spanish, "Buenos Aires." It is on the Plata River, which is another name that means silver. So we have the city of Good Airs on the Silver River in Silver Land.

In most of the other countries of South America there are many more Indians and Indians mixed with white men than there are white people, but in Argentina most of the people are white. That's another reason why it is like the United States; but Argentina was settled by people from Spain, not from England, so the people speak Spanish and not English.

Up the Silver River from Argentina, tucked in between the larger countries are two little countries called Uru- and Para- guay. Uruguay and Paraguay are similar to Argentina in many ways. They raise sheep and cattle and gauchos with ponchos. In *Para*guay they raise a tree from the leaves of which a kind of tea is made. It is called Paraguay tea or maté. It is the chief drink of the gauchos, and many people in South Amer-

ica drink it instead of real tea. It was thought so
good that they tried to sell it to other countries.
But other countries didn't care for it as much
as for regular tea or coffee. Grown people are
like children: what they like they like; what they
think they won't like they don't like. Most people
in the United States like soda-water, but people
in other countries usually do not.

The Andes Mountains separate Argentina
from a very long and narrow country on the Pacific shore named Chile. Argentina is called the
Silver Land. Chile is so long and thin it is sometimes called the Sliver land. Chile doesn't mean
chilly; it means Land of Snow, for most of Chile
is mountains, and the mountains are so high there
is snow on their tops all the time. Chile and Argentina were once going to war in spite of the
wall of mountains between them, but they made
an agreement, as Canada and the United States
did, that they would not fight. They set up on top
of the Andes Mountains a huge bronze figure of
Christ holding a cross—they melted their can-
nons to make it—and on the base they put words
which say something like this: "Sooner shall these
mountain crags crumble to dust than Chile and
Argentina shall go to war with each other—they
have sworn it at the foot of Christ." They have
had no fights since. What a pity such an easy way
to stop fighting cannot be used everywhere!

Chile is so long and so thin and has so many
mountains it hardly seems a country worth fight-

ing for, but in spite of what seems to be, Chile makes a lot of money. This may seem still more surprising when I tell you that the northern part of Chile is a desert where it often does not rain for ten years at a time. That doesn't sound like very good land, but it is one of the richest lands in the World. You would never guess why. Of course, nothing will grow there because it is a desert, and there are no diamonds nor gold. It is on account of something you probably never

THE CHRIST OF THE ANDES

At the foot of Christ, they have sworn not to fight

heard of. This something you never heard of is called Nitrate of Soda. It is a kind of salt that was once in the sea. The reason it is so valuable is because farmers all over the World buy it to put on their fields, as it makes vegetables grow so much better. Strange it doesn't grow anything where it is found; but that is because there is no rain there and nothing will grow without rain. But it is lucky there is no rain, for if there were rain the Nitrate of Soda would melt. This part of Chile is like a long narrow trough. It was once under the sea, then there was an earthquake, and this part of the bottom of the sea rose up and made land; the water in the trough evaporated and left this rough kind of sea salt called Nitrate of Soda. Iodine comes from there too; and who doesn't know that stinging brown stuff that your mother puts on cuts?

The Valley of Paradise is in Chile—only it isn't what you would think Paradise would be. It is the chief seaport of Chile, and it is not very lovely and not very healthful. In Spanish it is called Valparaiso.

The capital of Chile is up in the mountains where it is cool and healthy. It is called Santiago, which means St. James.

Columbus tried to go around the World, but didn't. The first man whose ship went around the World was named Magellan. Magellan sailed across from the other side of the ocean, as Columbus had done, but he went on until he bumped into America. Then he went along down South America, trying to find a way to get through to the Pacific Ocean. He sailed up the Amazon, thinking he might get through there, but he couldn't. Then he sailed up La Plata, thinking he might get through there, but he couldn't. Then when he had nearly reached the tip of South America he at last found a way through to the Pacific. This way through was quite crooked, but we call it a strait and we have named it after him

—the Strait of Magellan. He saw many fires on the land at his left, whether they were from volcanoes now no longer burning, or made by the Indians, no one knows. At any rate, he named it Fireland, which in Spanish is Tierra del Fuego. The Indians he saw on the right, which is now the southern part of Argentina, had such big feet he called them the big-feet people, which is "Patagonians."

For hundreds of years other ships followed this same way through that Magellan had taken, for though some went entirely around the outmost island at the tip of South America—the tip called Cape Horn—it was so stormy that way and so rough and dangerous that most ships used the strait. On this strait a little town grew up— a sort of filling station—just to supply ships with provisions they needed to keep on with their voyage, for there were no other places anywhere near, and it was a long voyage down South America on the Atlantic side and up again on the Pacific side. This little town was called Sandy Point, which in Spanish was Punta Arenas. It is the farthest south city in the whole World. As most ships now go through the Panama Canal, Punta Arenas does less business as a filling station, but a new business is taking the place of filling. They raise sheep on Tierra del Fuego, and the wool is brought to Punta Arenas to be shipped to other parts of the World.

24

The Bridge Across the Ocean

WHEN you go to Europe you have to take two things with you besides your ticket and your luggage. I wonder if you can guess what they are. You have to take plenty of money, but not of your country, as it wouldn't be any good, but of the kind used in the country to which you are going; and the second thing you have to have is a passport. A passport is a little book with only one picture in it—your own—and very few pages. The reading is not a story—it gives you permission to land in the country to which you are going. It is like a ticket of admission: Admit only the person whose picture is in the book. They won't let you go aboard the ship or airplane unless you have a passport, and they won't let you get off the ship unless you have a passport.

It is about 3,000 miles across the Atlantic Ocean from New York, the largest city in the New World, to London, the largest city in the Old World.

Columbus took over a month to cross the Atlantic Ocean from Europe to America.

We can cross in less than a week by ship.

We can cross in less than a day by airplane!

But there is something that crosses the ocean faster than that and does it every day and is always on time. You would never guess what it is. It's the sun. The sun crosses from London to New York in five hours and does it every day.

The people in London, when the sun reaches its highest point in the sky over their heads, set their clocks at 12 o'clock—midday. Five hours later the sun has reached New York and the people there set their watches at 12 o'clock too, because that's what 12 o'clock means: "when the sun is highest in the sky." While the sun has been crossing the ocean all the watches and clocks in London have been ticking along, so it is 5 o'clock in London when it is 12 o'clock here in New York. That is, London clocks are five hours ahead of our clocks.

When you sail for London you have to set your watch ahead each night when you go to bed, so that when you reach London your watch will be five hours ahead of the time you started with. You will then be just right with London time when you reach London. When you sail back you must put your watch back too. If you telephoned to London now at 10 o'clock in the morning and asked them what time it was they would say 3 P.M.

The clocks on board ship look the same as our clocks at home, but they strike differently. Our clocks, as you know, strike once for 1 o'clock, twice for 2 o'clock, and so on, but on board ship a clock strikes two bells for each hour from 1 o'clock to 4 o'clock, when it strikes eight times. It strikes one bell more for the in-between halves of the hour. Then it starts all over again—one stroke at 4:30, two at 5, and so on—never more than eight strokes altogether.

THE OCEAN

What is it that crosses the ocean in five hours and does it every day?

"A watch" on board ship doesn't mean only a watch that you put in your pocket. It means something else too. A ship doesn't stop going at night. A ship must keep on going, night as well as day, so the men, the officers and crew who run the ship, take turns at running the ship, as they can't stay awake all the time, and their turns are called "watches," because they must be wide awake and watching when it is their "watch." Some men are running the engines, some are steering the ship, and some are just watching out to see that they do not run into other ships while the others are sleeping.

How can the captain, when he leaves New York, know the way to go to London, when all the ocean in front of him as far as he can see on every side is just broad flat water or rolling waves or thick fog, with no sign-posts to guide him?

Right in front of the steering-wheel is a box in which is a little pointer that, no matter how much the ship rises and falls, or twists and turns, or rears and plunges, always points one way. The box with its pointer is called a compass. You know what a magnet is—a little thing like a small horseshoe that pulls needles and nails to it. Well, near the North Pole there is a spot on the World like a magnet and this spot pulls all the compasses on the World toward it. So that spot on the World that pulls all the compasses toward it is called the Magnet-ic pole, though there is no pole. This Magnetic pole is where the stem would be if the World were an orange or an apple, though there is no stem.

The captain knows from the way the compass points which way he must go to reach England. He doesn't follow the way the compass points— that would bring him to the Magnetic pole.

When it's fine weather at sea the passengers have a fine time too. They play games, they dance, they take photographs, they write letters and post-cards, they read books, they eat five meals a day, they lie in long steamer chairs wrapped up in rugs, and look out over the ocean or talk or sleep. Now and then porpoises, that look like big fishes, swim along the side or just ahead of the ship, and jump out of the water and dive in again, as if they were running a race with the ship. Occasionally a mountain of ice may be seen floating in the sea, many many times bigger than the ship, called an iceberg. It has broken away from the frozen part of the ocean far up north and floated down. And then at times a whale like a little island may rise out of the water, spout a fountain into the air, then sink out of sight again.

Sometimes, but not often, the sea is so smooth it is like glass, no wind and no waves except those which the ship itself makes. That's why the Atlantic Ocean is sometimes called "The Big Pond." But then again the wind blows, clouds rise, rain pours down, the waves rise up higher and higher until the sea is all moving hills and valleys of water, and the ship pitches up and down and rolls and tosses from side to side. It is necessary to put fences on the dining tables to keep the dishes from sliding off, and of course many people are seasick. The ship slides down one water hill and rises up the next water hill, and, big though it is, seems almost to turn over. But it seldom does turn over or sink unless it runs into an iceberg or another ship and smashes a hole in its side.

But it isn't rough weather that the captain fears most of all. It is a sea fog, especially when he knows there are other ships near, for when there is a fog he cannot see his way at all. It is like groping your way about in the dark at night, only the ship has no arms. The captain slows the ship down till it barely moves. He starts a big, deep horn a-blowing by clock-work, and it blows about once a minute regularly day and night as long as the fog lasts, which may be for several days, while sailors peer over the ship's side listening and looking. They can hear another ship's fog-horn some distance away, but often they cannot see another ship only a few feet away. When at last the fog clears off, land may be in sight— England.

We can tell land is near long before we actually see it. How do you suppose? Large white birds called sea-gulls come out to meet the ship, but not as friends come out to welcome you. They are looking for food that they know is dumped overboard from the ship's kitchen. Just before we do land a man comes out in a small boat to meet the big ship. The big ship doesn't stop; it lets down over the side a ladder made of rope and the man grabs hold of the rope, kicks the boat away, and climbs aboard. Who do you suppose he is?

Why do you suppose they take him aboard? He is the new captain of the ship. He is called the pilot, and it is his job to bring the ship into the harbor. A big ship is so big it can't sail into the dock itself; it has to have small boats called tugboats push and pull it. A broad gang-plank is laid like a bridge across from the dock to the deck and the passengers and their baggage go ashore. The people in England speak English, so you can ask questions and understand their answers, though their language sounds strange to us and our language sounds funny to them. They call it "an American accent." You must show your passport and you must open all your bags and let a man examine everything inside before he will let you go on. So you must have nothing you don't want him to see. This man is called a customs officer. You may have to pay for some things you have. This that you have to pay is called a "duty."

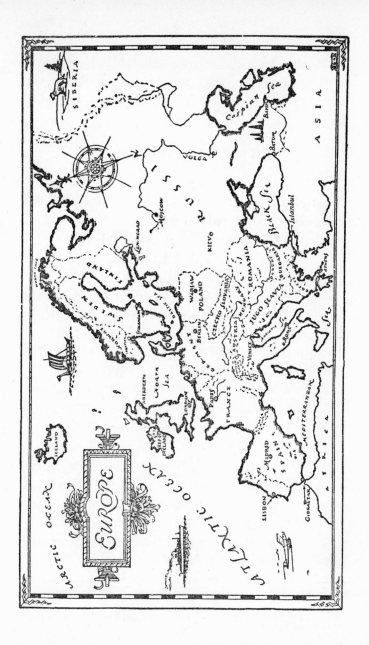

25

The Land of the Angles

ENGLAND is an island.

Angles once lived on the island—no, not Angels—but people called Angles.

So it was called Angle-land.
We now spell it Eng-land
But we call it "Ingland."

There are, however, two other countries on the island—Wales and Scotland—as well as England; so we should call the whole island "Great Britain." Next door to the island of Great Britain is another is-land. It is Ire-land.

A ship, when it reaches England, cannot land its passengers wherever it chooses. There are only certain places. The shore may be too shallow and the ship would run aground and turn over, or the shore may be too rocky or too high with cliffs. Most people who go to England usually land on the west side at a place called Liverpool—Liver pool: what a peculiar name!—or at Southampton, which we can tell from the name is on the south side of England; or at London, which is on the east side. If they land at London the ship must go up a river spelled Thames but called "Temz." English people spell many things one way and pronounce them another. The Thames runs right through London, but big ships cannot go up any farther than London Bridge. Have you ever played the game "London Bridge is Falling Down"? Well, London Bridge has fallen down several times, but each time it has been built up again; and the London Bridge that is there now I don't believe will ever fall.

"London Bridge is Falling Down"

London was a city when Christ was born, but it was then so small and so far off that Christ never heard of it. London is now the largest city i.t.w.W.

New York is tall, London is broad. New York buildings climb to the sky, fifty, seventy, a hundred stories high. London buildings seldom go higher than a few stories, but the city spreads out in every direction, mile after mile. People travel about London chiefly on buses, double-decker ones with seats on top as well as inside, but they also travel about London on trains that run under the ground.

London is the capital of England. The capit-o-l of England—the building—is, of course, in London and it is on the banks of the Thames. It is called the Houses of Parliament, which means the Houses of Talk. It is the place where people not only talk but make the laws for England. A king rules over England, but the English people send men to Parliament to make their laws. As I had lived in sight of our Capitol in Washington for many years, I thought all capitols had to have domes, just as all cows had horns. It was therefore a shock for me to see that the English Capitol, the Houses of Parliament, had no dome—only square towers with a large clock in one of them, with a huge bell, called "Big Ben," that strikes the hours.

He strikes the hours

There is, however, another great building in London that does have a dome like our Capitol. But that building is a church and it is called St. Paul's. Indeed, it is said that the dome of our Capitol at Washington was copied from St. Paul's, for St. Paul's was built long before there was a Capitol at Washington, long before there was a Washington, and even long before there was a United States. They once had a great fire in London—they still call it the Great Fire, for it burned up most of the city. That was about three hundred years ago. Then a man with the name of a bird, Wren—Christopher Wren—built up much of the city that had been burned down. He built beautiful churches and other buildings; so people say it was well the old city *was* burned down, for it gave them the chance to make a beautiful city. St. Paul's was one of the churches that Wren built.

It has a dome like the Capitol at Washington

During World War II thousands of buildings were destroyed by bombs dropped on London by the Germans. Many of Christopher Wren's churches were among the buildings burned or smashed by the bombs, but he had built so many that there are still some left. The people of London called these terrible bombings the Blitz. Great numbers of people were killed. The Blitz will be remembered, like the Great Fire, for hundreds of years to come, but no one can ever say, as they said about the Great Fire, that it was a good thing for the city. The only good thing about the Blitz was the bravery shown by the people of London.

A church that Wren didn't build, a very old one, is called Westminster Abbey. Westminster Abbey is not only a church; it is also a tomb for famous people. In it are buried the most famous English people who have ever lived and died— kings and queens, great writers, great poets, great musicians, great soldiers. After World

CORONATION CHAIR.

The king sits on two seats at the same time

War I a soldier who had died on the battlefield in France, but whose name no one knew, was buried in Westminster Abbey to honor all those who had died without name or fame for a great cause. The place is called the Tomb of the Unknown Soldier.

In Westminster Abbey is a chair in which all the kings of England sit when they are crowned kings. It is called the Coronation Chair. Underneath the seat of the Coronation Chair is a large stone. Why the stone underneath the chair seat? Well, hundreds of years ago the country North of England named Scotland was separate from England. When the kings of Scotland were crowned they used a large stone for a seat. So when England and Scotland became one country, the people took the stone of Scotland and

put it under the Coronation Chair of England,
so that the king could sit on both seats while he
was crowned king of both countries.

The oldest building in London, built long before the Great Fire, is one which from its name
sounds like only part of a building. It is called
the "Tower." In the times long ago the Tower
was a prison in which
were put many fa-
mous people. Even
princes and queens
were put in this
prison, and some of
them were put to
death. It is now a
museum where are
kept many interest-
ing curiosities of
those days—the steel
armor that soldiers
and their horses, and
even their dogs,
wore; the block and
ax with which pris-

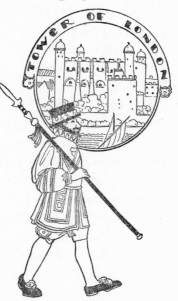

They are called "Beef-Eaters"

oners' heads were cut off; and wonderful jewels
which the kings wore in their crowns—huge diamonds and rubies as big as walnuts. The Queen's
crown is there on a white satin pillow. It is
studded with jewels and a huge diamond called
the "Koh-i-noor," which means "mountain of
light." This stone was supposed to bring bad

luck to any man who owned it, so a woman now owns it—the Queen. The guards of the Tower are called "Beef-Eaters" and should any one break into the cases in which are the jewels, the doors and gates of the Tower would automatically clang shut and the thief be caught a prisoner.

Did you ever collect stones or stamps, butterflies or coins? Well, grown-ups have collected treasures and curiosities from all over the World and brought them together in a wonderful museum, and the largest i.t.w.W. It is called the British Museum.

It is said that if all the streets in London were strung out in one line they would reach round the World. No one could ever know the names of all the London streets, not even the London policemen, who are called "Bobbies" and who are supposed to know everything. They may have to look for a street in a little book which they carry in an inside pocket. But every one knows the names of some of the streets—they are either so famous or so funny. There is Threadneedle Street and Cheapside. There is Pall Mall and Piccadilly, where are fine houses, hotels, clubs, and palaces. There is Fleet, Strand, Regent, and Bond Streets, which are shopping streets. There is Oxford Circus and Piccadilly Circus, but there is no "circus" there. A circus is simply a big open space where streets cross, and which we should call a Square or a Circle.

26

The Land of the Angles
(*continued*)

I ONCE asked an Englishman if he lived in London.

"Why does every American think that every Englishman lives in London?" he replied—and he sounded rather vexed. "There are other places in England besides London.

> There is *Chester* and Man *chester,*
> There is Nor *wich* and Har *wich,*
> There is Ox *ford* and Guild *ford,*
> There is Birm *ingham* and Nott *ing-*
>   *ham,*
> There is Cam *bridge* and Tun *bridge,*
> There is North *ampton* and South
>   *ampton,*
> There is Ply *mouth* and Yar *mouth* and
>   Wey *mouth* . . ."

And as he gasped for breath I cried, "Please don't tell me all the 'wiches and 'fords and 'mouths in England."

"Well," said he, "there are over thirty million people in England who don't live in London and I am one of them."

But nearly every Englishman, no matter where he does live, goes to London some time in his life. You can get to London in a day from any place in England, for the island is so small and trains are so fast.

Railroads were invented by an Englishman, and some of the fastest trains i.t.w.W. run in England. Their trains look different from ours. They seem much smaller and lighter and the cars are divided into rooms instead of being one long room like ours. Each room has half the seats facing forward and half facing backward, so that half of the people have to ride backward. Some of these rooms are labeled "1st class," but most are "3rd class." People pay more to ride in a 1st class room than they do in a 3rd class room. The 1st class has cushioned seats and there is more space for each person. The 3rd class has wooden seats without cushions, and more people are put in a room. The English railroad trains run on the left hand side of the road. Most Americans are right-handed, and we say "Keep to the Right," but most Englishmen are right-handed too, yet they say "Keep to the Left." You would be arrested in England if you drove or rode on the right hand side as we do here.

Our country roads usually have fences alongside, but in England the country roads usually have hedges. Sometimes the hedges are like those that grew up round *Sleeping Beauty's* castle, so thick and so high that you cannot see through them or over them, and the houses behind them are hidden, all except perhaps the roof. Some-

times the roofs are quite different from ours—
made of piles of straw, which are called "thatch."
You would hardly think thatch roofs would keep
the rain out, but they
do; and you would
think they would burn
up easily, but they
don't. The houses
themselves are seldom
built of wood, because
there is very little
wood in England to
build them of. Almost
all of them are built
of stone which comes
out of the ground, or
brick made out of the
ground. In America
there is a great deal

You would be arrested if you
drove on the right side of the road

of wood, but in England there is little wood, for
there are very few forests, hardly any big ones,
and they are usually kept like a park. The country is so old the trees have nearly all been cut
down. The trees that are left are so valuable that
people do not often cut them down to use them
for building houses. In America a wood house is
cheaper than a stone or brick house. In England
a stone or brick house is cheaper than one made
of wood.

Among the sights which people go to see in
England are the churches and cathedrals. Few

churches in America are a hundred years old. There are few churches in England that are *not* a hundred years old, and many of the cathedrals are more nearly a thousand years old. Most of the people in England are Episcopalians, so most of the churches in England are Episcopal. In fact, the Episcopal Church is called the Church of England.

SALISBURY CATHEDRAL

It's the loveliest spire in England

Two of the greatest universities in the world are in England. They play each other football, but not baseball. Instead of baseball they play a game called cricket, and they have rowing matches. One of these universities is on River Thames where oxen used to wade across or "ford" the river, and so is called Ox-ford; the other university is by the River Cam where a bridge crosses, so this is called Cam-bridge.

Many of the World's greatest writers whose stories you read and whose poetry you have learned lived in England, and the greatest

English writer i.t.w.W., William Shakspere,
lived there at a place called Stratford-on-Avon.

But the chief business of England is "making
things"—as the chief business of *New* England
in America is "making things." In *New* England
there is neither coal nor iron to make the things
with; both have to be brought from somewhere
else; but in Old England there is a great deal of
both coal and iron. Coal makes the fire to run the
machinery and iron makes the things; so in England they make everything that can be made of
iron, from huge engines to small penknives. At
Sheffield they make a great quantity of table
knives and silver-plated ware called "Sheffield."
Look at your own table knives and silver-plated
ware and see if any of them have the label "Made
in Sheffield" stamped on them.

In England they also make a great deal of
cloth—cloth made of wool from the backs of
sheep that are raised in England, and cloth made
from cotton which is not grown in England but
brought there all the way from the United States.

There are farms in England too, but not
enough is raised on the farms to feed the English
people one day a week. Most of the food has to
be brought to them from other countries across
the sea. The English eat a great deal of mutton
and roast beef. "The Roast Beef of Old England" has been celebrated in song and story. One
story is that a certain King of England thought
steak from the loin of the beef was so good

that he called it "Sir Loin," as he would a knight
or a lord, and that's why we still call it sirloin
steak to-day. It's a good story but I'm afraid it
isn't a true story.

The King of England is king of many more
people than just those who live in Great Britain.
Englishmen explored and conquered and settled
in far-off places all over the World in times gone
by. England owned countries in every continent
and at first the laws for all these countries were
made in London. Now, however, many of these
countries that belonged to England govern themselves and make their own laws. They have become independent countries but they have kept
the King of England as their king. This big
family of countries all over the World with the
same king, the king of England, is called the
British Commonwealth of Nations. The country
of Canada, that I told you about earlier, is a
member of the British Commonwealth of Nations.

27

The Englishman's Neighbors

HERE is the longest name I know. It has fifty-eight letters. It is LLANFAIRPWLLGWY-NGYLLGOGERYCHWYRNDROBWLL-LLANTYSILIOGOGOGOCH. It looks as if a child had been playing on a typewriter and had pounded out the letters at random. But it is a real name, the name of a town in Wales—a little country on the same island with England. It means "Church of St. Mary, in a hollow of white hazel, near a rapid whirlpool, and near St. Tysilios Church, which is near a red cave." People who live there or direct letters there usually call this place simply "Llanfairpwll," for short—and that's long enough. I'd rather call it "Gogo-goch"! Wales is now a part of England, but once upon a time it was not. The people in Wales spoke a different language—a difficult language with many long names hard to pronounce, with many "ll's" and "w's" and "y's" all mixed to-gether.

An English king at last conquered Wales, and in order to make the people he had conquered satisfied and happy he told them he would give them a ruler who was born in Wales and couldn't even speak a word of English. The people in Wales were pleased at that, for they thought the king would give them one of their own countrymen to rule over them. But the king's own son was born in Wales—of course, he was a baby and he couldn't speak a word of English, nor of any other language either. So the king made him the ruler of Wales and the king called him the Prince of Wales. Ever since then the King of England's

TO THE TOWN OF
LLANFAIRPWLLGWYNGYLLGOGERY-
CHWYRNDROBWLLLLANTYSILIOGOGOGOCH.

A little town in Wales has the longest name I know

first-born son, the one who will be king when his father dies, has been called the Prince of Wales. Nowadays few people of Wales can speak their own "mother-tongue," for all the children learn English in the schools. Many people study other languages besides their own, but it isn't necessary to know Welsh in order to travel in Wales, for every one speaks English even if he speaks Welsh too.

The game of golf first started in Scotland, the

country north of England, on the same island, and some of the finest golf-courses i.t.w.W. are there. Scotland is the land of the Scots and it once had a separate king. The Scotch men used to wear—and some do to-day—shawls of bright-colored squares, and skirts instead of breeches, and stockings rolled down, leaving their knees bare even in the coldest weather—and they have a great deal of cold weather in Scotland. The Scotch families are called Clans and each Clan has a special design called a plaid in which its shawls and skirts are woven. A great many Scotch names and words are different from English, and yet similar. They call a baby a bairn, and boys and girls they call lads and lassies, and a pretty girl they call a bonnie lassie.

The Scots have a peculiar musical instrument called a bagpipe. It's a bag made of a pig's skin and it has a pipe to blow it up as you would a balloon, and there are several horns attached to the bag. The player puts the bag under his arm, keeps blowing it up to keep air in it, and at the same time squeezes out the air with his arms so that it blows the horns, making a peculiar squeaky music like a "dying pig."

Some of the greatest ships in the World such as those that cross the ocean are made in Scotland, at a place called Glasgow on the River Clyde, on the west side. Glasgow is the second largest city on the island, but the capital of Scotland is on the other side, the east coast. It is called

Edinburgh. The Presbyterian Church started in Scotland and most of the people in Scotland are Presbyterians, just as those in England are Episcopalians.

We call white potatoes "Irish" because they raise and eat so many potatoes in Ireland, the island to the west of Great Britain. In fact, Ireland is shaped something like an Irish potato. But they had no potatoes at all in Ireland and no one there had ever seen or heard of a potato before Columbus discovered America. Potatoes were born in South America and were brought over and raised in Ireland.

He makes a squeaky music that sounds like a "dying pig."

The island of Ireland is divided into two parts. The small northern part is called Northern Ireland and is part of the United Kingdom of Great Britain and Northern Ireland. That means the King of England is king of Northern Ireland as well as of England, Scotland, and Wales.

The Irish are great story tellers and fairy-tale tellers, and they say that once upon a time long ago a giant in the north of Ireland built a magic bridge from Ireland all the way across to Scotland; and to prove the story true they show you thousands of stone posts from the shore out into

the sea—all there is left of the bridge—that look
as if they had been driven down into the sea by
a pile driver. These stone posts running out into
the sea are called the Giant's Causeway, which
means the Giant's Bridge.

Have you a handkerchief in your pocket? Is
it made of linen or cotton? If it's a "party" handkerchief it is probably made of linen and came
from Ireland. Linen is made from the fiber of a
plant called flax. Flax is much stronger and more
silky than cotton, but it costs more. Flax grows
especially well in the country around Belfast,
which is the capital and chief city of Northern
Ireland. In Belfast, they make more linen, and
especially fine linen, than anywhere else i.t.w.W.
—handkerchiefs, napkins, and table-cloths.

Most of the people of Northern Ireland are
Presbyterians like the Scots or Episcopalians like
the English, for their ancestors, many years ago,
moved to Northern Ireland from Scotland.

The other part of Ireland, the south part, used
to belong to England too. But the Irish people
there never liked being ruled by the English and
so they started a country of their own, with a
city named Dublin for its capital. It is often said
that the people in Dublin speak better English
than even the people in England do. There is
another language used in southern Ireland besides English. It is called Irish and is the language spoken long ago by the ancient Irish
people before they spoke English. Some of the

Irish coins and postage stamps have Irish words on them.

The country that the Irish formed is a republic with a president, and the King of England now is no longer their king, as kings of England used to be.

Farther south than Dublin is another city with the strange name of Cork, and at some distance another place called Kilkenny. The Irish are famous for their quick wit. Once a man named Kenny was drinking a bottle of ginger-ale, when he swallowed a piece of the cork and nearly choked to death. Some one said to him, "That's not the way to Cork." "No," said Kenny, between coughs, "that's the way to Kilkenny."

Near Cork is an old ruined castle called Blarney. There is a certain stone high up in the wall of this old castle, and the story goes that if you kiss this stone you will be able to say very pleasant and nice things to people. People go long distances to kiss this Blarney stone, although they can only do it by lying on their backs almost upside down. So when a person says something to us that is very flattering, we reply, "Oh, you must have kissed the Blarney stone."

Almost all the people of the Republic of Ireland are Roman Catholics, for their families have lived there since before the time of Christ, and missionaries from Rome taught them Christianity over a thousand years ago.

Ireland is often called the Emerald Isle be-

cause an emerald is a very beautiful green stone
and Ireland has so much rain the country is very
green. That's why green is the national color.
Their flag is green, white, and orange, and a kind
of clover, called the shamrock, which grows there,
is their national leaf.

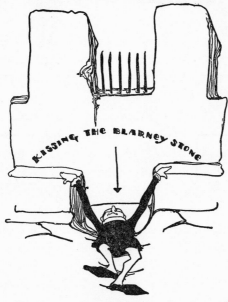

People come from all over the World to kiss
the Blarney Stone

You have all heard of St. Patrick, who was
supposed to have driven the snakes out of Ireland. Well, the British flag has three crosses
worked together like a monogram. One is the
cross of St. George of England, the second is the
cross of St. Andrew of Scotland, and the third is
the cross of St. Patrick.

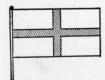

**The Cross of
St. George**

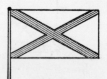

**The Cross of
St. Patrick**

**The Cross of
St. Andrew**

28

Parlez-vous Français?

I KNOW a boy who has never been to school and who has never had a French lesson in his life, but who can speak French fluently. He's no brighter than you are, either. How do you explain that? It's because he was born in France. He is a French boy. But there was a time when every one who was anybody, no matter in what country he was born, could speak French. The English kings and nobles and educated people all spoke French; they spoke English only to their servants, who were not supposed to know anything better.

France is only two dozen miles from England —twenty-four miles—but there is water between the two countries and no bridge. The water between England and France is called the English Channel. It might just as well have been called the French Channel, for it doesn't belong to either England or France. The finest swimmers in the World, both men and women, have come from all over the World just to try to swim across the English Channel. But only a very few have been able to do it. A boat takes only about an hour to cross and an airplane takes even less time.

When you cross over to France you usually leave a place on the English side called Dover and land at a place on the French side called Calais, because this is the shortest distance. It's short, but often so very rough that every one is seasick—then it seems very long. Some day perhaps a tunnel will be made underneath the English Channel. People usually speak of this as the Calais-Dover route, and there is an old catch question, "What is the shortest route from England to France?" One usually answers "Calais-Dover," but that is wrong, for the shortest way *to* France is "Dover-Calais." Some people cross a longer way, landing at other places on the French side. Havre is one of these places. Havre is at the mouth of a river spelled "Seine," but called "Sane."

When you land in France you see French flags flying; they are red, white, and blue, the same colors as our own flag, but their flags have only three stripes and the stripes are up and down, not from side to side, and the colors are backward—blue, white, red, instead of red, white, blue. The street signs and signs on the buildings are in a different language, the people are talking a different language, and of course the money is different too. It is called "francs."

You have probably heard some one say, "You look like your father or mother," but they don't

say that your father or mother looks like you.
Well, up the River Seine is the capital and largest city of France, spelled "Paris," but called
"Paree" by the French people. Some call it the
most beautiful city i.t.w.W. People often say
some other very beautiful city looks "like Paris,"
but they never say Paris looks like any other
city.

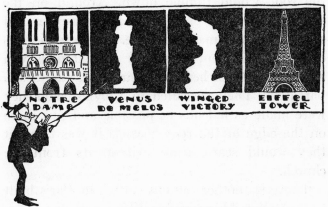

Here are some of the "sights" of Paris

London is up a river too, but it is only a short
way and quite large ships can get up to London. But Paris is a long distance up the Seine,
and the river is too shallow and too narrow for
large steamships to go up so far, although
smaller boats can do so. The Seine runs straight
through Paris, or rather I should say it runs
crooked through Paris, for it curves as it passes
through.

On a small island in the river is a great church

—a cathedral, built to the Virgin Mary, whom the French call Notre Dame, which means Our Lady. Notre Dame was built many hundreds of years ago of stone and stained glass, with two towers in front and a thin spire in the center "like a finger pointing to heaven." Long props made of stone hold up the roof. They are called flying buttresses, and if these props were taken away the roof would tumble down. Around on the edge of the roof of Notre Dame are perched strange animals made of stone. They are hideous creatures, different from any real animals you have ever seen or heard of, part bird, part beast, part devil. They are called "gargoyles," and they were made as hideous as possible and put there on the edge of the roof because it was thought they would scare away evil spirits from the church.

There is another famous church in Paris built to that other Mary in the Bible known as Mary Magdalene. This church to Mary Magdalene is called simply "The Madeleine," which is the French for Magdalene. It is a much newer church than Notre Dame but it is much older-looking. It is built like the old temples they used to build before Christ was born—before they had any churches. The Madeleine has stone columns all around the outside, but it has no windows, no towers, no flying buttresses, no spire, no dome.

Once upon a time France had kings and queens

and princes and princesses, and along the Seine
are many beautiful palaces in which they lived.
Now, however, France has no more kings and
queens or princes. It has a President as we have,
for France is a republic as we are. So the old
palaces are now used for museums or art gal-
leries or libraries. One of the greatest of these
palaces is the Louvre, and in the Louvre are
many famous pictures and statues.

A photograph is never worth much—even
though it may be a good likeness and the
person famous. But a painting, even though not
a good likeness and the person unknown, may
be worth a fortune. One of the great pictures in
the Louvre is the painting of a smiling woman
called Mona Lisa. It is one of the most valuable
paintings i.t.w.W., but it was once upon a time
stolen right off the wall in the Louvre where it
was hanging. It was a foolish thing to steal, for
the thief could not sell it nor even show it to
any one. All the World looked for the picture,
but it was a long time before it was found in another country and put back again in the Louvre,
where it is once more.

Before Christ was born people believed there
were many gods who were like good and bad
fairies, and statues were made of them as they
were supposed to look. Two of the greatest statues i.t.w.W. are in the Louvre. One is a marble
figure of the goddess Venus. Venus was the goddess of Love, and this statue of her was made

more than 2,000 years ago, but was found not many years ago on an island called Melos, so it is called the Venus of Melos. The other figure, like an angel with outspread wings, is called "Victory." Victory too was made before Christ was born. Venus has lost her arms and Victory has lost her head, but, in spite of that, both figures are more beautiful than most real people who have both arms and head.

The Capitol of France has neither a dome like our Capitol nor towers like the English Capitol. There is, however, a building in Paris with a dome something like that of our Capitol and St. Paul's in London, but it is neither a church nor a Capitol. It is the tomb of France's two greatest soldiers. One was named Napoleon, and he lived at the same time as our George Washington. He was at one time emperor before France had presidents. His bones are in a large marble chest under this dome. The other soldier is General Foch—the leader of the armies in World War I.

The tallest tower in the World is in Paris near the banks of the Seine. It is called the Eiffel Tower and it is about a thousand feet high. It is made of iron and stands on four tall iron legs. You can look between its legs and see whole buildings as if the tower were a giant straddling them.

29

Parlez-vous Français?
(*continued*)

THERE are two French words which I know you know, even if you don't speak French. One is "Boulevard" and the other is "Avenue." You have probably always thought they were English words, but they are both French words. Paris has many Boulevards and one of the finest Avenues in the World. This Avenue is lined with trees and runs directly toward the setting sun, and was thought beautiful enough to be a street in Paradise, so it was called the Champs-Elysées, which means "The Fields of Paradise."

In London a square is called a Circus, but in Paris it is called a Place, as if spelled "Plass." The most beautiful Place in Paris is the Place de la Concorde. In the center of this Place is a monument made of one single tall stone standing on end. It is called Cleopatra's Needle. The Place de la Concorde is at one end of the Champs-Elysées and at the other end is a beautiful arch like a huge gateway across the avenue. It is called "L'Arc de Triomphe," which it is easy to guess means The Arch of Triumph. No automobile nor carriage may pass through this Arch of Triumph, however, for underneath it in the pavement is the tomb of the French Unknown Soldier, and from this tomb a flame flickers day and night—a flame to be kept burning forever to the memory of the brave Frenchmen who died in the World Wars.

Underneath the Arch of Triumph is the tomb of the French Unknown Soldier

The French people love beautiful things. They love beautiful pictures and beautiful sculpture and beautiful buildings, and they know how to make them; so young men and women from our country and from other countries go to Paris to learn from the French how to make beautiful things—to become painters and sculptors and architects.

But the French love beauty in everyday things as well—in such everyday things as hats and clothes and cooking and manners. French hats and French clothes and French cooking and French manners are famous. Strange to say, the most famous French dressmakers are men. Also, strange to say, the most famous French cooks are men too. We call them "chefs." Our dressmakers go to Paris to study and copy the fashion in clothes and the style in hats, and we get French chefs for our finest hotels and restaurants. Perhaps you have noticed that the bill of fare in many of our restaurants is printed in French. That is because our cooks copy not only the way the French cook but the names of the dishes they cook. The French can make delicious soup out of a piece of bread and a bone. In America soup is just soup, but in France soup is called potage or consommé instead of soup—it sounds better,

The most famous French cooks are men

and anything that sounds better you expect will taste better, too, and it usually does.

When we eat our meals we almost always do so indoors, where we can see no one else and no one else can see us. But the French often eat out-of-doors, on the sidewalk or overlooking the sidewalk, where they can see every one and every one can see them, and that's where many of their most famous restaurants are placed.

The French drink a great deal of wine with

their meals, much as we drink milk or coffee or tea, and there are many great farms in different parts of France where they raise grapes from which they make the wine. These farms are vine-yards—called "vinyards."

Cloth is made out of several things—linen, cotton, wool, and silk; linen, cotton, and wool are chiefly for use, but silk is chiefly for beauty. In Ireland cloth is made out of linen, in England cloth is made out of cotton and wool, but in France cloth is made out of silk for beauty's sake. Linen and cotton are made from plants, wool is made from sheep, but silk is made from a little caterpillar. We call this caterpillar a silkworm, but he is not really a worm at all. A worm is born, lives, and dies always a worm, but a caterpillar turns into a beautiful moth or butterfly if let alone. Most caterpillars, however, we try to kill, for they eat the leaves of trees and other green things. But silkworms are so valuable that people feed them leaves and raise them as our farmers raise chickens. The silk caterpillar likes a special kind of leaf—the leaves of the mulberry-tree. So in the valley of a river in France called the Rhône the French people grow mulberry-trees—not for the mulberries but for the leaves, which they gather and feed to the silkworms.

After the silk caterpillar has eaten, he spins a fine thread of silk almost a quarter of a mile long out of his own body, as a spider spins a spider web out of his own body. The silk caterpillar winds himself up in this thread as he spins it round and round and round until he is completely covered up and looks in his cover of silk thread something like a peanut. Then he goes to sleep inside, and if he waked up he would come out a moth; but they don't let him wake up. They boil him while he is asleep, till he is soft, and then they *un*wind the thread which he has wound round himself and use it to make silk cloth, silk stockings, silk ribbons, and all the silk things that women love. On the River Rhône is the greatest place in Europe for making silk. It is called Lyons.

The River Rhône flows south into a gulf called the Gulf of Lyons, which is a part of the Mediterranean Sea. The chief city on the Gulf of Lyons is Marseilles. It is the next largest city to Paris, but it was a city long before there was any Paris, for it was a port for ships that sailed the sea long, long ago, and it still is one of the great ports for ships. It is near, but not quite at, the mouth of the Rhône.

Another thing that women love is perfume— sweet perfume! The French are famous for making perfume from flowers and from sweet grasses and even from weeds. French perfume is very expensive, because it often takes a whole field of flowers to make but a very few bottles of perfume. A dollar for a thimbleful! It always seemed wonderful to me that both flowers and their perfume come out of the ground—that the beautiful colors and sweet perfume are both made from mud!

French farmers raise other things, of course, besides grapes and silkworms and flowers for perfume. They raise many of the same things that our own farmers raise. Most of the people in France are farmers, but they don't live in farm-

Ladies go to Paris to buy hats and clothes

houses on their farms; they live in houses in a village and walk out and back to their farms, which often are a long way off.

When I was five years old I was given a penny bank, "to save for my old age." When, at the age of twelve, I had a hundred dollars, I felt like a millionaire. The French are very saving. Even a man who earns very little saves some of that little, so that even poor people have money saved up for their old age when they can no longer work.

A girl saves her money so that when she marries she will have enough to buy furniture and perhaps a house or even more. This is called her "dot." Sometimes her father and mother give it to her, and sometimes the girl earns it herself;

sometimes her "dot" is only a few hundred dollars, sometimes it is thousands of dollars, but seldom can a girl marry who hasn't some "dot." "And they lived happily ever afterward."

30

The Land Below the Sea

Bells and Battle-fields don't seem to go together, but north of France is a land of Bells and
Battle-fields, called Belgium.

The bells are in the towers of churches, of town
halls, and of other buildings. The bells in Belgium
strike the hour, but they do more than that—
they play a tune every hour or oftener. And on
Sundays and holidays a bell-ringer, seated at a
keyboard as at an organ, plays all sorts of hymns
and tunes on the bells, so that every one in
the town can enjoy the music without leaving his
own home. The music is broadcast without a
radio. Some of the bell sets have as many as fifty
bells of different sizes and sounds—little bells
that make high notes, and big bells, as big as a
man, that make deep, low notes. The bells themselves don't move; the bell clapper moves instead. The clappers are fastened by wire to keys
like those of a piano or organ, and as the player
touches the keys the clappers strike the side of the
bell. When a bell concert is being given, all
noises in the streets near-by are forbidden—no
honking of horns nor loud shouting allowed—so

that nothing will spoil the music for those who are listening.

Bells and Battle-fields! Belgium has been the battle-field of Europe—not battles fought by the Belgians themselves, but by other countries of Europe. In the two World Wars Belgium was a chief battle-ground of the French and German soldiers, and thousands of buildings were wrecked and an immense amount of damage done. A little over a hundred years ago a great French General named Napoleon, who I told you was buried in Paris, fought one of the greatest battles in history at a place in Belgium called Waterloo. Napoleon was beaten at Waterloo, and beaten so badly that we now use the word "Waterloo" to describe almost any big defeat, whether it is a defeat of an army in battle or of a team in a game. We say "A tennis champion has his Waterloo" or "A football team has its Waterloo."

B. B. B. The capital of Belgium also begins with a "B." It is Brussels. Perhaps you have heard of Brussels lace, Brussels carpets, or Brussels sprouts. They all come from Brussels.

Another city of Belgium beginning with a "B" is Bruges. Bruges has many streets of water with bridges crossing them, and boats instead of carts, although there are paved streets also. See how many things in Belgium begin with a "B":

Belgium
Bells
Battle-fields

Brussels
Bruges
Bridges
Boats

Belgium is hilly on the side near France, but on the opposite side it is very low. On this low side it joins the land of the Dutch people, which is called Holland. Holland means "hollow land," and it is so named because in many places it is even lower than the sea. Banks or walls called dikes had to be built to hold the water back, and windmills with big sprawling wings had to be built inside the dikes to pump the water out and keep it out. Water won't run off the ground in Holland, for there is no low place for it to run to; it would have to run uphill. So it has to be pumped off.

The dikes that hold back the sea have to be very big and very strong to stand the pounding of the waves against them, for the slightest break or hole in the dike would soon burst open and the water would flood the country, and cover houses and drown the people, so they have men to watch the dikes all the time to mend any broken places as soon as they are made.

But long, long ago—about seven hundred years ago—there was a terrible storm, and the North Sea did break through and it drowned thousands upon thousands of people and the villages and houses in which they lived. Ships now sail and fish now swim where these drowned villages lie, and this inland water is called the South Sea, which in Dutch is the Zuyder Zee. But the Dutch people are planning to build dikes and shut off the North Sea once again and pump the water out. This will make dry land where the Zuyder Zee now is; so some day, not many years from now, there will be no Zuyder

Windmills with big sprawling wings were built to pump the water off the land

Zee, no South Sea, and where fish now swim and ships now sail will be houses and farms.

Where we have roads and streets, in Holland they have canals. In the summer, boats sail on the canals and in the winter the people skate on them. Children skate to school and men skate to work. What fun!

In Holland they don't have many horses; they use dogs to haul and bicycles to carry. Dogs eat less than horses, they don't have to have stables, and bicycles don't have to have garages. Dogs can be trained like horses to haul small carts, large enough to carry milk cans. Sometimes, however, when a cat comes along, there is trouble.

Though there are few horses in Holland, there are many cows. They have black and white cows called Holsteins. Holstein cows give a great deal of milk, more milk than any other kind of cow. The milk is used for making cheese, for which

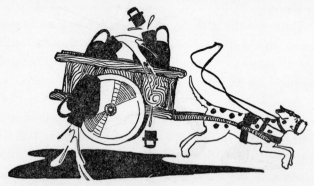

Sometimes when a cat comes along there is trouble

Holland is famous. The cheese is made in big pieces and then varnished so that it will keep a long time. They have markets in which nothing but cheese is sold—cheese markets.

The Dutch keep their houses very clean. The kitchen is usually the living-room and dining-room too. They scrub and scrub and scrub, outside as well as inside, even the sidewalks, and in some towns even the street. The cow sheds are often part of the house and are kept just as clean as the houses, with white curtains at the windows, and hooks to hold up the tails of the cows while they are being milked. People wear wooden shoes, because Holland is such a damp country, and they take them off and leave them at the door, as we do overshoes, before entering the house. In some places in Holland the men wear trousers as big as pillow-cases and the girls wear very big skirts and white bonnets. In the large cities, however, the people dress about the same as we do.

Dam means a dike, and as there are so many dikes in Holland there are many towns' and cities' names ending in "dam." Amsterdam and Rotterdam are the two largest cities.

Amsterdam is a city of diamonds. The diamonds are not found in Holland but are brought there from Africa. When they are taken out of the diamond mines in Africa they don't look like diamonds but look like pebbles, and you would never guess they could be made into anything beautiful. But at Amsterdam they are made into the beautiful sparkling jewels that we know. A diamond is the hardest thing in the World. You cannot cut it with a steel tool nor grind it on a grindstone; you cannot scratch it with sandpaper nor make a mark on it with a file. The only thing that will cut a diamond or scratch a diamond is another diamond. So in Amsterdam they chip one diamond with another diamond and polish it into a many sided jewel with diamond dust.

31

Castles in Spain

WHEN-I-WAS-A-BOY I used to plan the kind of home I would have when I grew up and had plenty of money. It was to have a gymnasium in the attic, a zoo for pets in the cellar, a museum of curiosities in the parlor, and a soda-water fountain in the dining-room. My mother used to say that was my Castle in Spain, and when I asked her what a Castle in Spain was, she said, "Any wonderful home—in your mind."

But Spain is a real place, a real country, and there are real castles there even now.

The map of Europe is like a puzzle-picture. If you turn it around or look at it sideways you will see a little old woman with a big head, a humpback, and a long leg kicking a football into the sea. The head is called Spain, and the cap that Spain is wearing on the front of her head is called Portugal. Where the head joins France there is a collar of mountains called the Pyrenees.

At one time Spain not only looked like the head of Europe, she really was the head of Europe, for she owned a great part of Europe. Then there came a time just after Columbus discovered America when Spain was the head not

only of Europe but of all the World. She then
owned a great part of North America and all of
South America, except Brazil. So she was the
greatest country i.t.w.W. Now, however, Spain
doesn't even own all of Spain. On the map Spain

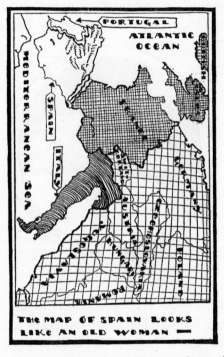

THE MAP OF SPAIN LOOKS
LIKE AN OLD WOMAN —

seems to be rubbing her nose against the nose
of Africa, as some savages rub noses when they
meet. This nose of Spain is called Gibraltar, but
Gibraltar does not belong to Spain; it belongs
to England.

Gibraltar looks like a nose on the map, but if
you were in a boat out on the Mediterranean Sea,

Gibraltar would look like a long, high rock. Between it and Africa there is a narrow strip of water called the Strait of Gibraltar. It is only about thirteen miles across. It is about half as wide as the Strait of Dover, but powerful currents are pulling and pushing in and out from the Atlantic Ocean, and only recently has any one

Hidden in this rock is a huge fort
with soldiers and big guns

been able to swim across it. Inside of the Rock of Gibraltar, England has cut hallways and rooms and windows with long-distance guns in them, and placed her soldiers there to watch out over the water, and in time of war to fire on any one England does not want to pass through the water-gate.

Long years ago most all of the World that people knew was chiefly around the edge of the Mediterranean Sea. Sailors at that time thought it dangerous to go outside this gate, the Strait of Gibraltar, into the great ocean, and—so the story goes—they set up Pillars on each side of the Strait like gate-posts. They called them the Pillars of Hercules, and they put up a sign to warn sailors that it was dangerous to go beyond these Pillars. The sign said "Non Plus Ultra," which meant "Nothing More Beyond." It was supposed that not far outside the Pillars of Hercules the ocean came to an edge where you would tumble off down, down, down to bottomless nothing. Columbus did not believe any such foolishness; he was not afraid. He sailed from Spain, starting from a place outside the Pillars of Hercules called Palos. He sailed on and on and on until, as you know, he came to America.

Just before Columbus sailed from Spain there were people living there called Moors, who had come across from Africa and made their home in Spain. The Moors were different from other people in Europe. They did not believe in Christ; they were not Christians. They believed in a man named Mohammed and a god whom they called Allah. The Moors built beautiful palaces, but they were different from Christian palaces. The Moorish princes lived in one of these palaces on a hill in the city of Granada, which is not far from Gibraltar. The palace in Granada was called the Alhambra.

The Christians in Spain didn't like the Moors,

so they fought them, and at last the Christians drove the Moors out of Spain, drove them across the Strait of Gibraltar back into Africa whence they had come. The Spanish Queen received Columbus in the Alhambra and bade him good-by

before he started out for the New World, but no one now lives there. It is still there on the hill at Granada and Spain keeps it as it once was, so that people may visit it. The walls, instead of being plastered or painted, are covered with colored tiles. The doorways, instead of being square, are shaped like a horseshoe, and its court-yards have splashing fountains and walled-in pools where the

She wears a tall comb in her hair and a veil over her head and shoulders

Moorish princesses used to bathe instead of in bathtubs.

A city in Spain called Seville has a great Cathedral, the second largest church in the World. It was built, of course, after the Moors had been driven out of Spain, as it is a Christian church, built where there once was a Moorish church. In this Cathedral are buried what are supposed to be the ashes of Columbus, though we think, as I told you before, that they are not his ashes at all, but the ashes of his son, and that his real ashes are in Haiti.

Moorish women used to wear veils over their faces. It was thought immodest for them to go out on the street with their faces uncovered. The Spanish women often wear veils too, but they wear them over their heads instead of hats, and some of the veils made of lace are very beautiful and very costly. They also wear very big and high combs in their hair and bright-colored silk shawls over their shoulders, and in summer carry beautiful fans, for it gets very warm in Seville —so warm that during the middle of the day no one goes out-of-doors who doesn't have to. In our country young children take naps during the day, but in Spain grown-ups take naps too, after their midday meal, only they call a nap by the very pretty name "siesta."

32

Castles in Spain
(*continued*)

WHEN-I-WAS-A-BOY I once climbed over a
fence into a field, and before I knew it a bull
was dashing toward me. I barely had time to
scramble back over the fence again—a narrow
escape; I didn't see any fun in it at all. But in
Spain on Sundays and holidays great crowds of
people go to an outdoor theater called the bull-
ring to see men fight bulls.

The people sit on seats outside a fence that
shuts in a sandy field, and from that safe place
they watch the bull-fights. A gate is opened into
the field and a big, wild bull rushes in. A man
called a bull-fighter goes to meet him with a red
cloak in his hand and waves it in the face of the
bull. This makes the bull mad, so with lowered
horns he charges the red cloak. The bull-fighter
jumps to one side just as the bull reaches him,
and the angry bull, unable to turn quickly, passes
him by. The bull-fighter teases the bull in this
way again and again. After worrying him in
various ways, as a cat plays with a mouse, the
bull-fighter kills the bull with a thrust of a long

sword. It seems to us very cruel, but in Spain they say *we* kill bulls for meat and do not give any one the fun (?) of seeing them killed.

A bull-fighter has to be very brave and very skilful, and his foot must not slip on the sandy ground, or he cannot dodge the bull and *he* will be killed. Almost every city and town in Spain

The bull-fighter teases the bull with a red cloak

has a bull-ring, as almost every city in the United States has a baseball field or a stadium, for bull-fighting is a national sport, as baseball or football is our national sport. Even boys play bull-fighting, one making believe he is the bull and the other the bull-fighter.

Every country seems to have certain games they like to play best. In Spain the girls do not jump rope, but they dance instead, and keep time by clicking little clappers on their fingers, often singing as they do so. The clappers look like big chestnuts and so are called castanets, which means chestnuts. They dance in twos and fours on the sidewalk, in the parks and squares, wherever our children would jump rope or play hop-scotch. Even in the great Cathedral of Seville the choir boys dance with castanets in front of the altar at certain church festivals. It is the only place in the World where any one dances in church.

Instead of jumping rope they dance with castanets

Spanish houses have no front yard nor back yard nor side yard, but an inside yard with the rooms all around it. This inside yard is called a patio and it is often a living-room and dining-room for all who live in the house.

As you ride through Spain on a train you can see from the car window a very peculiar looking tree—different from any tree that grows in our country. This is the cork-tree. The little and big corks we use for bottle stoppers don't grow on trees as cherries or peaches do. They are made from the bark of a kind of oak. The bark is cut off from the tree in large pieces and cut up into big and little corks. The tree then grows another coat of bark, but it takes nine years to grow a thick enough bark to be cut again. So every cork you use is nearly as old as you are, or older.

Cork-trees live to a great age, much longer

than people do. But another tree you see in
Spain grows to be still older. It is the olive-tree,
which bears a fruit that looks something like
green cherries. It is said that olive-trees have
been known to live and bear fruit for a thousand
years! Olives have been used as food since Bible
times and long before that, and yet many people
have to learn to like them. Olives are also pressed
to make olive oil, which we use in salad dressing,
for no other kind of oil is quite as good for food.
In Spain they often use it instead of butter, and
it is also made into a very pure soap called Cas-
tile soap, which you may have used.

Winners of games long ago used to be crowned
with a wreath made of olive leaves, and in time
of war, messengers bringing peace used to carry
an olive branch. In certain parts of Spain you
can ride all day long on a train and see olive-
trees, olive-trees, olive-trees, from morning to
night, till you wonder what the people can do
with so many. They use a great many olives themselves, for olives are often bread and butter, meat
and vegetables to Spaniards, but they send millions of bottles of olives and olive oil all over the
World to other countries that have none.

One of those cities that says it is like Paris is
the capital of Spain. It is near the center of the
country. It is called Madrid. Old Madrid had
narrow streets and small houses. New Madrid has
broad boulevards and big buildings, and if you
did not hear the people speaking Spanish you

might think you were in Paris or even in New York. In old Spain men used to say all the time "Manyana," which means "to-morrow," for they put off everything they could until to-morrow. New Spain says "Do it now." When you are in Madrid and say you live in America, they think you mean South America, and that of course you speak Spanish, for to a Spaniard "America" means South America. A Spaniard who has made his fortune in South America comes "home to Madrid" to live on what he has made, for a house in Madrid is his "Castle in Spain."

Sometimes two brothers have families and live in the same house, but usually they get along better if they live in separate houses. Portugal and Spain are like two brothers. They speak a language that is alike and the people are alike in other ways, but they have never been able to get along together, though they tried it once for a little while. In both countries they like dancing and music. In both countries they raise cork and olives. In both countries they like bull-fights— though in Portugal they do not kill the bull, and they wrap the points of his horns so that he can't kill.

33

The Land in the Sky

THE lowest country in Europe is Holland.

The highest country in Europe is the land of the Swiss people, called Switzerland.

There is hardly a hill in the whole of Holland. The country is as flat as a ball-field.

There is hardly a hill in the whole of Switzerland. The hills are all mountains—the highest mountains in western Europe—mountains so high that there is snow on their tops all the year round, in summer as well as winter. They are called the Alps.

But you can't have a hole in a doughnut without the doughnut, and so you can't have a mountain without a valley. The mountain tops in Switzerland are white, but the valleys are green, and cows with tinkling bells graze over the fields. The melting snow from the mountain tops makes beautiful waterfalls and babbling, tinkling brooks in the valleys.

Have you ever seen the snow on the roof of a house suddenly slide off and fall to the ground? That is called an avalanche. But suppose the roof of the house were a mile long like the side of a mountain, and suddenly the snow covering it slipped and fell into the valley beneath. That is an avalanche such as they have in Switzerland; and sometimes avalanches bury people and houses and even whole villages beneath.

Some long and wide valleys are filled with snow that has turned to ice. The ice filling these long valleys, like a river frozen to the bottom, is called a glacier, and the biggest of these glaciers have names just as rivers have.

Most rivers start from springs, but in Switzerland they usually start from the melting ice under a glacier. One of these big glaciers in Switzerland is called the Rhône Glacier. From under the end of the Rhône Glacier, as from an ice cave, flows a cold stream of melting ice. This stream grows larger and larger as it flows on down the valley and is joined by other streams of melted snow and ice. It is then called the Rhône River. It runs on until it reaches a big, broad valley, which it fills and forms a lake— the largest lake in Switzerland—called Lake Geneva.

The Rhône flows out again on the other side of Lake Geneva, down through France past Lyons and the mulberry-trees and silkworm farms and silk manufactories I told you about, and at last empties into the Mediterranean Sea.

Another river with the same name as the Rhône, all except one letter, is the Rhine. It, too, starts from underneath a glacier, but flows north between France and Germany, through Holland, and empties into the North Sea.

There are many people in the World who think it great sport to climb mountains—the higher the mountain and the more difficult and the more dangerous it is, the more they like to climb it. Now the highest mountain in the Alps is Mont Blanc, which means White Mountain. Part of it is in Switzerland, but the top is in France. Every summer many people climb Mont Blanc and other mountains in the Alps. These mountain-climbers use long poles with spikes on the ends to catch on the ice, and they wear heavy shoes with hobnails; and they take along guides who know the way to go and the way to climb, and they are tied together so that if one slips over a ledge the others may pull him back. But every summer people lose their lives in such mountain-climbing. They slip and fall and are dashed to their death or they are covered by an avalanche and buried alive under the falling pile of snow.

Probably the hardest of all Swiss mountains to climb is a mountain that looks like a huge horn. It is called the "Matterhorn." Only the most skilled and the most daring ever attempt to climb it, though the only thing you can do after you have risked your life to reach the top is to admire the view. The reason most people climb it, however, is simply so they can say "I've done it."

So many people go to Switzerland to see the giant snow-covered mountains, even if they do not climb them, that the Swiss people have built hotels wherever there is a fine view of a mountain, or a waterfall, or some other wonderful or beautiful sight. There are thousands of such hotels all through Switzerland, so that the chief business of the Swiss people seems to be hotel-keeping, and they keep them very well indeed. In fact, it is said they are the finest hotel-keepers in

Men risk their lives climbing to the top

the World. They are famous for other things too: Swiss milk chocolate, which you have probably eaten; Swiss cheese with big holes in it, which you may have eaten; Swiss watches; Swiss wood-carving, and cuckoo-clocks and cowbells and music boxes.

Most countries have an army and a navy as we have police and a watch-dog to keep out burglars. But Switzerland is one of the few countries in the World that has no seashore. So she can't have a navy, and she doesn't have to have much of an army either, because the mountains are like great walls to keep out the enemy. Switzerland kept out of both World Wars, although every country around her was fighting.

Switzerland is completely surrounded by other

countries. On one side is France, on the other Germany, and on another Italy. So the Swiss have no language of their own. On the side nearest Italy they speak Italian, on the side nearest Germany they speak German and on the side nearest France they speak French. In fact, many Swiss people speak all three languages.

To get into Switzerland or out of Switzerland, or from one part of Switzerland to another, you don't have to climb the mountains. You can go over the low places between the high mountains, but many of these low places are a mile or more high, so they are not so very low at that. These low places are called passes. One of these passes is named the Simplon; and Napoleon, the French general I told you about, once crossed the Simplon Pass with his army into Italy. But you can now go under and through the mountains, for in many places long tunnels have been built.

One of the longest tunnels is St. Gothard. The men who built it started to dig from both sides of the mountain, and the two holes they dug exactly met in the middle. Some people said it was wonderful that two tunnels, each miles long, dug from opposite sides of a mountain, should meet. The men replied, "Not at all. It would have been wonderful if the tunnels hadn't met. We are not moles digging blindly. We had figured it out beforehand and we knew where we were digging."

But the longest tunnel in the World is under

the Simplon Pass. At one end of this tunnel is Switzerland and at the other end is Italy. It is over twelve miles long. I have been under the pass riding in a train through this tunnel and I have been over the top of the pass carried by my own two legs. It takes sixten minutes to go through the tunnel. It took me part of two days to climb over.

Near the top of the Simplon Pass is a house called a hospice where I once spent the night. It is a house where certain priests, called monks, live, and the reason the hospice was built there and the reason the monks live there is to provide a shelter for travelers and a place where they may rest safely in case they should be caught in a storm.

Few people now cross the pass, for it is so easy and so quick and so safe to go through the tunnel; but before the tunnel was made underneath there was no other way for people to go from Italy to Switzerland but over the top of the pass, and many people were traveling that way all the time. Snow-storms and blizzards were likely to happen almost any time, summer or winter, and often travelers would be lost and frozen to death. These good monks living in the hospice were the life-savers of the mountain pass. They had built little huts along the mountain pathway and they had large, strong, intelligent dogs called St. Bernards who were trained to go forth from the hospice when there was a storm,

and search for travelers who might have been
overcome, lost their way, or fallen in the snow.
A dog would carry, strapped to his neck, a barrel
filled with bread and wine. His sense of smell was
so strong he could find a man even though buried
in the snow, shake him back to his senses, and
drag him to the nearest hut, to wait for food and

He won't hurt you. He is a good friend

drink until the storm should stop. The Simplon
Hospice is one of the few places in the World
where any one, whether he be rich man or poor
man, saint or sinner, will be housed for the night,
fed, and taken care of for nothing, without question and without charge.

Do you know the story of William Tell? Well,
Switzerland has many lakes, but the most beautiful one is called the Lake of Light—Lake

Lucerne—and on the shore of Lake Lucerne is a little church marking the spot where William Tell is supposed to have shot the apple off of his young son's head.

34

The Boot Top

You've heard of the "old woman who lived in a shoe, who had so many children she didn't know what to do." Well, there is a boot in which live not only many children but millions of children and millions of men and women too. It is called Italy. It is the largest boot in the World and yet it is not large enough to hold all its children, so a great many of them have come over to America. The very first one of them to come over was Christopher Columbus, over four hundred years ago. He sailed from Spain, but he was born in Italy and lived in a city at the top of the boot, called Genoa. A part of his house is still standing in Genoa, and there is a statue of him just outside the railroad station. Ships still sail from Genoa to America, but they know where they are going now and Columbus didn't.

On the other side of the boot top is another city. It is not *near* the water, nor *by* the water, nor *on* the water, but *in* the water. It is built on many little islands, and the streets are water with bridges across them. This city is called Venice. The water streets are called canals, and the main street, which would be a broad avenue if it were paved, is called the Grand Canal. Instead of automobiles or carriages, the people have to use boats. These boats are painted black and in the center there is a little cabin like a closed automobile. In the very front there is a queer thing with teeth which looks something like a big comb standing on end. These boats are called gondolas, and a man called a gondolier stands back of the little cabin and rows the gondola with one long oar. There are no "stop" and "go" signs at the canal crossings, so the gondoliers, as they come to a crossing, call out a funny "ooh," and if there is a gondolier coming from the cross canal he calls back so that they will not run into each other. There are no honking horns, no rumbling wheels —Venice is almost silent except for singing and music.

Long ago where Venice now is there were many little islands but no city. Some people, called Veneti, were troubled by a wild tribe from the north. So they moved to these islands to get away from these annoying tribes. The Veneti cut posts made of cedar wood, which does not easily rot, and drove them down into the water, and on top of these posts they built their houses. The Veneti lived chiefly on fish, which they caught in large numbers, because all they had to do was to drop a line or net out of the front door. In fact, they caught so many fish they could not eat them all. So they gathered salt by drying sea-water and salted the fish so that they would keep.

As the Veneti lived on the water they had to be good sailors, and they were. So they sailed to all corners of the Mediterranean Sea, selling their salt fish and selling salt too, and bringing back in payment silk gowns and rugs and jewels. Then people from all over Europe came to Venice to buy these things which the Veneti had brought back in exchange for this fish and salt, and Venice became the greatest shopping-place, the greatest market, in Europe. So the Venetians, as the Veneti came to be called, kept on getting richer and richer. They built beautiful palaces along the canals, and as they believed a certain saint had brought good luck to them and their city, they built a beautiful church to him. This saint was St. Mark. They found his bones and buried them in this church underneath the altar. St. Mark's Church is different-looking from any of the churches I have told you about so far. It has five domes, one on each side and one big dome in the center, but these domes are not like those of St. Paul's or the Capitol—they are shaped like an onion.

Pictures are usually painted with paint, and you have probably never seen colored pictures made without paint. But the inside of St. Mark's, and the outside too, is covered with hundreds of pictures, not made with paint but out of bits of colored stone and gold and colored glass. Such pictures are called mosaics. They will not fade nor peel off, nor wash off, as painted pictures might do.

As you might have a dog for a pet, St. Mark was supposed to have had a lion for a companion, so on top of a column, out in front of his church, the Venetians put a bronze statue of a lion with wings. Over the door of the church there are four horses. They are not live horses, yet they have traveled far. They were made about the time of Christ, out of bronze, and they have been carried away by one ruler and another from one place to another, and finally back again to Venice.

They built this church to St. Mark because they believed he brought them good luck

The largest piece of land in Venice is a paved square in front of St. Mark's. In this square there are flocks of pigeons, and they are so tame they will alight on your hand or shoulder to be fed. People have pictures taken of themselves with pigeons on their head and shoulders and at their feet. Once upon a time Venice was saved from an enemy by a message brought by a carrier-pigeon, and ever since then Venetians treat pigeons as sacred, and they would arrest and punish any one who harmed a pigeon.

Did you know that a pigeon discovered America? Yes, that's a fact, for in Italian "Columbus" means "pigeon." So his real name is Christopher Pigeon.

Venice is now only a city, but it used to be like a little country all by itself. It made its own money and it had its own ruler, who was called a Doge (dozhe), which means Duke. A Doge ruled like a president and lived in a palace like a king, and punished people who had done wrong, like a judge. Just across the water street from the Doge's palace was the prison, and connecting his palace with the prison was a covered bridge. When a man was sent to prison by the Doge he crossed over this bridge, sighing and groaning, so it came to be called the "Bridge of Sighs."

Theaters are sometimes named "The Rialto," but *The* Rialto is not a theater. It is a bridge in Venice over the Grand Canal. It has shops along its sides. Venice was the shopping-place of Europe, and the Rialto was the department store of Venice, where every kind of thing was sold. There is a play written by William Shakspere, the English author, called "The Merchant of Venice." The story is about a man who had a shop on the Rialto.

The Venetians made their living in the first place out of two commonplace things right at hand—fish and salt. That was the start of their fortune. There was also a great deal of another commonplace thing right at hand too—this was sand. Sand seems to have very little value, but the Venetians found out that they could make glass out of sand by melting it in a furnace with something else. They found out too that they could blow this melted glass as one blows soap-bubbles, and by blowing the glass in this way into different shapes they made wonderfully beautiful bottles, vases, beads, and drinking-glasses. The glass-blowers became as famous as any artist who could make beautiful paintings or beautiful music, and the glass-blowers made fortunes besides, for people everywhere sought their work and paid high prices for it. They were the most important people in Venice. A specially fine glass-blower was as important as the Doge himself—one glass-blower was made a Doge—and some of their daughters even married princes.

VENETIAN GONDOLA

WINGED LION OF ST. MARKS

BRIDGE OF SIGHS

Venice is now no longer a country by itself. It is now only one city in Italy, but people go from all over the World to see St. Mark's and the Doge's palace, to bathe at its wonderful beach nearby called the Lido, to ride in gondolas on its canals, and listen to musicians who on warm moonlight nights sing and play on stringed instruments. Venice is one of the places in the World where every girl thinks she would like to spend her honeymoon when she is married.

An American girl once sent a postal card home: "Here I am in Venice. It is wonderfully beautiful—the golden palaces, the gorgeous sunsets, the enchanting music. I am sitting in a gondola on the Grand Canal and drinking it all in!"

We speak of a person "thirsting" for knowledge or beauty, but one would have to be very thirsty to drink in the Grand Canal.

FEEDING THE PIGEONS

The "Boot" lies in the Mediterranean Sea, but the part of the sea that borders Venice is called The Adriatic. Venice is so beautiful it is known as the "Queen of the Adriatic." Fame and fortune made from fish and salt and ships and sand!

35

The Gates of Paradise and the Dome of Heaven

Down the length of Italy like the back of a sea monster is a ridge of mountains called the Apennines. To get from one side of Italy to the other side you have to go over, under, or through these Apennine Mountains, and trains do all three; over, under, through, winding in and out of one tunnel after another. There are forty-five tunnels in going just from Venice to a city across the Apennines called Florence.

Florence is a girl's name meaning "flowering," but Florence is also the name of this city. As the train comes into Florence it curves around the city and you see above the housetops, near the center of the city, a large dome that looks like the hub of a wheel about which the train is turning. Next to the dome is a big, square tower. Both the tower and the dome were built before Columbus was born. The dome looks like the dome of St. Paul's in London, but, as a matter of fact, this dome is not like St. Paul's. The dome of St. Paul's is like *it,* and so is the dome of the Capitol in Washington like it, and so are all the other domes of that kind in the World like it, for this dome in Florence was the first one of that kind ever built and all others are copies.

Little domes and flat domes had been built before, but when the people of Florence were building a cathedral they wanted a different kind of dome on it, a dome that would be bigger and better than any other dome i.t.w.W. They wanted a dome so big that no one knew how to build it. Now a dome is built out of pieces of stone, and the stones have to cover a space beneath without falling, just like a bridge or an arch. No cement is strong enough to stick stones together so that they will not fall when placed across an open space, but if the stones can be held up by some wooden framework until every stone is in place, the wooden framework underneath can then be taken away and the stones will not fall, for all the stones push downward at the same time, and as all push downward together they get wedged in so tight that none can fall through. It is like a jam of people all trying at once to get through a door: they get so wedged in that none can go through.

But the dome on the Cathedral of Florence was to be so big no one knew how to hold it up while it was being built. It would have taken a whole forest of trees to build a big enough framework underneath. Some one said, "Let's pile up a mountain of dirt and put pennies all through the dirt, then build the dome on top of this mountain. After the dome has been built people will cart away the dirt in order to get the money out of the dirt and that will leave the dome standing alone." But this very foolish scheme was never tried.

At last two artists who were rivals said they knew a way to build the dome, but neither one would tell how he would do it. One artist was named Brunelleschi. As Brunelleschi is such a long name, I'm going to call him Mr. B. for short. The other artist was named Ghiberti, and I shall call him Mr. G. Mr. B. got the job and Mr. G. was made his helper. Mr. G. didn't like to be only a helper, so he went about saying that Mr. B. did not really know how to build the dome at all, and would never finish it.

Mr. B. and his men went on with the work for some time, until the sides of the dome reached the place where the stones had to be built over the center to cover the vast space beneath. This was the hard part, for the sides of the dome had to meet in the middle with nothing underneath to hold them up. Mr. G. kept on with his talking against Mr. B., and even made fun of him, until Mr. B., tired of being nagged in this way, made believe he was sick and stopped work. Time went on and Mr. B. staid home—still sick—and the dome stood unfinished. Mr. G. said, "Oh, Mr. B. isn't really sick; he is only making believe he is sick—as a school-boy sometimes does—because he doesn't know how to go on." So the people of

Florence went to Mr. B.'s house and begged him to go on with the dome.

"I'm sick," said Mr. B. "Mr. G. knows so much about building a dome, let him go on with it."

So the people went back to Mr. G. and told him to go ahead. Then Ghiberti tried, but he was able to go only a little way and couldn't go any farther.

Mr. B. was the only one who knew how to build this "Dome of Heaven"

So then the people went back to Brunelleschi again.

"If you'll make that Ghiberti keep still and not say another word," said Mr. B., "I will go on as I started," and he did, finishing the first and one of the most beautiful domes of its kind i.t.w.W., and no one to this day knows exactly how he did it.

Although Ghiberti was such a poor "sport," he was, however, a great sculptor. Right across the street from the cathedral with the dome which Brunelleschi built is a low, six-sided building called a baptistery, because they baptized children there. The doors of this baptistery are made of bronze, and on these doors Ghiberti made bronze figures and scenes of some of the Bible stories. One of these pictures in bronze shows Abraham about to sacrifice his son on the altar as he was told to do by God.

"They are fit to be the gates to Paradise!" said another great Florentine artist when he saw these doors. The artist who said this was named Michelangelo, and he lived in Italy at the same time as Columbus. Columbus was never at home; he was away from Italy almost all his life, discovering new countries. But Michelangelo never left Italy; he stayed at home. He spent his whole life there making beautiful drawings, paintings, sculptures, and buildings, for an artist in those days did every kind of artistic work, from making necklaces to churches, as well as painting and sculpture.

One day Michelangelo found a block of marble which some one had thrown away because it had a crack in it. Michelangelo said that he saw in this block of marble the figure of young David, so he set to work with his chisel and cut the figure of the young shepherd boy out of the marble. In Florence there are two huge copies of this statue several times bigger than a man, and in thousands of other places in the World there are small copies in plaster, and you may have one of these copies in your own home.

Many of these beautiful works of art are kept in buildings that used to be palaces. The palaces in Florence look more like prisons than palaces.

The shops on the Old Bridge sell souvenirs

They were built that way, not to keep people in, but to keep people out. In olden times rich families lived in these palaces, and they were not good neighbors, for one family frequently quarreled or fought with another, so the palaces had to be strong as forts.

There are no water streets in Florence like those in Venice, but through Florence flows a river called the Arno, and across it are several bridges. On one of these bridges, called the Ponte Vecchio, which means the Old Bridge, are shops as on the Rialto in Venice. Most of the shops sell ornaments and souvenirs made out of silver, mosaic, leather, and tortoise-shell, for this is the kind of art work that present-day Florentines make to sell to the thousands of travelers that visit the city.

Towers are built to stand erect—straight up and down—as boys and girls are. But not far

THE LEANING TOWER
OF PISA
Some day it may fall

from Florence is a city named Pisa, which has a very peculiar tower that leans to one side. It is called the Leaning Tower of Pisa. The tower was built to stand straight, but the foundation has sunk on one side, so that the tower slants over as if it were going to fall. It has stood that way for hundreds of years, but is gradually leaning more and more, and if it cannot be stopped, some day it will fall.

You remember I told you that marble was made from the bones of sea animals; but all marble is not alike—some is so coarse you can even see the bones in the stone. But near Pisa are stone mines called quarries, from which are cut blocks of stone of a very fine and smooth kind of marble called from the name of the place, Carrara. Ever since the time of Christ men have been cutting out blocks of marble from these quarries, and people send all the way to Carrara from this country and other countries when they want especially fine marble for a building or a mantel or a piece of sculpture.

36

The Dead and Alive City

Two thousand years ago you could start out on any road anywhere, and if you kept on going far enough you would at last come to a great city in Italy called Rome, for at that time "all roads led to Rome." Rome was then the largest, the richest, the most beautiful, the most important city in the World. It was the capital of the World.

Rome was built on seven hills, and seven was supposed to be a lucky number. Through Rome runs a river called Tiber, whose waters the Romans thought were ruled over by a god called Father Tiber, to whom they prayed to save them from drowning and shipwreck.

. The old Rome of that time is now dead, mostly in ruins, but there is a saying that Rome will live forever—that it is "Eternal"—and though old Rome is in ruins, there is a new Rome. The new Rome, however, is no longer the capital of the World. It is now only the capital of Italy.

Rome is still the capital, however, of all Roman Catholics in the World, and the head of all the Roman Catholic churches in the World lives

there. He is called the Pope, which means
"Papa."

St. Peter is supposed to have been crucified
and his bones buried in Rome. It is said that on
this spot a religious service has been held every
single day since the time of St. Peter to the present—that is, for about 1,900 years. At first
these services had to be held in secret at night,
for most of the Romans did not believe in Christ,
and any one who did was likely, if caught, to be
thrown into prison or even put to death. But over
this same spot, many hundreds of years later,
was built the largest church in the World. It is
called St. Peter's.

On the top of St. Peter's is an immense dome
copied after Brunelleschi's dome in Florence,
but much larger. It was built by that great artist
Michelangelo, who, I told you, was an architect
as well as sculptor and painter. St. Peter's is so
large that on the roof is a village of small houses,
a village in which live the caretakers of the
church.

The front door of St. Peter's is never closed
night or day, but just to the right of that door
is another door of bronze that is never opened
except every twenty-five years. It is called the
Holy Door and it is walled up with stone. At
the end of every twenty-five years this wall has
to be taken down in order to open the door.

St. Peter's is so large that thirty services can
be carried on at one time without one interfering

with another. Inside the church everything is huge, to match the building. The statues of angels are the size of giants and the doves are the size of eagles. There is a bronze statue of St. Peter himself seated on a throne. This is one of the few statues there of natural size. Good Catholics from all over the World, when they come to St. Peter's, kiss the statue's bronze foot. So many millions have kissed it that they have kissed away all his toes.

THE DOME OF ST. PETER'S

St. Peter's is the largest church in the World

At Easter and at other celebrations the inside walls of St. Peter's are hung with crimson silk, thousands of candles burn, choir boys chant and altar boys swing smoke of burning incense to the high roof, while hundreds of priests in gorgeous robes and cardinals in red caps and red gowns and the Pope himself, the head of all the Catholics in the World, in glistening white, move in stately procession down the main aisle to the high altar, over the spot where, 1,900 years before, St. Peter himself was crucified and a Christian would have been afraid to show himself for fear of being killed.

The Pope lives next door to St. Peter's in an immense house called the Vatican. Your house may have a dozen rooms, or perhaps even a score, but it is said that the Vatican contains more than a thousand rooms. There are so many rooms that probably no one has ever counted them all. Many of the large rooms are filled with famous pictures and sculpture. They are art museums which people may visit. One room is the Pope's private chapel. It is called the Sistine Chapel. Michelangelo painted pictures on the ceiling and walls of this chapel. In order to see the pictures on the ceiling comfortably you have to lie flat on your back or look at them in a mirror held in your hand.

Before the time of St. Peter, when people believed in many gods, another church was built in Rome "To All the Gods." This building is still standing. It is called the Pantheon, which means "All Gods." The Pantheon too has a dome, but it is not like St. Peter's. The dome of St. Peter's is like a giant cup turned upside down. The dome of the Pantheon is like a giant saucer turned upside down. There are no windows at all in the Pantheon, but there is a large hole in the top of the saucer called an "eye" which looks toward heaven, and through this eye the sun shines and the rain falls. It is so high above the floor, however, that the rain scarcely wets the floor beneath, but evaporates before reaching it.

Most of the buildings in Rome that were built about the time of Christ are in ruins, but the Pantheon is still almost the same as it was when first built. Around and about the very old buildings the dust and dirt and rubbish of the city had collected for two thousand years and had grad-

ARCH OF TITUS
It was built to honor Titus because he destroyed Jerusalem

ually piled higher and higher until the ruins were twenty feet or more lower than the present city, so that it has been necessary to dig them out.

In those days long ago there was a great market-place in Rome called the Forum. Around the Forum were beautiful palaces, court-houses, temples, and arches. The arches were built so that generals, when they returned from the wars they had fought and won, might ride in triumph through them. One of these arches is called the

Arch of Titus. Titus was a Roman Emperor who
destroyed the capital city of the Jews called
Jerusalem and this arch was built to celebrate the
event. Another arch is the Arch of Constantine.
Constantine was the first Emperor of Rome to
believe in Christ. That was not until three hundred years after Christ had died.

The old Romans had a peculiar idea of fun.

The ghost of a lion that used to kill Christians in the
Colosseum

They liked to watch fights between men and wild
animals such as lions and tigers, and they liked
to see the men and animals kill each other.
Sometimes the men were prisoners who had been
captured in battle, sometimes they were just
Christians whom the Roman Emperors wanted
to put to death. So a great stadium was built
where the Romans could sit in safety and watch

these fights as we watch football or baseball games. This stadium is called the Colosseum and, though it is partly in ruins, most of it is still standing and you can still see the dens where the wild animals were kept before they were let loose into the arena.

As the Christians were afraid to worship above ground where the Romans would see them, they hid in secret cellar-like places where they could worship as they pleased. Just outside of Rome, underneath the ground, are miles upon miles of these cellar-like rooms where they worshiped and where they were buried when they died. They are called Catacombs. Millions of the Christians were buried in the Catacombs.

INSIDE OF THE ROMAN CATACOMBS

37

A Pile of Ashes a Mile High

A PILE of ashes is not usually very beautiful, and if it is in your back yard it is usually very ugly. But in Italy there is a pile of ashes which every one thinks beautiful, though it is nearly a mile high and though it is in the back yard of a city called Naples. It is on the beautiful Bay of Naples, and people have built their homes and hotels around the bay so as to get a view of this pile of ashes, which is called Mount Vesuvius, though it's not really a mountain at all.

In olden days when grown-up people believed in fairy-tales they said that a lame blacksmith lived down under the ground, that he kept a huge furnace burning there to heat the iron with which he worked. His name they said was Vulcan, and the smoke and flame that came out of the ground and the ashes that piled up above the ground were from his fires. So we call these mountains of ashes, through the top of which fire and smoke pour forth, volcanoes, after Vulcan.

There are volcanoes in many places in the World, but Vesuvius is the best known of all. We now know that volcanoes are huge fiery furnaces beneath the ground, but we also know that no man nor fairy nor god is down there keeping them burning. Some volcanoes in other parts of the World have burned out, but the fires of Vesuvius have not. Vesuvius is always smoking and burning. We can see smoke or steam coming out of its top in the day and we can see the firelight come out of its top at night, but

MT. VESUVIUS AND THE BAY OF NAPLES

Near the Bay of Naples is a pile of ashes almost a mile high

usually it does no more damage than a huge smoking chimney would. But every now and then the fires start burning fiercely and rock and ashes are shot up into the air, and pieces of rock are blown to such fine powder that they float in the air like dust. This dust may float for months in the air and for thousands of miles to other countries far off from the volcano from which it comes. Strange to say, it is this dust from volcanoes that often makes the sunsets such brilliant colors.

The fire in volcanoes is hotter than any fire

we can make. We can make a fire so hot that it
will melt copper and iron, but we can't make a
fire so hot that it will melt rock. A volcano fire
melts rock as easily as if it were butter. The rock
that the volcano melts flows over the top like a
pot boiling over and runs down the sides in
streams that gradually harden into rock as they
cool off. This rock is called lava, and as there is
plenty of lava around Naples the people there
use blocks of lava to pave their streets.

Some years ago I was in Naples after Vesuvius had been firing up. The streets of Naples
were filled with what looked like gray snow. The
gray snow was dust that had fallen from the volcano, but it would not melt like snow and had to
be carted away and dumped into the Bay of Naples. I wanted to see what the inside of a volcano looked like. There had been a railway
almost to the top, but it had been wrecked. So I
climbed from the bottom to the top, though it
took half a day to do so, for at each step my feet
sank deep into the ashes. I looked over the edge,
down into the fiery mouth of the volcano. Every
now and then pieces of rock would shoot high
into the air and, looking up, I would dodge those
that fell near-by. Entirely too many were falling
around me, so I started back down the side of
the volcano. I didn't walk down, I jumped, for
each step I took was like jumping off a house,
and at each step I fell, only I didn't hurt myself
when I fell, for I sank into the ashes up to my

knees, up to my waist, up to my neck. It was great fun, like jumping into a pile of hay, only it was oh, so dirty! It took me half a day to go up—it took me about ten minutes to come down—but hours to wash off the ashes when I was down, and my clothes were utterly ruined.

Some birds build their nests on the tops of chimneys, but it seems strange that people should

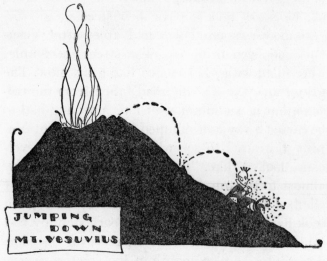

JUMPING DOWN MT. VESUVIUS

It got too hot for me at the top so I jumped down the side

build their homes at the foot of a volcano that may blow up and destroy them at any time. Yet long, long ago people built a city at the foot of Vesuvius, nearer even than Naples. It was called Pompeii. All of a sudden one day Vesuvius began to burn and boil and then blew up. Before any one in Pompeii knew what was going to happen, before any one had time to move from the spot where he was working or playing, Vesuvius had poured down on this little city its deadly fire and smoke and gas, and every one was killed where he stood and buried deep in dust and ashes. There the city and its people lay buried for almost two thousand years. Not so very long ago the city was dug out, its houses and temples and theaters were uncovered, and travelers can now visit the ruins, walk through the streets, and go into the houses and shops where once upon a time people went about their daily tasks and pleasures without a thought that the end of the World was coming to them in the twinkling of an eye.

No one knows when Vesuvius may do the same thing again, but the people in Naples never seem to think of such a thing; they don't worry; they go about the streets singing happily; in fact, it's one of the few cities in the World where people sing on the streets.

We may hear people whistling on the street in this country, but seldom, if ever, do we hear them sing on the streets. Singing may not be a sign of happiness at all, but people in Naples sing and sing, especially at night. Taxi drivers sing, ragged street urchins sing, beggars sing, and they sing songs you hear at concerts or in the opera. One of the greatest singers that ever lived, who now is dead, but whom you can still hear singing on the phonograph, was once a street urchin in Naples. Then he came to America. His name was Caruso.

The Italian language is the language of singing, the language of music. Some one has said you can't help singing if you speak Italian. Even the sheet music we use in this country is usually written in Italian and the directions for playing are given in Italian. In Italian almost every word ends in a vowel, that is, in a, e, i, o, or u. Piano and 'cello, soprano and alto are Italian words. Even Naples ends in a vowel, for in Italian it is called Napoli.

The name "Goat" is neither pretty nor musical and it wouldn't sound well in a song, but across the Bay of Naples is an island the name of which in English is goat; but in Italian it is "Capri," and songs are sung about "Bella Capri"—the beautiful Capri—the beautiful Goat Island.

In the rocky shore of Capri there is a sea cave which you can only enter in a rowboat through a low opening. The opening is so low you have to duck your head, and if the waves are high you can't go through at all. The cave is called the Blue Grotto, for inside this rocky cave the water is such a beautiful clear blue that it seems almost as if your boat were floating on sky instead of on water. What makes it so blue? If you dip some of the water up in a bottle to take home as a souvenir—as I have known people to do—the water is just as colorless as the water in your own bathtub.

38

Wars and Fairy-Tales

Though Italian is the language of music, the people of Germany are quite as musical as the Italians. But their music is very different from the music of the Italians. Some of their music is warlike, big and loud, and yet some of it is gentle and sweet, and the most famous cradle songs and Christmas carols have been written by Germans. "Silent Night, Holy Night" is one. Musical plays are called operas. Some of the greatest operas in the World have been composed by Germans.

Cradle songs and Christmas carols don't seem to go well with fighting. But the Germans, besides being very musical, have also been very warlike. You have all heard of the two terrible World Wars, World War I and World War II. Most of the countries of the World took part in these two wars. In each war Germany fought almost all the other countries in the World and, even with almost all the rest of the World against her, she nearly won both times.

After World War II the countries that had beaten Germany divided Germany up to keep her from starting any more wars. Russia took Eastern Germany. The United States, Great

Britain, and France ruled Western Germany.
So there came to be two Germanies, West Germany and East Germany.

Which do you like better, fairy-tales or true
stories? Some of the World's best fairy-tales have
been made in Germany. Stories, poems, songs,
and operas have been written about fairy people
and real people who once lived on the hills and
in the caves by the side of a river in Germany

Some of the World's best fairy-tales come from Germany

called the Rhine. The Rhine starts from a glacier
in the Swiss Alps and runs north along the west
side of Germany and through Holland.

On both sides of the Rhine are steep hills and
rocks and on top of these hills are castles built
many years ago. The men who built these castles
were called robber barons, and they built their
castles on these hills so that they could rob and
would be safe from their enemies. The poor people, who lived down in the valleys, had to give

part of the things they raised to the barons; if
they did not do so, the barons would swoop down
on them with their men and take what they
wanted and destroy the people's homes. The
people knew it was useless to attack the barons
because of their strong castles. Most of these
castles are now in ruins, because it is too hard to
get to them and to keep them in repair, and no
longer can any one treat the poor people the way
the barons did.

CASTLES ON THE RHINE

Robbers once lived in these castles

Cologne is a kind of strong perfume. It is
named for a city on the Rhine called Cologne.
Cologne means colony, for it was once a colony
of Rome. The house in which I live took seven
months to build, but there is a Cathedral in
Cologne that took seven hundred years to build!
—the longest time of any building in the World.

Cologne is a city famous for its Cathedral but
the most famous German city is Berlin. Before
World War II Berlin was one of the finest and

cleanest cities in the world. It had broad tree-lined avenues, great handsome stone buildings, parks and statues. It was also the capital of Germany. But by the time World War II was over, much of Berlin was a wreck. Many of its finest buildings were in ruins, destroyed by bombs

It took seven hundred years to build Cologne Cathedral

dropped from airplanes during the war. Berlin is in Eastern Germany, the part of Germany ruled by the Russians after the War, but the United States, Great Britain, and France as well as Russia govern Berlin. The Russians had fought on our side during World War II, but after the War was over they became very unfriendly to the United States and Great Britain. They even

said that the countries ruling Western Germany
could not use the railroad or auto roads to Berlin.
The people of Berlin had to be fed, so the United
States and Great Britain flew tons and tons of
food and coal into the city by airplanes day after
day for a year and a half. Finally the Russians
realized they could not keep out the Americans
and British and opened the railroad again. This
carrying of supplies to Berlin was called the
Berlin Airlift because the supplies were lifted
through the air from Western Germany to Berlin.

Sticking up off the map of Germany like a
thumb is a little country called Denmark. On
one side of it is the North Sea; on the other side
is another sea called the Baltic. Germany fronts
on the North Sea and on the Baltic Sea too, but
this little thumb of land does not belong to Germany. The Germans had to go all around this
country in order to get from the cities on the
North Sea to the cities on the Baltic Sea, so they
cut off the thumb by digging a canal across the
bottom of it. It is called the Kiel Canal.

39

The Great Danes

WHEN anything annoyed my uncle he used to cry out, *"Skagerrack and Kattegat!"* It sounded terrible, for I didn't know then that Skagerrack and Kattegat were merely the names of the narrow waterway around Denmark from the North Sea into the Baltic Sea and that Kattegat simply meant "the cat's throat" and Skagerrack meant "Skager throat."

There are two chief pieces to Denmark. One piece is the thumb-like land called Jutland, because a people called the Jutes used to live there. The other piece is a little island right alongside of Jutland called Zealand. You don't have to be a good guesser to know that Zealand means "Sea Land." On this island is Copenhagen, the capital of Denmark. Copenhagen means "Merchants' Harbor," because merchants with their ships used to stop there on the way from the North Sea to the Baltic. But there are not as many ships now as there used to be, for instead of going through the Skagerrack and Kattegat, many ships take the short cut through the Kiel Canal. Copenhagen is the only big city that Denmark has—there are no other large cities.

You probably have heard of a "Great Dane," a kind of big dog that comes from Denmark. But the people in Denmark are called Danes, and there is one great Dane whom you probably know and whose stories you have probably read. He wrote "The Little Match Girl" and "The Ugly Duckling." The man who wrote those fairy-tales lived in Copenhagen. His name is Hans Christian Andersen. The Danes like the name "Christian." Ten of their kings have been named Christian.

But over a thousand years ago the Danes were not Christians, and many were pirates who sailed the seas and robbed other lands. They are now, of course, no longer pirates; but they are still great sailors. In some towns almost every person is either a sailor, a ship-builder, or connected with shipping in some way.

The Danes who stay at home are chiefly engaged in the butter and egg business. They raise cows to make butter and chickens to lay eggs and they send butter and eggs to other countries that haven't enough. Danish eggs have the date when they are laid stamped on them, so that every one may know how fresh or how old they are. Danish butter is so good and brings such high prices that the Danes send most of it away, and they themselves usually eat an imitation butter made out of fat or grease.

Denmark is one of the healthiest countries in the World. People live longer there than in almost any other country; so the moral of this is, if you want to live long, go to Denmark.

Denmark, though such a little country, used to own two islands that were perhaps ten times as big as itself. These two islands are far away from Denmark in the cold north; one is a little island called Iceland and the other is a big island called Greenland. Greenland still belongs to Denmark, but Iceland no longer does. Most people cannot see why Denmark should want either island, for Iceland is full of volcanoes and many hot springs—which seems strange, for ice and fire do not seem to go together—and Greenland is chiefly ice. I think it would be more exact if Greenland were called Iceland and Iceland were called Volcano Land. I used to know a boy who was very fat, but all his friends called him "Skinny." That is like calling this ice-covered land Greenland, so I think it was called Greenland for a joke. Only along one edge of Greenland do we find any land at all showing. The ice in Greenland is about a quarter of a mile thick, covering the land, and where the ice comes down to the water's edge big chunks often as big as a church break off and float away in the sea. They are then called icebergs, which means ice mountains.

There are Eskimos living in Greenland. You may well wonder what the Eskimos in Greenland live on, for they can't raise any of the vegetables we have to eat. They live chiefly on fish out of the sea and animals and birds. There are millions of birds called "auks" which fly so low and so thick over the land that the Eskimos catch them with a net as you would catch butterflies. They can catch enough to last them for many months, and as all out-of-doors is a refrigerator the birds that are caught can be kept on ice without having the ice man call every day. Eskimos use the auk's soft feathers to line their clothes to keep themselves warm and comfortable, for the thermometer sometimes goes to seventy degrees below zero. Another bird, the eider-duck, has still softer feathers. They are called "down." Eider-down is one of the softest and lightest things imaginable and makes the best filling for bed quilts, as it is both light and warm. Eskimos eat the eider-duck's eggs, too, and they gather thousands of them at a time.

Instead of beef, the Eskimo eats the flesh of an animal called the musk-ox. The musk-ox has hooklike horns and a shaggy long-haired coat to keep himself warm in the terrible cold. His coat makes him look big, but when he is killed and the coat removed, there is only a poor little lean animal left inside.

There is another animal which the Eskimo hunts. It lives both in the water and on the land and has tusks like an elephant. It is called a walrus. It is also caught for meat, but chiefly for its ivory tusks, which are two big teeth that hang far down out of its mouth.

What the Eskimo likes best to eat, however, is not lean meat but fat. A big, greasy strip of fat to him is as delicious as a banana to us. Fat food keeps people warm, and nature in its wonderful way makes fat taste good to the Eskimo because it makes him warm. People in warm countries don't like fat food because it would make them warm when they want to be cool.

One of the most valuable furs that ladies wear is made from the coat of the seal, another animal that lives both in the water and on the ice. The Eskimo uses the sealskin to make his tents in which he lives in the summertime. The winds are so terribly strong in parts of Greenland that a tent has to be anchored down by heavy stones to keep it from blowing away. In the wintertime, however, the Eskimo makes his hut of blocks of stone—if he can find any; but if he can't, he cuts blocks of snow and makes a bowl-shaped house of that instead. Of course, his house is hardly large enough to stand up in and has only one room and no windows, so that he has to light it inside with a fire built right on the ground, or by a lamp made out of a hollowed stone with a wick soaked in the grease or fat of the animals he has killed.

The only tame animals the Eskimo has are the Eskimo dogs, which look very much like wolves and may be cousins of the wolves. The Eskimo uses dogs hooked up to his sled, instead of a horse and carriage or automobile. Four or eight or more dogs are harnassed together and make a team. Almost all of our dogs love water; they will run and jump into a pool or into a river if given half a chance. But the Eskimo dog is afraid of water, and though he can swim he will not go into it unless he is whipped into it, and not even then if he can run away. The Eskimo, however, is not afraid of the water even when blocks of ice are floating in it. He has a canoe called a kayak which is completely covered, all except a place in the center where he sits and paddles. It is water tight, so that even when upset no water can get in. The Eskimos are experts at paddling, and they have water sports in which an Eskimo upsets his kayak on purpose and rolls over and over in the water just to show off.

ESKIMO IN
HIS KAYAK.

40

Fish, Fiords, Falls, and Forests

HAVE you a good imagination? I mean, when there are clouds in the sky, can you see giants or galloping horses or rabbits with long ears or other things? Then look at the map on page 260 and tell me what it looks like:

Turn it on the side. Do you see what I see? A WHALE, with his mouth open, ready to swallow little Denmark. Skagerrack and Kattegat are the whale's throat.

My geography calls this whale the "Scandinavian Peninsula"—that's a big name, but then a whale is a big animal. The geography calls the back of the whale Norway, and it calls the other side Sweden. Norway plus Sweden equals Scandinavian Peninsula.

Perhaps the reason I thought of a whale was because there are so many real whales in the sea near Norway. Now a whale is the largest fish there is, you know, only it isn't a fish. Fish lay eggs as chickens and birds do, only much smaller and many more, but a whale mother doesn't lay eggs. She has babies as a cat has kittens. Besides, a whale has to have air to breathe and must come

up to the top of the water as you would have to
do if you were swimming under the water. A fish
wouldn't do that, for he couldn't do that, so you
see a whale is not a fish.

The whale eats little fish called herring, lots of
them at one gulp, bones and all. There are millions, billions, trillions of herring in the sea,
and millions, billions, trillions more than that.
They live together in enormous crowds called
"schools," but one school of herring has more pu-
pils than all the schools in the World; so, although the whales eat some herring, there are
plenty of herring left for us to eat. The Norwegian people catch herring in nets, then they salt,
smoke, or dry them to make sure they will keep
almost forever without spoiling. Then they send
these dried herring all over the World to be sold.
I had a herring for breakfast this morning which
may have been swimming round Norway years
and years ago—it has been kept all that time.

I also ate a thousand eggs for breakfast this
morning. That sounds impossible, but it's really
so—only they were not *hen's* eggs, but herring
eggs, for the mother herring carries her eggs inside of her—thousands of them. The herring's
eggs we call "roe."

The seashore of Norway is not smooth and
level like a bathing beach. There are mountains
all along the edge right in the water and the sea
fills the valleys between these mountains. These
valleys filled with water are called "fiords."

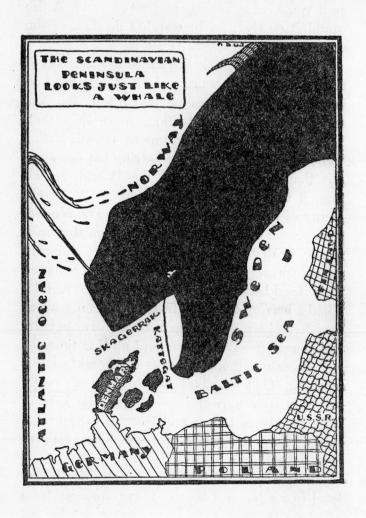

Norway is so far north we would expect the water in these fiords to be very cold in the winter; and we know what happens when water gets very cold—it freezes and turns to ice. But, strange to say, the water in these fiords does not freeze. The reason it doesn't freeze is because the sun shines down on the water in the Gulf of Mexico, several thousand miles off. You may wonder what the Gulf of Mexico several thousand miles off has to do with Norway. Well, the boiler way off in my cellar heats the water in the pipes and that heats the radiator in the farthest room in my house. In the same way the sun heats the water in the Gulf as if it were a big boiler and from this Gulf a warm stream of water, called the Gulf Stream, flows as if it were a river in the ocean, all the way across the ocean from the Gulf of Mexico to the shore of Norway and warms the fiords. In the warm water of the fiords the herring schools have a fine recess until a whale or a fisherman comes along.

The north*est* city in the World is in Norway and the name of this city ends in *est,* too. It is Hammer*fest*. The Gulf Stream seems to end at Hammerfest and it dumps on the shore sticks of wood, some of which have floated like toy boats in a river all the way from the Gulf of Mexico. The people gather this "driftwood" and use it to make fires. Ordinary wood burns with a yellow flame, but wood that has drifted for a long time in the sea-water gets filled with salt from the water and when dried and burned gives off flames colored blue and green and purple, so that driftwood makes especially beautiful fires in open fireplaces.

You have probably tasted cod-liver oil—and hated it—but you were told it was very good for you, and it is. The cod is a much bigger fish than the herring, but of course not nearly as big as the whale. One of the playgrounds of the cod is near Norway, round some islands called "The Lofodens." Fishermen catch shiploads of cod, press the oil out of their livers, and bottle it for your good health. The bones of the cod they have no use for, so they take them out—and this is quite a job, for there are a great many—and then they dry the flesh of the cod to make food. Here is a sentence that sounds funny unless you put in a period where it belongs, and then it makes perfect sense: "A codfish was swimming round the Lofoden Islands a month after all its bones had been taken out." Where would you put the period to make sense?

41

Fish, Fiords, Falls, and Forests
(*continued*)

THE "fishiest" city in the World is in Norway on a fiord. The city and the fiord are both called Bergen. The fishermen from the Lofoden Islands and the fiords bring their catches to Bergen—boatloads of big fish and little fish, thick fish and thin fish, white fish and black fish—to sell and to ship everywhere.

Bergen is also another "est" besides the "fishiest." It is the wett*est* city in Europe. People carry umbrellas or raincoats all the time, for you scarcely ever see the sun, and when it is not raining it is getting ready to. It takes a lot of rain, if caught in a bucket, to make as much as an inch deep of water. Perhaps you have seen it rain so hard that the streets were flooded and at the crossings the rain has been over your shoe tops, but probably it has rained less than an inch in any one spot, such as in a bucket. Of course, when rain runs off the roof and pours down on to the street the water has run together from a large space, but very few cities have a rainfall of more than a few feet in a whole year. Bergen however has a rainfall of six feet in a year. This is enough rain to drown every man, woman, and child in the city if it all came down at once, but fortunately it does not.

As nearly every family in America has an automobile, nearly every family in Norway has a boat. The Norwegians always have been famous sailors.

Long, long ago the Norwegian sailors were called Vikings, which, however, does not mean Vi-"kings," but "Vik"-ings, and that means "fiordmen." One of the greatest of these Vikings was a man named Leif, son of Eric, called Leif Ericson. Leif Ericson lived about a thousand years ago. He and his men sailed across the ocean and landed in America five hundred years before Columbus discovered America, but he didn't think much of the country, and when he went back to Norway he said little about it.

In later times there have been famous sailors and discoverers too in Norway. Men up there live so near the top of the earth that they have tried to go all the way to the top, to the point where if you stood still you would turn exactly around on the spot where you stood once every twenty-four hours. That point is the North Pole. Such men have risked their lives—and many have lost them—in trying to reach the poles. Two famous Scandinavian explorers, Nansen and Amundsen, tried—they didn't lose their lives, but they didn't reach the North Pole either. An American named Peary was the first man to

reach the North Pole. Amundsen, however, tried
to reach the South Pole and he succeeded. He
was the first man to reach the South Pole. Since

Peary was the first man to reach the
North Pole

then airplanes, and a Norse airship too, have
crossed the North Pole, but they didn't stop
there. Later Amundsen started for the North
Pole in an airplane and was never heard from
again.

You have overshoes to wear when you go out
in the snow, but every one in Norway and Sweden has a pair of long wooden runners called
"skis," which he straps to his shoes when he goes
out. With these on his feet he coasts over the
top of the snow, making a sled of himself—sliding down slopes and pushing himself along on
level ground with a pole, as if it were a cane.

Have you ever seen a white blackbird? No one has. Have you ever seen white coal? They have a lot of it in Norway and Sweden. On the tops

He makes a sled of himself

of the mountains there are vast fields of snow and ice like frosting on a huge cake, but as this snow and ice sinks down to the valleys it melts and the water falls in streams like rain running off a roof down a waterspout. This water falling is used in Norway and Sweden to turn wheels and the wheels turning are used to run sawmills and machinery, just the same as if the wheels were turned by steam-engines run with coal fires. Norway and Sweden have no black coal, but the waterfalls do much the same thing; they run machines, and so people speak of their water-falls as "white coal."

But white coal won't do one thing that black coal will do—it won't heat. In the northern part of Sweden there are iron mines. This iron is particularly good for making tools that have to have sharp edges, like knives and razors. But there is no black coal to melt the iron out of the ore, so they ship most of the ore to England, where there is plenty of coal, and there the English make fine cutlery from it.

Perhaps you have seen pictures of pine-trees in the snow or covered with snow. Anyway, pine-trees and snow seem to go together, and a great part of Norway and Sweden is covered with forests chiefly of pine-trees. Pine-trees—tall, straight ones—make fine masts for ships, flag and telegraph poles, and lumber for building. They also make fine match-sticks, and millions of match-sticks can be made out of a single tree. If you will look on a box of matches that you may find at your home, you will probably see the words "Made in Sweden" printed on it. The smaller trees the Swedes grind up into pulp, which is used to make paper, for almost all paper nowadays—whether it is newspaper, wrapping-paper, or the paper you write on—is made of wood-pulp rolled thin. So the people in Sweden cut down trees, saw them up into logs, slide them into the streams, and float them down to the sea, and there they ship them all over the World. But they take good care to plant little trees for every large tree cut down, so that there will always be more trees.

42

Where the Sun Shines all Night

In "Through the Looking-Glass" the story of "The Walrus and the Carpenter" starts this way:

> The sun was shining on the sea,
>   Shining with all his might: . . .
> And this was odd, because it was
>   The middle of the night.

Sun shining at midnight! You probably think this can't be true and is only a joke, but it *is* true up at the top of Norway and Sweden. At the top of Norway is a great rock sticking out into the Arctic Ocean. It is called the North Cape, and although there is no town there, people make long journeys from other lands to the North Cape to see the sun shining on the sea in the middle of the night.

You have always been told that the sun rises in the east and sets in the west, and probably you have never seen it do anything else; but the boys and girls in the north of Norway and Sweden know differently, for up there the sun doesn't rise in the east and set in the west. It goes completely round the house low down in the sky near the ground and keeps on going round and round this way every day for six months and in that time never sets—is never out of sight—there is always daylight for six months. But the sun gradually gets closer and closer to the ground as it goes round the sky and then at last sinks out of sight below the edge of the World, and there it stays out of sight for another six months and for six months it is night.

How can such a thing be? Isn't it the same sun we see here?

Yes, of course it's the same sun; there's only one sun. But we are living on the *side* of the World and we can't see the sun when it goes round to the other side of the World. If, however, we climb up the side of the World to the top where the North Cape is, we can see the sun go all the way round. It is as if you lived on the side of a hill and some one went round the hill and came back on the other side. You could see him go off one way and come back the other way, but you couldn't see him when he was on the other side. If, however, you went to the top of the hill you could see him all the way round.

The land at the top of the World is often called "The Land of the Midnight Sun," because the sun shines at midnight. It might just as well be called "The Land of the 10-o'clock-at-night Sun," for the sun shines at every hour of the night as well as every hour of the day. And it also might be called "The Land of the Midday

Night," for when the sun is going round out of sight below the edge of the World it is dark every hour of the day as well as of the night.

This "Land of the Midnight Sun" is the land

A LAPLANDER WITH
HIS REINDEER.

It's Santa Claus Land

of the Reindeer—Santa Claus Land. In this land of snow and ice very little grows except moss, and the Reindeer is the only animal that can live on moss. The people that live there are called Lapps. They look something like Eskimos, and both look like the Chinese, so we think they probably were Chinese long, long ago. The Lapps and the Reindeer live together in the same hut— the Reindeer is like a horse, a cow, a sheep, and a dog all in one. The Lapp harnesses the Reindeer to his sled, he gets milk from her, he kills her and eats the meat, and then he uses her skin to make himself and his family fur coats and tents.

But the people who live in the rest of Norway

and Sweden are the same kind of people as you
and I, only some of them are much smarter and
better educated. I know a Swede who speaks
twelve languages, I know of a Swede who invented a way of separating cream from milk
without skimming it, and I know of two Swedish
boys who invented a machine for making ice
with heat.

Sweden and Norway used to be one country
with one king, but now they are separate countries and each has a separate king and a separate
capital.

In the geography your grandfather used, the
capital of Norway was named Christiania, but
the name was changed. You will find it on the
map way down the throat of the whale. It is now
called Oslo. The capital of Sweden begins with
an "S," as Sweden does. It is Stockholm. Both
Oslo and Stockholm are on the water, but they
are not touched by the Gulf Stream, so the
water in their harbors is frozen over nearly all
winter and ships cannot go and come at that
time. Stockholm is often called the Venice of the
North, because like Venice it has many streets
of water.

Mary and John are our commonest names.
The Scandinavians like some names for their
children better than others. Ole is one name they
like especially well. Hans is another, and Eric
and Peter are others. We sometimes make a
family name by adding "son" to John to make

Johnson. The Scandinavians add "son" or "sen" to their names to make family names, as Ericson, Oleson, Hansen, Petersen, Nansen, Amundsen. If you were in Wisconsin or Minnesota and looked in the telephone book you would find thousands of such names. That is because many, many Swedes and Norwegians have come to our country and settled in that part of our country which is most like their country.

Many common Norse words look like English words misspelled:

> lamp is lampe
> house is hus
> cow is ko

They haven't copied us, we have copied them, for long ago Norse sailors settled in England, and after thousands of years we still use some Norse words changed very little.

Long years ago the men of Scandinavia were fierce fighters, who drank a strong liquor called "mead" and used the skulls of their enemies for cups. They believed in fairy-tale gods and goddesses. Thor, they believed, was a god who made the thunder and lightning. Tiu was the god of war. So they named some of the days of the week after their gods; Tiu's day, Thor's day, Woden's day, Fria's day. Strange to say, four of the seven days of our week are still named after these Scandinavian gods, for those wild people who believed in those gods are the great-great-grandfathers of many of us. Tuesday is Tiu's day,

Thursday is Thor's day, Friday is Fria's day and Wednesday is Woden's day—that's why we still have a "d" in Wednesday which we might forget in spelling, as we do not sound it now. Most people have forgotten that our week-days are named after heathen gods, but some think that we should not use such heathen names, so they use numbers instead of names for the days of the week, as in Bible times.

Dynamite, you know, is something used to blow up things. It was invented by a man who lived in Sweden some years ago. When he died he left a lot of money and said that the interest from this money was to be given every year to the men or women who, no matter in what country they lived, had done the most for the World during that year. So each year judges go over all the things that have been done and choose those men or women who have done the most for the good of the World and give them the money. This man was named Nobel and the money is known as the Nobel Prize. Two of our Presidents —Theodore Roosevelt and Woodrow Wilson— won the Nobel Prize for Peace and so did an American Negro, Ralph Bunche. You yourself could win the Nobel Prize if you ever did something big enough and fine enough. Do you think you ever will?

43

The Bear

WHEN-I-WAS-A-BOY the story I liked best was
one about wolves in Russia. Some Russians in
a sleigh were driving across the snow, when they
were attacked by a pack of hungry wolves. The
men whipped up their horses, but the wolves
drew nearer and nearer. When the wolves were
just about to spring upon the sleigh the men
threw out food, which the wolves stopped a mo-
ment to devour, allowing the sleigh to get ahead.
But the wolves caught up and again food was
thrown out and again and again, till there was
no food left. See if you can guess the end of the
story, or make up an ending of your own.

Naturally, I used to think of Russia as a land
of wolves, though for some reason people call
Russia "The Bear."

Russia is a huge country—it is the largest
country in Europe—it is as large as all the other
countries of Europe put together, and in the far
north there are wolves, snow, and sleighs. But
there is also a middle Russia which is not so cold
and a southern Russia which is quite warm.

In the north of Russia it is so cold that even in
summer when the snow has gone and the ground

has thawed out on top, the ground underneath remains frozen stiff, and, though grass
and even flowers grow above, the ground below remains hard and icy. These frozen lands
are called "tundras," and there are thousands of
miles of such tundras across the north of Russia.

At the top of Russia is a sea called "White"
and at the bottom of Russia a sea called "Black."
The White Sea, I suppose, is called "White"
because it is frozen over most of the year and
covered with snow—and yet, during a few months
of the summer when the ice in it has melted, great
ships sail into the White Sea, bringing in loads
of all sorts of goods to the one great port on this
sea—a city called Archangel—a name that makes
one think of heaven.

You may wonder why people live in such far-
off places, why they don't move to other places
that are more comfortable. But people live where
they can make a living, and cities usually start
with a few houses and more and more houses
are built until there is a city. But there is a great
city farther south than Archangel which was
built all at once—to order. It was built by a man
named Peter, who was one of the rulers of Russia. They were called "czars." Peter wanted to
live by the water so that he could sail ships, just
as you might like to go to the seashore to sail
boats, so he built a city by the sea, with streets,
shops, houses, and palaces, and then, as he was
a czar who could make people do what he wanted,

he made people come and live in this city. Peter
had been named for St. Peter, so he called his
city St. Petersburg, which meant St. Peter's
City. That was two hundred years ago.

When Russia was fighting in World War I
the people of St. Petersburg said that they
wanted a real Russian name for their city, for
"burg" was the German name for city, and they
were fighting the Germans, so they called it
Petrograd, which was the Russian name for
Peter's City. But the people got tired of the war
and all of a sudden they said they would not fight
any more; they had a revolution, killed the
czar and set up a government of their own.
They wanted the city of Petrograd called for
the leader of the revolution, a man named
Lenin, so they changed the name of the city
again to Leningrad, which meant Lenin's City.

St. Petersburg ⎫
Petrograd ⎬ was built to be the capital of
Leningrad ⎭

Russia, but it was so cold there they moved the
capital to a city still farther south near the center
of Russia that had been the capital before. This
city is called Moscow.

The revolutionists took the palaces and homes
of the wealthy and turned them into hospitals and
public buildings. They took the land of the rich
and lent it out to farmers and workers. These
revolutionists were known as Communists. The
provinces and districts of Russia combined as the

Union of Soviet Socialist Republics, which is governed from the capital at Moscow.

In Moscow there is a big walled-in place with houses and palaces and churches called the Kremlin. It is from the Kremlin that Russia is ruled, so the Kremlin is really the capitol, though it is not just one building like our Capitol in Washington. The churches in the Kremlin are not used as churches now for after the Revolution the Communists turned them into museums and government buildings just as they did the palaces of the wealthy.

Near the walls of the Kremlin is a great open paved space called Red Square. On one side of Red Square is a flat-topped building which is the tomb of Lenin. The Russians have the largest army i.t.w.W. and they often have parades of soldiers which pass through Red Square past the chief Russian rulers who stand on top of Lenin's tomb to see the soldiers march by.

The square is called Red Square because red is the color of revolution and the people who govern Russia adopted it as their color. Russia's flag is red and the Communists themselves are often called Reds. The Communists are not Christians. They don't believe in any religion.

There are still some Christians in Russia, but the Communists have done many things to make it hard to be a Christian there.

One thing the Communists believe is that all countries must sooner or later be made Communist countries. Communists have seized many of the small countries that are next to Russia. Communists even try to overthrow the governments of countries that do not like Communism and want nothing to do with it. There are a few Communists in England, in France, in the United States—in fact in almost all countries, and these Communists plot and scheme against these countries all the time. A person doesn't have to be a Russian to be a Communist, but the chief Communists are Russians.

In a Communist country the people must do whatever the Communist rulers tell them. People can be put in prison, or sent to work as slaves in the mines, or even killed by the Communist police without a trial. When they are taken away by the police their families may never hear from them again. Almost no people from other countries are allowed to visit Communist countries, especially the chief Communist country of Russia. "VISITORS NOT WANTED. KEEP OUT" would be a good sign to paste on the map of Russia.

Russia is more than twice as big as any other country i.t.w.W. It's hard for us to understand why Russia wants to take over more and more countries when it is already so big. But it does. The Russian Communists would like Moscow to be the capital of the whole World, not just the capital of the Union of Soviet Socialist Republics.

The Russian people love music and they love

their land of Russia. Some of the best music in the whole World has been written by Russians. Whenever a group of Russians are working together they are apt to sing. Russian soldiers sing on the march, workers in the fields sing together as they work, sailors sing on their ships. Even those poor people who are kept like slaves in prison camps sing, though their songs are not gay but sad.

44

The Bread-Basket

In the north of Russia the ground is white with snow.

In the south of Russia the ground is black—almost as black as coal—because the soil is so rich, probably the richest in the World. So this part of Russia is called the Black Earth Land. In parts of our country the rich soil usually goes down only a few inches before there is rock or clay, on which nothing will grow, but in Russia the rich soil is so deep that you could dig down in some places three or four times your height before striking rock or clay in which nothing grows. In America many farms *wear out,* because there is such a thin layer of the rich soil that it is soon used up. This is the case on many farms in New England that were in use two hundred years ago but are now used up, and so little will grow on them that the farmers move away and leave their farms, for they are no longer any good. In Russia, however, the rich soil never seems to wear out. Their farms are thousands of years old and still there is enough of this soil to grow food.

In the Black Earth Land they raise great quantities of wheat and, as bread is made from wheat, this part of Russia is often called the Bread-Basket. There is one thing the farmers raise that may seem strange—that is, sunflowers —acres and acres of them. But they do not raise them for their flowers; they raise them for their seeds. They eat sunflower seeds as we eat pea-nuts; but the chief thing they do with them is to press the oil out of the seeds, for this oil is good for salad, for making soap and other things.

The largest lake in the World is in the corner of Russia next to the Black Sea. Rivers run into it but none run out of it, and so the lake is salt. It is called the Caspian Sea, for it is like a little ocean.

As the *March Hare* in "Alice in Wonderland" said, "You can draw water out of a water-well, so I should think you could draw treacle out of a treacle-well," and in the same way you get oil from an oil-well. At the city of Baku on the side of the Caspian Sea there are so many oil-wells and so much oil that it seems to get into everything. You see it, smell it, feel it, and taste it. As there are no rivers flowing out of the Caspian Sea, no ships can get to the ocean from Baku, so a way had to be found to carry the oil to a place where ships could come and get it. The nearest place where a ship could come was over seven hundred miles away, a place called Batum on the Black Sea, so they laid a huge pipe seven hundred miles long to carry the oil from Baku to Batum, where it is put into boats called oil tankers and carried away.

The highest mountains and the longest river in Europe are both in Russia. The mountains are the Caucasus, on the southern edge of Russia, between the Black and the Caspian Seas. They are higher than the Alps.

Most rivers we say "run," but the longest river in Europe is also the slowest. It is the Volga. It moves so slowly it is hard to tell whether it is going or coming. It "walks" into the Caspian Sea. In the Volga River big fish are caught called sturgeon. The sturgeon's eggs are called caviar, and caviar is considered a great delicacy, though one usually has to learn to like it. Caviar is probably the most expensive food there is—a very little costs so much: a pound of caviar costs almost a hundred times as much as a pound of beefsteak—perhaps that is one reason why people like it.

The most precious metal in the World is not silver, not gold, but a metal called platinum. Platinum looks something like silver, but there is so little of it that it costs more than gold. On the eastern edge of Russia, which is also the eastern edge of Europe, there is a range of mountains called the Ural Mountains; they are not very high, in fact they are not much more than hills. In these mountains platinum is found.

There is a peculiar kind of rock found in Russia. The rock is like bundles of silky threads, which can be made into a kind of cloth. It is called asbestos. As asbestos cloth is made from rock it will not burn. A king long ago had a table-cloth made of asbestos. People didn't know about asbestos at that time, so the king used to amaze his dinner guests by throwing the table-cloth into the fire after dinner was over, then after awhile taking it out unburned. We use asbestos to cover hot pipes, for firemen's suits, and for roofs of houses, as it will not burn, no matter how hot it is heated. Asbestos is also found in parts of the United States and Canada.

45

The Iron Curtain Countries

THERE are thousands of cities and towns in the World that neither you nor I have ever heard of, yet millions of people call these cities and towns *home*. These same people probably have never heard of the town or city where you yourself live.

Between Russia and the rest of Europe are nine little countries, some of them not very important, but all of them most important to the people who live in them; and yet many people may live their whole lives and perhaps never hear of some of these places—unless they collect postage stamps. Six of these countries end in "ia" and two end in "land."

All but two of these countries are run by Communists. These Communists are the same kind of people who rule Russia. In fact many of them were trained in Russia. Communist countries don't like people from other parts of the World to visit them and they don't let their own people travel in other countries. It is as if they were separated from the rest of the World by a fence of iron, or, as a great Englishman once called it, an Iron Curtain. For this reason we call them the Iron Curtain countries.

The Iron Curtain is an invisible curtain. Its iron is really the iron of the weapons of Communist soldiers who guard the border and keep people who are out out and people who are in in.

The two countries next to Russia that aren't run by Communists are Finland and Austria. Finland is the largest of these in-between countries. It lies between Russia and the Scandinavian Peninsula. Finland means Marsh Land, for it is a land of marshes and lakes. It is like Norway and Sweden in some ways—it has fiords and it makes paper and matches. It is a republic with a president.

The other "land" country is Po-land, which means Flat Land. It is almost as large as Finland. Poland has much farm land and there are iron and coal mines. Many famous musicians have been Poles.

Are you a good speller? How would you spell a cough or a sneeze? South of Poland is a long thin country with a name which sounds funny to us—something between a cough and a sneeze—Czechoslovakia. I have a set of china dishes that has stamped on the bottom MADE IN CZECHOSLOVAKIA, for there they used to make a great deal of china, and glassware too. Perhaps they still do but I can't tell you for sure because, after my dishes were made, Czechoslovakia became an Iron Curtain country.

There used to be a country called Austria-Hungary. Now there are two countries—Austria and Hungary. Through Austria and Hungary runs a famous river—almost as famous as the Rhine. It is called the Danube; and, like the Rhine, the Danube has castles overlooking it, castles in which once lived robber barons. Fairytales and poems and music have been written about the Danube too. One of the most famous waltzes ever written is called "The Blue Danube." The *Blue* Danube runs into the *Black* Sea. The capital of Austria is Vienna. Vienna used to be famous for its restaurants and cooking. Perhaps you have eaten Vienna rolls or been to a Vienna restaurant, even if you have never been to Austria, for we have Vienna rolls and restaurants in the United States too.

The name Hungary makes you think of food, or rather lack of food, but the name doesn't mean *hungry*. It means Land of the Huns. In fact, Hungary should not be hungry, for a great deal of wheat for making bread is raised there. Have you ever eaten a kind of hash called Hungarian goulash? It is very highly seasoned with pepper and spices, and some restaurants in our country serve it. In some of these restaurants orchestras play Hungarian music. It is a kind of music such as the Gypsies dance to—slow and sweet, then fast and furious, with a hop, skip, and jump time. In Hungary many of the peope are, strange to say, related to the Chinese way back. They are called Magyars.

Have you ever had your palm read or your fortune told? Gypsies are people who wander over the country doing that for a living. Most of the Gypsies come from a country next to **Hungary** and bordering on the Black Sea called Romania — nowadays frequently spelled R*u*mania.

She will tell your fortune

It is supposed that long ago people from Rome settled in that country and called it Romania from Rome. The language of Romania is still something like the Roman or Italian.

Bulgaria is an Iron Curtain country next to the Black Sea. It has forests and mountains as well as farm land. In the forests live bears, wildcats, and wild boars. The ibex, a kind of wild goat, lives there too. And in the mountains there is a goat-like antelope called the chamois. We get our name for chamois or "shammy" cloths, used for washing automobiles, from this animal. Once chamois cloths were really soft leather from the skin of the chamois, but now we make the cloths from other materials.

An important business of the Bulgarians is perfumery. They raise fields of roses from which they make a very fine and expensive perfume called "attar of roses." It takes a whole roomful of rose petals to make only a tiny bottle of attar of roses, so you can see why attar of roses is expensive.

Albania is a little country where most of the people raise farm crops or cattle and sheep. In parts of Albania the men wear skirts that reach to their knees and stick out all around like a dancer's. The skirts that the men wear in Scotland are made of dark-colored cloths but the skirts worn by Albanian men are white.

Jugoslavia is a country just across the Adriatic Sea from Italy. It has many forests. It also has copper mines. In fact more copper is mined in Jugoslavia than in any other European country.

When I hear the name of a place or a person, some one thing usually pops into my head, though that thing may not be at all important.

If I hear "George Washington," the first thing that pops into my head is "cherry-tree."

If I hear "New York," the first thing I think of is "sky-scrapers."

So when I hear "Finland," I think of marshes.

When I hear "Poland," I think of music.

When I hear "Austria," I think of Vienna rolls.

When I hear "Hungary," I think of the Blue Danube.

When I hear "Romania," I think of Gypsies.

When I hear "Bulgaria," I think of chamois and perfumes.

When I hear "Albania," I think of men with skirts.

When I hear "Czechoslovakia," I think of china and glass.

When I hear "Jugoslavia," I think of copper.

What do you think of when you hear "Iron Curtain"?

46

The Land of the Gods

THE first book I ever read was Æsop's Fables. Æsop was a slave who lived in a little country called Greece. Æsop the slave wrote such famous fables that his master set him free. The book I read was in English, but the Fables were first written in Greek.

Greece is so small that if I pointed to it on the map down at the corner of Europe it would be entirely covered by the tip of my finger. But small as it is, it was at one time the greatest country, its people were the greatest people, and its language the greatest language in the World. When the rest of the people in Europe were ignorant savages the people in Greece were writing the greatest books, building the most beautiful buildings, making the most beautiful statues, and teaching the most famous schools that have ever been. There is one Book that was first written in Greek but is now printed in over eight hundred languages, and more people have read it than any other book in the World. It's the Bible—the New Testament part.

But the people of Greece didn't at first believe in the Bible or Christ. They didn't believe in only one god but in many gods, who they said lived above the clouds on the top of a mountain called Olympus. The mountain is still there, but if you should climb to the top you wouldn't find any gods. When the sun shone the Greeks said that the god Apollo was driving his golden chariot across the sky. When the rain fell they said another god, Jupiter, was watering the earth, and when the lightning flashed they said he was angry and throwing thunderbolts. They believed that there was a god of love and that there was a god of war and that there was a god of almost everything in the World.

Greece is in two chief parts, like a tiny North and South America, which were once joined by a thin stem of land called the Isthmus of Corinth, only four miles across. In the northern part was, is, and probably always will be a great city called Athens. The people in Athens thought that one goddess in particular looked after their city. She was the goddess of wisdom called Athene Parthenos, so they named their city Athens, after her first name; and on the top of a high hill they built the most beautiful temple in the World to her and called it the Parthenon, after her last name. Inside of this temple they placed a huge statue of her, made of gold and ivory. The statue has now disappeared, nobody knows where, and the building itself was blown up in a war and is now in ruins. The beautiful sculptures on this temple were taken down and carried away to London and are now in the British Museum. So if you want to see what beautiful statues the Greeks once made, don't go to Athens—go to London. On the side of the hill on which is the Parthenon and all through the city of Athens are other temples to their many gods. These temples had no domes nor spires like Christian churches, but columns around the outside.

The most beautiful temple in the World is now in ruins

The marble for these buildings and statues they got from a hill near Athens called Mount Pentelicus. Some one has said the reason the Greeks long ago made such beautiful statues and buildings was because they had such beautiful marble to work with; but there is still beautiful marble on Mount Pentelicus, and yet no one seems able to make such beautiful things of it any more.

People long ago used to go to a place called

an oracle to have their fortunes told. At Delphi not far from Athens was one of the most famous oracles. There was a crack in the ground from which gas was always escaping. Over this crack in the ground sat a goddess called a Sibyl and over the goddess a little temple was built. The escaping gas put the goddess to sleep, just as the gas a doctor or dentist uses puts people to sleep so they won't feel any pain; then the goddess began to talk in her sleep and would mumble answers to the questions asked her. People came from all over the World to hear what the oracle had to tell them. The Delphic Oracle, like the statue of Athene, has now gone—no one knows when, nor how, nor where.

Did you know that you could speak Greek? Well, when you say "music," "museum," or "amusements" you are speaking Greek, for all three words are named from nine beautiful goddesses called "Muses," who used to live near a spring at Delphi. This spring was named Castalia, and it was supposed that those who drank from the spring would be able to write music and poetry. The Castalian spring is still there, and sheep and goats as well as men drink its cool waters, but now it does no more than quench the thirst of men and beasts.

Long before the time of Christ, athletic meets used to be held in Greece once every four years. These were called Olympic Games, and champions in running and jumping and other sports from all over Greece used to compete for a prize, which was a simple crown made of laurel leaves. There is a huge stadium in Athens where such games and races were held, but it had fallen to ruins. Not so many years ago a Greek who had made a fortune and wanted to do something splendid for his home city repaired and re-covered the old stadium with marble, and again the Olympic Games were held there.

Near Athens there is another hill called Mount Hymettus, where was found a very delicious kind of honey. It is said to taste like flowers and it was supposed to be the food the gods lived upon—they called it "ambrosia." You can still get the same honey in the restaurants in Athens, but there are no more gods to feed on it.

Greece of to-day is famous for—what do you suppose? For poetry? No. For music? No. For sculpture? No. For beautiful buildings? No. My geography says it is famous for "currants." Cur-rants are little dried grapes that are used in cakes and puddings. Currants are named from Corinth, the stem that joins north and south Greece, or rather, I should say, the stem that used to join them, for the Greeks have cut a canal four miles long straight through the isth-mus so that boats can now sail across Corinth without going all the way around Greece.

There is a lunch-room downtown kept by a young Greek who has come to America to make his fortune. He calls it the Delphi Restaurant. Last week I went in for luncheon, and just for fun I asked him if he had any ambrosia. "No," said he, "we have corned beef and cabbage to-day."

47

The Land of the New Moon

EVERY place is east of some other place. America is east of China. Europe is east of America. But the only place called "THE East," with a capital THE, is the land east of Europe. This land east of Europe is the continent of Asia. It's the biggest continent of all.

Long years ago in fairy-tale days a god in Asia was in love with a beautiful girl whose name was Europa. Now a god was not supposed to love a human being, so the god turned himself into a snow-white bull and, persuading Europa to get on his back, he ran away with her. At last the bull came to a strait of water and swam across it with Europa still on his back. On the opposite side of the strait where the bull landed with Europa on his back was a great new continent, and to-day we call this continent Europe —after Europa.

People who do not believe in fairy-tales say, however, that Europe is a name that simply means The Land Where the Sun Goes Down, and they say that Asia, the land from which Europa and the bull came, means The Land Where the Sun Gets Up.

The strait across which the bull carried Europa we still call Bull-Carry Strait, for in the Greek language "bull-carry" is Bosporus, and Bosporus is the name on the map.

EUROPA AND THE BULL

The god changed himself into a white bull and ran away with Europa

People built a city where Europa landed, and about a thousand years afterward a Roman Emperor named Constantine, who was the first Christian emperor, moved his capital from Rome to this city and it was called after him, Constantinople.

After another thousand years Constantinople was captured from the Christians by some people from Asia called Turks, who had a ruler called the Sultan. Most of the people in Europe are Christians, but the Turks are not Christians. They do not believe in Christ. They believe in a god whom they called Allah and a man named Mohammed who they say was Allah's messenger on earth. So we call the people who believe in Mohammed Mohammedans or Moslems.

One dark night many years ago an army was approaching Constantinople, but it was so dark the people in the city did not see it and did not know they were about to be attacked. Suddenly the moon shone out from behind a cloud. By the light of the moon the watchmen saw the enemy, sounded the alarm, and the city was saved. Ever since then the Turks have used the new moon on their churches as we do a cross and a new moon and a star on their flag, as these had brought good luck. A new moon is called a "crescent." The Turks have a society, the same society as our Red Cross; but as a cross is a Christian sign, they don't use it, so they call their society the Red Crescent.

One of the largest churches in the World was built in Constantinople before the Turks came. It was called the church of Holy Wisdom, which in Greek is Santa Sophia. Perhaps you may know a girl named Sophie. Well, she may be wise or she may not, but her name means wise. When the Turks captured the Christian city of Constantinople they changed Santa Sophia and all the other churches in the city to Mohammedan churches, which are called mosques, and they tore down the crosses on top of the churches and put up in the place of each a crescent. There are now over eight hundred mosques in the city. Finally not very many years ago they changed Constantinople's name to Istanbul.

You might think it would be better if I hadn't told you the old name of Istanbul. Then you would have one less long name to remember. But Constantinople was the name of the city for a much longer time than Istanbul has been. Even now Constantinople is a better-known name than Istanbul. I won't, however, tell you what the city was called before it became Constantinople. Two names are enough to learn about any city. So if you want to know Istanbul's earliest name you'll have to ask some one or find it in some other book.

The Turks also built, close to each mosque, one or more candle-shaped towers, called minarets. About midway of a minaret is a balcony, and five times a day a priest appears on this balcony and calls the people of the city to prayer. This is done instead of ringing church bells as they do in Christian churches, for Mohammedans do not use bells, even in their own homes. When they want to call a servant they clap their hands. The first call to prayer is about five o'clock in the morning—sort of an alarm clock—when the priest says, "Come to prayer. Prayer is better than Sleep."

Not many people get up at that time to pray, however. When he calls out, a very good Mohammedan goes into the nearest mosque to pray, or he gets down on his knees and bows his head till it touches the ground. Whenever he goes into a mosque he must first wash his face, hands, and feet, so almost every mosque has a pool or fountain, sometimes on the steps, sometimes in the

They turned the church into a mosque

courtyard, where the people can wash before they enter. For this reason also there are a great many fountains throughout Istanbul. They are not for drinking—they are not for beauty; they are for washing. The mosques are for men only. Women used to be allowed in little hidden cells in the mosque, where they could not be seen, for women and children were supposed neither to be seen nor heard. The Mohammedans' Sunday is our Friday. The Mohammedan goes to the mosque every day if he can, but always on Friday.

An inlet from the Bosporus cuts into Istanbul in the shape of a horn. It is called the Golden Horn, and across the entrance a great chain used

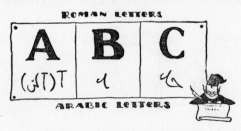

Turkish writing has been changed

to be stretched to keep out ships which the Sultan did not wish to enter. Across the Golden Horn is a bridge called Galata. I have told you of some of the most famous bridges in the World: Brooklyn Bridge, London Bridge, the Rialto and the Ponte Vecchio. Galata bridge is one of the oldest and most famous bridges of the World. All day and all night people of every nationality, every color, every dress, and every language pass in an unending stream. Every one on one side seems to want to get to the other side, which makes me think of the old riddle, "Why does a chicken cross the road?"

Turkish writing looks something like shorthand and is very hard to read and to write. But because it is so difficult and so different from the letters of Europe, Turkey began to use an alphabet like ours, and every one under forty years of age is now required to learn the new writing.

In fact, Turkey has been made over into a new Turkey. The old ruler of Turkey, the Sultan, ruled alone and whatever he said had to be done whether it was right or wrong. Turkey now has a ruler who rules not alone but with others chosen by the people to rule with him. The women used to think it immodest to go out on the street with their faces uncovered, so they wore veils. Now, however, they wear hats and dresses as Christian women do. The Turks used to have

Turkish styles have been changed too

many wives, and every house had a separate apartment, called the harem, where all the wives lived together.

You may wonder why the bird we eat at Thanksgiving and Christmas is called a turkey. Turkey was first brought to our country from Mexico, but people thought it had come from Turkey, so they called it a Turkey bird.

48

The Ship of the Desert

THERE are a few camels in Istanbul, but camels don't belong in Europe. They have to be carried across the Bosporus from Asia, for a camel is said to be the only animal that cannot swim and cannot learn to swim. Most animals, like dogs, swim naturally; they don't have to learn. The camel may not be able to swim, but he can cross deserts, which no other animal can do as well.

The camel is an animal of the desert, and when we see camels we know there must be deserts somewhere near. The camel loves heat and dryness, the sun and sand. Men and most animals, when it is hot, like the cool shade when they rest, but a camel when he rests lies down in the hot sun. He is often called "the ship of the desert," for he is the only "boat" that can carry passengers across the sea of sands. His feet are made like cushions so that they do not sink into the sand. A camel has several pouches inside of his body in which to store up water, as in tanks, for in crossing desert lands he may have to go days at a time without a drink, so he fills up these tanks inside of him.

The camel in Asia has one hump and is called a Dromedary. There are other camels that have two humps. The hump is not a broken back, as it looks—it is made of fat, and when the camel can get no outside food, the fat in his hump helps to feed him as the food in his stomach feeds him.

The camel "follows the leader," almost as in the game, for wherever the leader goes he goes —so when a number of camels are used to carry loads long distances they are tied head to tail in a line, like a train of cars hitched together, often with a donkey at the head of the train like a locomotive to lead them. The donkey has sense, but a camel has little sense; that's why the donkey is made the leader. Such a train of camels is called a caravan. The camel looks very superior—as if no one were as good as he—but he is really a stupid animal with a very small brain. He has, however, an even temper—always mean, ugly, and nasty. He grunts as he walks slowly along on his stilt-like legs. He is trained to kneel and a load is then put on his back, and he will carry great loads with his driver on top of that. If too big a load is put on his back, when kneeling, the camel will not get up at all; but once he gets up he never gives up, no matter how heavy the load. You can then pile anything on him until it crushes him to the ground. When he has all the load he can carry, one straw more may be enough to break his back. So when you give some one too much work to do, people say, "It's the last straw that breaks the camel's back."

THE CAMEL AND THE LAST STRAW

"It's the last straw that breaks the camel's back"

The camel carries loads for his master, but the camel does more than that. The mother camel gives him milk, and sometimes young camels are used for food. The camel's hair is woven to make blankets and clothes and tents. In our country the best paint brushes are made of camel's hair.

49

A "Once-was" Country

WE call a small boy a "minor" until he grows up. The corner of Asia on the other side of the Bosporus is only a small part of Asia, so we call it Asia Minor. Asia Minor does not touch Europe, although it comes so close to it in two places that a giant could stride across. One of these crossings is the Bosporus; it is only about half a mile wide. The other crossing, called the Dardanelles, is only about a mile wide at the narrowest point. People have swum across the Dardanelles, and floating bridges have been made here by tying boats together, but there are now no bridges from Asia to Europe, and men and animals have to be carried across in boats if they want to get from Asia to Europe or from Europe to Asia.

Asia Minor is a "Once-was" country. It once was the richest part of the whole World; it is now one of the poorest.

Crœsus, who once was the richest man in the World, lived in Asia Minor.

Helen, who once was the most beautiful woman in the World, was stolen away from her home in Greece and brought to a place called

Troy in Asia Minor. Here the Trojan War was fought on her account.

Homer, one of the greatest story poets who ever lived, was said to have been born in Asia Minor.

St. Paul—the Apostle—was born in a little town in Asia Minor, a town called Tarsus, where he made tents for soldiers.

You have probably heard of the Seven Wonders of the World. They were supposed to be the seven most wonderful things made by the hand of man in Ancient Times. Three of the Seven Wonders were in Asia Minor:

The Temple built to the Goddess Diana was one of these wonders. This Temple was at Ephesus in Asia Minor, and silversmiths made little copies of this wonderful temple to sell as souvenirs to visitors. St. Paul preached against Diana, for whom the Temple was built, because she was a heathen goddess. The silversmiths at Ephesus who made a living out of their souvenirs of the Temple were afraid St. Paul would hurt their business, so they tried to mob him. Nothing is now left of this wonderful Temple of Diana except the floor, and the silver souvenirs have all disappeared; but the letters which St. Paul wrote to men at Ephesus are still read by millions of people, for they are in the Bible.

The greatest tomb in the World was in Asia Minor. It was built by a woman named Mrs. Mausolus, for her husband, Mr. Mausolus. This was another Wonder of which little is left. And yet nowadays we call a very handsome tomb a "Mausoleum" after this tomb of Mausolus.

There is a little island off Asia Minor, called Rhodes. A huge brass statue of the Sun God was built there. It was called The Colossus of Rhodes, for Colossus means huge. It was as tall as a ten-story house. This was a third Wonder, but an earthquake upset the quake upset the statue and its pieces were sold to a junk dealer.

An earthquake upset the statue into the sea

Almost all of the old glory of Asia Minor has gone. We can see the ruins of the wonderful old buildings, but most of the houses now, except those in a few big cities, are made of mud with one door and no windows, and grass often grows in the mud on the roofs.

Asia Minor now belongs to Turkey—in fact, it is about all there is left of Turkey except Istanbul, although before World War I, Turkey owned much more land.

You have probably seen Angora cats—beautiful cats with long hair and bushy tails. They come from Angora, the capital of new Turkey. In the country round Angora is raised a peculiar kind of goat which has long silky hair. The hair from this Angora goat is used to make lovely rugs and shawls which can be bought here in America. Mohair suits which men wear in hot summer weather because they are so thin and cool are made of Angora goats' hair—if genuine.

In Asia Minor is a very crooked river that flows lazily along to the sea, turning this way and that way as if it had no particular place to go. Its name is the "Meander." So when a boy goes lazily along to school, turning this way and that, or when he goes along on an errand and does not go straight there but wanders along as the Meander goes to the sea, we say he "meanders." Girls sometimes "meander" too.

Figs grow in the valley of the Meander River and dates grow in many parts of Asia. Figs and dates are brought on camel back across to a beautiful city called Smyrna on the Mediterranean Sea, and from there are shipped to us in America. You can probably get at your corner grocery store a package of Smyrna figs or "Dromedary Dates" that have been picked far away in Asia, carried by caravan to Smyrna, and shipped here. Another thing sent us from Smyrna is sponges. Sponges grow in the sea near Asia Minor. Naked men dive for the sponges and pull them off the rocks, where they grow on the bottom of the sea. They gather as many as they can at a time, as long as they can hold their breath.

50

A Land Flowing with Milk and Honey

In Sunday school I used to hear of Bethlehem and Jerusalem and other places in the Bible, but I had no idea then that there were any such places with people living in them to-day. But there are. We call the land where these places are Bible Land, because so much is told about them in the Bible. Bible Land is at the east end of the Mediterranean Sea. The northern part of Bible Land is called Syria, the southern part is called the Holy Land, or Palestine.

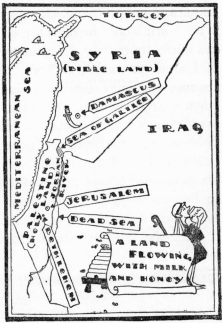

There are a great many cities in Syria

and Palestine that were alive when Christ was
born and are still living, and there are a great
many places that are now dead—nothing left of
them but ruins. But there is a city mentioned in
the Bible that was a thousand years old when
Christ was born and yet is still very much alive.
It is the old*est* city i.t.w.W. Its name is Damascus.

The main street in Damascus was called
"Straight," because it was not quite as crooked
as its other streets. On both sides of Straight
Street are shops, for Damascus was once the
greatest shopping city in the East; the shops are
called bazaars. Some of the bazaars are not big
enough to hold a piano. One department store in
New York would hold all the bazaars in Damascus many times over. In these bazaars the people
of Damascus used to sell only things they made
themselves. They sold gold and silver jewelry,
rugs, shawls, swords, and silks, and they made
everything by hand, for there was no machinery.
Now there is machinery to make all these things,
but it is not in Damascus. Many of these things
are now made by machinery in England and sent
to Damascus to be sold. Often a traveler buys
something in a Damascus bazaar only to find on
it later the tell-tale words "Made in Birming-
ham."

A white picture painted on white paper or a
red picture on red paper would not show, but in
Damascus they used to make a beautiful kind

of cloth with designs of the same color as the cloth woven into it by hand. This kind of cloth is called damask, after Damascus. White damask has white designs on it and red damask has red designs, and they do show. You probably have in your own home linen damask table-cloths and napkins or silk coverings on chairs, but the damask that we buy now is made by machinery and does not come from Damascus.

The people in Damascus also used to make a kind of jewelry of iron, with gold designs laid in the iron. This was called Damascene work. Damascene work was much used in decorating swords, and they used to make wonderful swords and knives with edges so sharp they could cut through a bar of iron, so they say. These were called Damascus blades. Soldiers no longer use swords except for show or ornament. Wars are now fought at long distance and soldiers seldom get close enough to use swords.

South of Syria is Palestine, which is also called the Holy Land. On my map there is no room to print the names of even a very few of the places you know. They would run out into the Mediterranean on one side and into the desert on the other, and would be so crowded together that they would cover the little country completely.

You see how small the Holy Land really is. There is a town at the top of the Holy Land with a name like a boy's—Dan. Down at the bottom of the Holy Land is another town called

Beersheba; so people often say "from Dan to Beersheba," meaning from top to bottom or from one end of something to the other. Between these two towns the distance is only one hundred and fifty miles and the distance across Palestine is only about fifty miles, so that it would be possible now in one day to go in an automobile up and down and across Palestine.

There are two lakes in Palestine; one is in the north and one is in the south, but both are called Seas. The one in the north is called the Sea of Galilee. The one in the south is known as the Dead Sea, for nothing can live in it nor grow around it.

The Sea of Galilee is where Christ walked on the water and where the miraculous number of fish were caught. Many of Christ's close friends were fishermen, and He asked them to help Him teach others, saying He would make them "fishers of men." So a club of Galilee fishermen was started and they used a drawing of a fish as the sign of their society, for, strangely enough, the first two letters of the Greek word for fish were Christ's initials. As in Bible times, they still have sudden storms on the Sea of Galilee and a great many fish are still caught there.

Running from the Sea of Galilee into the Dead Sea is a zigzag river called the Jordan. It was in the Jordan River that John the Baptist baptized Christ, and people go from all over the

World to see the spot where this took place, and some to be baptized there themselves. There is always a clergyman on hand, ready and waiting, to baptize those who come. Many people fill a bottle with some of the muddy water and take it home to use as "holy water," or in order

The Christians used a fish as the sign of their society

to baptize their children with water from the same river in which Christ was baptized. The Jordan is very muddy, because it flows very swiftly and washes the mud from the banks and bottom. It empties its yellow water into the Dead Sea, but the Dead Sea, strange to say, is as blue as the Mediterranean.

The Dead Sea is in the bottom of a very deep valley, so low that no water can run out of it, as water cannot run uphill. You might think the Dead Sea would fill up and overflow, but it does not, for the air is so hot and dry that the water in the Dead Sea evaporates as fast as it runs into it. But the river is always bringing in salt, and as salt does not evaporate, the Dead Sea, like Great Salt Lake, is getting saltier all the time. It is saltier than Great Salt Lake, it is ten times saltier than the ocean, and of course no one could drown in it. People don't bathe in the Dead Sea, however, because the water is so salty that if it splashes into one's eyes or touches any scratches or broken skin it stings like iodine put on a cut. There is so much salt around the Dead Sea that nothing will grow there, and even salt-water fish cannot live in the water. We think that the two most wicked cities in the World, Sodom and Gomorrah, were by the Dead Sea. The Bible

Lot's wife disobeyed the Lord and looked back

says they were so wicked that the Lord destroyed them. There is nothing now left of them but desert, with a crust of salt over all. You remember, the Lord told Lot to take his family and flee from Sodom before he destroyed it, and ordered him and his family not to look back. Lot's wife disobeyed and she was turned to a pillar of salt. And a guide will point out a mound of salt that he says is Lot's wife!

51

The "Exact Spots"

THERE are three most famous places in Palestine. The first is the place where Christ was born, the second is the place where Christ lived, and the third is the place where Christ died.

Christ was born in Bethlehem, which is a dirty little village, not at all like the heavenly place with angels hovering over it that you see in pictures and on Christmas cards. Christ's father and mother were traveling and happened to stop in Bethlehem over night when Christ was born. A church was built over the place where Christ was supposed to have been born, and a silver star is in the floor to mark "the exact spot." The fact is that no one knows "the exact spot," but we do know that the church over the supposed spot is the *oldest* church in the World.

Though Christ was born in Bethlehem, He spent most of His early life in another town in Palestine called Nazareth, for Nazareth was His home town and there His father, Joseph, lived and worked. Joseph was a carpenter, and in Nazareth guides point out Joseph's carpenter shop, the work-bench where Christ worked with the saw and hammer and other tools He used. They also point out the kitchen where Christ's mother, Mary, cooked the meals for the family. But just as we cannot believe what the guides tell us about the "exact spot" in Bethlehem, so we cannot believe what they tell us about most of the "exact spots" in Nazareth. There is, however, one exact spot which we can believe. That is a well where

THE WELL OF MARY IN PALESTINE

The women of Nazareth still draw water from this well to-day

they say Mary went to get water, and this may actually be the same well, for there never has been any other place in Nazareth where one could get water. There was no such thing as running water in each house.

The last most important place in Palestine is the city where Christ died—Jerusalem. Christians call it their Holy City. But, strangely enough, the Mohammedans call it their Holy City too, and it was once the capital of the Jews. Mohammed lived about six hundred years later

than Christ, and Mohammedans believe some of
the same things about Mohammed that Christians
believe about Christ. Mohammed was supposed
to have died in Jerusalem and to have ascended
into Heaven from there. The Moslems captured
Jerusalem and kept hold of it for more than a
thousand years. During that long time the Christians have tried time and again to get Jerusalem
away from the Moslems. Time and time again
the Christians from all over Europe formed
armies and marched on Jerusalem, trying to take
it away from the Moslems, but they were usually
beaten; and though they have held the city for a
time, the Moslems have always recaptured it,
until at last in World War I the English captured Jerusalem.

Jerusalem has probably been destroyed and
built up again more times than any other city in
the World. King David built Jerusalem about a
thousand years before Christ was born. Then
Solomon built his magnificent temple there, but
not very long afterward Jerusalem was captured
and destroyed. Every once in a while Jerusalem
has been captured and destroyed and then built
up again, so that they say there are really eight
Jerusalems, one on top of the remains of the
other. That is one reason why it is impossible to
know "the exact spots" where so many things
mentioned in the Bible took place.

Men say they have found in Jerusalem the
tomb of Adam, the first man. They have also

found the tomb of Christ—His sepulcher—and right near Christ's tomb they have found in the rock a hole which they say is where the cross was put when Christ was crucified. Over these places they have built a church, called the Church of the Holy Sepulcher. There is one thing, however, that they could not put under this Church of the Holy Sepulcher—that is, the place from which Christ ascended into Heaven, for that spot is on a hill just outside of Jerusalem, called the Mount of Olives.

The Moslems say Mohammed ascended into Heaven too, and not very far from the Church of the Holy Sepulcher is the place. Over this place the Moslems have built a building called the Mosque of Omar, though it really is not a mosque at all and was not built by Omar.

MOSQUE OF OMAR

Underneath the dome is a huge rock on which oxen used to be sacrificed

It is much more beautiful than the Church of the Holy Sepulcher, however, and, indeed, some even say it is one of the most beautiful buildings in the World. It is built over the spot where the wonderful temple of Solomon stood. It is made of

beautiful marble and tile and has a bowl-shaped
dome.

Underneath the Mosque of Omar is a huge
rock on which oxen used to be sacrificed. On
this same rock Abraham, so they say, was about
to kill his son as he was ordered to do by the
Lord, who wanted to test him, when an angel

sent by the Lord stopped his hand. From this
same rock Mohammed ascended to Heaven—so
they say. The stone tried to follow him, but the
archangel Gabriel held it back; and finger prints
of archangels are shown you to prove the story
true.

Part of the Temple of Solomon is still standing. It is a piece of the foundation wall. Ever
since the temple was destroyed Jews have gone
there to weep and to pray that their country,

which the ancient Romans took from them, would be restored to them. It is called the Wailing Wall. Jews lived in many countries but there was no Jewish country that they could call their own. After World War II, however, the United Nations voted to divide Palestine into two parts. One part, they said, should be for Jews and would be the country that Jews for two thousand years had prayed to have. The other part, the United Nations said, should be for the many Arab Mohammedans who lived in Palestine. So at last the Jews had a country of their own. They named it Israel. Israel is the part of Palestine on the east next to the Mediterranean Sea. The western part of Palestine became part of the Arab country of Jordan. Jerusalem, which is the holy city for both Mohammedans and Jews, was divided also. The western and newer part of Jerusalem belongs to Israel and the eastern and older part belongs to the Mohammedans.

Israel is a republic. Though some of the oldest cities in the World are in Israel, the Jews made one of the newest cities in the World the capital of the new country, the city of Tel Aviv. Tel Aviv has modern buildings and wide straight streets and it is very clean and neat, much different from the old cities with their narrow, dirty streets. Many Jews from other countries have gone to live in Israel. They are welcome there, for Israel is the home land of the Jews.

52

The Garden of Eden

OF course, you have heard of the Garden of
Eden, haven't you? When-I-was-a-boy I thought
that when I was old enough to travel I should
like to go and see it for myself. I should like to
see whether or not the angels with fiery swords
were still there. So I asked my Sunday school
teacher where the Garden of Eden was. "It's in
the Bible," said she. That didn't help me much.
But grown-up people have been looking for the
Garden of Eden for a great many years and
some say they have found it, or rather that they
have found the place where it once was, for it
does not look like a garden now, much less like
a Paradise.

If you were in Damascus and asked a man
on the street, "How do you get to the Garden of
Eden?" he might think you were crazy, or maybe
he might say, "I'm a stranger here myself." But
if he did know the way, he would point to the
east and say, "You cross the desert and keep
going straight ahead toward the rising sun. In
about a month, if you are going by camel, or in a
couple of days, if you are going by automobile,
you will come to a muddy river. This river is

called the Euphrates. Cross the Euphrates and
go on a short distance and you will come to a
second muddy river. This second muddy river
is called the Tigris. These two rivers flow into
each other, and near the place where the two
rivers join, there you'll find the Garden of Eden.
You can't miss it."

There is no garden there now and you may

wonder how there
ever could have
been a garden
there, for most of
it is now mud,
and, when there
has been no rain
for a long time,
just baked mud
ground, which
looks as little like
a Garden of Eden
as you could possi-
bly imagine. Nev-

Some say they have found the Garden
of Eden

ertheless, people think this is where the Garden
of Eden once was. They even point out an old
apple-tree that once bore some apples and say,
"That's the original tree." They think the Great
Flood took place between these rivers. They
think that Noah lived down there somewhere,
that he built his ark down there, and that the
Flood came and flooded all this valley between
the two rivers, and when the Flood was over, the

Ark was left high and dry on the top of Mount Ararat, a mountain way up above where the rivers rise. This valley between the two rivers was called Mesopotamia, because "Meso" means "between" and "potamia" means "rivers." But it is now called Iraq, and that is the name you will see on the map.

On the Tigris River, high up, there used to be a big city called Nineveh, and on the Euphrates, farther down toward where the two rivers meet, there used to be another big city called Babylon. I say "used to be," for although these two cities were the largest cities in the World before Christ was born, they have almost completely disappeared.

Have you ever built on the beach or in a sand pile a town of houses and streets and then some big bully has come along, tramped on it, stamped on it, and kicked it to pieces? Well, Nineveh and Babylon look as if some giant had come along and stamped all over them and kicked them all to pieces, for about all there is to be seen of them now are piles of dirt. Men have been digging in the piles for many years and they have found buried under the dirt some of the things the people of these cities once had in their homes and shops and schools and palaces, for these cities had some of the finest houses and palaces ever built. The walls and gardens of Babylon were once one of the Seven Wonders of the World, but practically nothing is now left of them.

Though Nineveh and Babylon are gone—their names are not even on the map—there are to-day two big cities on the Tigris that are very much alive, with people living in them. One of these cities is just across the river from where Nineveh used to be. It is called Mosul. You know what muslin is, don't you? Well, muslin was first made in Mosul, so this kind of cloth was called "Mosulin," which became muslin.

Not many years ago people discovered oil in the country round Mosul, enough oil to run all the automobiles in the World. The difficulty was to get the oil to the automobiles. Pipe lines were built from the oil wells to the Mediterranean Sea miles away. The oil is pumped through the pipes and then is loaded on ships. The ships are really floating tanks and so are called tankers. The tankers carry the oil to America and to Europe.

Mosul is a Moslem town. On the great mosque there is a minaret that leans, something like the Leaning Tower of Pisa. People say that Mohammed was once passing this minaret and it bowed to him and was never able to get entirely straight again—it's still leaning.

Have you ever read the stories of *Ali Baba* and *Sindbad the Sailor?* Down the Tigris River below Mosul is another big city called Bagdad. The people you see there on the streets look like the people you see in the pictures in the

"Arabian Nights." Bagdad in summer is one of the hottest places you can imagine. It is sometimes 125°, and you know that 100° is about as hot as we can stand. The streets used to be like narrow alleys, dirty and smelly. But after World War I, England ruled over Iraq and Bagdad and the English made great changes. They built a wide street right through the city and called it New Street. They put in electric lights and ice factories which Bagdad had never had before. Then they had the people vote for a king, and Iraq has been a kingdom ever since. It is still under the protection of England, however, and a few Englishmen stay there to help train the army of Iraq.

A STREET IN BAGDAD

Puzzle: Find Ali Baba and the
40 Thieves

53

The Land of Bedtime Stories

HAVE you ever been thirsty—really thirsty? Very few people in our country ever have. Have you ever gone for more than one whole day without a drink of water? Some people have gone without food for days and even weeks, but no one ever has gone without water for as long as a week. Suppose that you lived in a country where there is not a single river nor lake in the whole land, where it seldom, if ever, rains, where there is practically no water to drink and even less for washing—a country that is almost surrounded by water, but water you can't drink because it is salt—a country that is a desert except for a little fringe around the edge and damp spots here and there. That country is Arabia, the home of the Arab people. How can any one live there? The answer is that people can only live along the edges or in those few spots where there is water. These spots are called oases. Dates are bread and butter, meat and dessert to an Arab. Dates grow on palm-trees, so the Arabs plant palm-trees in deep holes in order that their roots may be far down where the ground is a little damp. The well-to-do Arab has a camel, be-

cause that is the only animal that can stand hard-
ships such as lack of food and water for any
length of time; also, he has a few goats or sheep
and a horse. The Arab horses are small but they
are swift runners. Some say they are the finest in
the World, and many of our race-horses have
come from Arab stock.

ARABIAN HORSE, SHEEP AND GOATS

The Arabs are very much like all boys and
girls in one particular—they love to listen to good
stories, especially at night. They can't get
enough of them. Once upon a time there was a
king in the old days long ago when kings could
put to death whomsoever they wished. This king
had a wife whom he was going to put to death
the next morning, but she told him a bedtime
story which so interested him he wanted to hear
another. So, on condition that he would spare her
life one more day, she promised to tell him another story the next night. And again, day after
day, he postponed putting her to death in order
that he might hear another story at night. This
she kept on doing for one thousand nights and
one night more for good measure until the king

could no longer live without her stories, so his queen was saved. Some of the most famous of these stories have been translated into English. They are called the "Arabian Nights."

Arabia was the birthplace of Mohammed, the man who started the Mohammedan religion. Mohammed was born in a place called Mecca about six hundred years after Christ was born. He was a camel-driver for a rich widow, who fell in love with him and married him. Mohammed thought he was called by God to be His messenger. His wife and friends believed in him, but his neighbors did not, so they ran him out of Mecca. He fled to the next town, Medina, where he preached to the people, and before long there were millions who followed him and obeyed his teachings, and now to-day there are about one third as many people who believe in Mohammed as believe in Christ. Mohammedans think Mecca is the center of the World. Jerusalem is one of their holy cities, but Mecca is their holiest of holies. Medina, which means simply "The City," is second only to Mecca in holiness. The Mohammedans think that one prayer said at Medina is worth a thousand prayers said anywhere else, so Mohammedans send long distances to have prayers said for them in Medina.

The Mohammedans have commandments as the Christians do. We have ten; they have four or more. One of their commandments is to pray five times a day; another is to give a present to

every beggar who asks—it doesn't matter how
little—it may be less than a penny; a third is to
fast for a month each year—that's something like
Lent; and a fourth is to make a trip to Mecca
some time during their lives. Such a trip is called

The whole way—hundreds of miles—was covered with carpet
for the king to walk on

a pilgrimage, and every Mohammedan, no matter
where or how far off he lives, hopes to make a
pilgrimage to Mecca some time before he dies.
A great Mohammedan king named Aaron the
Just once made the trip from Bagdad to Mecca
—hundreds of miles—all the way on foot, but
as he was a king, the whole way was covered with
carpet for him to walk on!

Have you ever seen a "shooting-star" in the
sky? Most shooting-stars usually burn up before
they reach the ground, but some do not. At
Mecca there is a mosque and inside this mosque

is a black stone called The Kaaba. The Mohammedans say this stone was sent down from
heaven, and that may be true, for it is probably
a shooting-star that fell to the ground before it
burned up. The Mohammedans think, if they kiss
this stone, all their sins are forgiven and they
will go to Heaven and have a high place there
when they die. They say this stone was once
white, but it has been turned black by all the sins
that have gone into it from the countless kisses of
Mohammedans. A railroad one thousand miles
long has been built from Damascus to Medina,
and there is now a bus line from Medina to
Mecca, but this railroad and bus are only for pil-
grims, for none but Mohammedans are allowed
in either city—Mecca or Medina.

I have told you of a White Sea and a Black
Sea. Here is a Red Sea. It is a long, narrow sea
bordering Arabia. I don't know why it's called
Red, unless it is because it's red hot, for I have
been there, and the water is as blue as the Mediterranean. There is a little strip of land that
used to separate the Red Sea from the Mediterranean, but men have dug a canal through this
strip of land so that ships may pass from the one
sea to the other. This strip of land is the Isthmus
of Suez and the canal across it is called the Suez
Canal.

The Suez Canal is one of the most important
canals ever dug. It is important because, before
it was dug, this little isthmus that tied together

the two big continents of Africa and Asia, barred the way to ships and they had to go all the way round Africa to get to the east side of the World. It is a water gateway to the east part of the World and England owns it.

The driest city in the World is at the lower end of the Red Sea. It is called Aden. Aden is often called the Gibraltar of the East, for the English own Aden too, and they hold on to it even though it is so dry, because then they can say who shall or shall not pass through the Red Sea. Three gateways for ships between the Atlantic and the Indian Oceans—Gibraltar, Suez, Aden—and England owns all three!

There are no springs nor lakes nor rivers at Aden, and often it does not rain there for years, so the people cannot get drinking-water in any of the usual ways. But the English have found a way. They boil the sea water to get the salt out of it and store it in huge tanks so that they have plenty of fresh water all the time.

You may never have heard of Arabia till now, yet you write Arabic every day of your life, for all the figures we use are Arabic—1, 2, 3, 4, 5. There are only ten figures, as you know, but with those ten figures you can make any number from one to a billion, or more.

Arabia seems far away—a dry and desolate land that could have no connection with us—and yet if there had been no Arabia we should have no figures and no "Arabian Nights."

54

The Lion and the Sun

HAVE you ever seen a Persian cat? They are big, beautiful animals with soft thick hair. They come from Persia.

Persia is one of those "once-was" or "used-to-be" countries too. It used to be the greatest country i.t.w.W., yet many people now do not even know exactly where Persia is and can't even find it when they look for it on a map—for the Persian name for Persia is Iran and most maps now say Iran instead of Persia. As I look around me in my home where I'm writing this, I find, to my surprise, I can count nearly a dozen things that have come from Persia or are connected with Persia, though before I began to count I should have said not a single thing Persian did I own.

The rug at my feet was made in Persia, entirely by hand. It was woven of woolen threads in beautiful colored designs and must have taken some Persian many months, perhaps a year or more, to make. Some Persian rugs are said to have taken one person the whole of his lifetime to make.

My wife has a silken shawl also woven by hand in Persia. The silkworms were raised there, the cocoons unwound, the silk spun into thread, dyed in many colors, and then woven into this shawl.

She has a ring set with greenish blue stones, called Turquoises. A turquoise is the birth-stone of December, and they too come from Persia. In some countries of the East people wear turquoises to keep away what is called the "evil eye." They believe that some persons can do them harm by looking at them, and the turquoise prevents this "evil eye" harming them.

On my wife's dressing-table is a small thin bottle of perfume called attar of roses. In some parts of Persia they grow the most beautiful and fragrant roses and from their petals this perfume is made.

I have a scarfpin in which is a pearl that came from an oyster that was brought up from the bottom of the Persian Gulf by a naked diver.

My bath slippers—big, sloppy slip-ons, with heels turned down—are Persian.

The electric light I am writing under is a Mazda lamp, and Mazda was the old Persian god of light.

In my bookcase is a book called "The Rubái-yát." It is a book of poetry written by a Persian named Omar Khayyám.

For breakfast I might have had a melon, and melons were first grown in Persia. Our melons are grown from seeds brought many years ago to this country from Persia.

What I did have for breakfast were peaches, and these too were first grown in Persia. Peach-stones were brought to this country and from these our first peach-trees were grown.

If I had a Persian cat this would complete the picture, but I have a dog instead.

Persia is called the Land of the Lion and the  Sun, and the Persian flag has a lion and a sun on it. I do not know why there is a lion, but the sun is on it because the people of that country used to worship the sun. The sun was their god. They also worshiped the stars, moon, and fire, so we call them fire-worshipers, but they call themselves Parsees. The fire-worshipers' chief god was called Mazda and that is where we get the name for our electric-light bulbs. According to their religion, everything that was light was good and everything that was dark was bad. A few Persians are still fire-worshipers, but most are now Mohammedans.

The good part of Persia, like the little girl who had a little curl, is very, very good, but the bad part is horrid. In the part that is good, beautiful roses, fine melons and peaches grow, but much of Persia is desert. Most rivers get bigger and bigger as they flow along, but the Persian rivers get smaller and smaller and at last dwindle away to nothing. There are a great many mountains in Persia, and when the melted snows come down from these mountains they form streams, but many of these streams do not empty anywhere; they just dry up; they have no mouths.

Did you ever play charades? Here is a word we used to act out when I played charades, though we pronounced the word incorrectly. In the first act two girls would play drinking tea. In the second act a boy would run across the room. The two acts made the capital of Persia. Can you guess it? It is "Tehran." Another charade can be acted out in only one act. A boy runs across the room and then points to himself. Can you guess this one? It is "Iran," the Persian name of the country.

The ruler of Persia is called, not a king, but a Shah. Once upon a time the Shah could do anything he wished with his people. He could take all their money away from them and put them to death, if he wished to do so; but all that has long been changed. In Tehran is the most famous jeweled throne in the World. It is called the Peacock Throne. It is made of solid gold and the back is in the form of a peacock's tail studded with rubies, emeralds, and sapphires—red, green, and blue precious stones.

All jewels, such as diamonds, rubies, and emeralds, come out of the ground—all except one.

But one jewel does not come out of the ground.
It comes out of the water, out of an oyster. This
jewel is the pearl. The oyster makes a pearl
around a grain of sand that has gotten into his
shell and annoys him. So at the center of each
pearl is a tiny grain of sand. It takes an oyster
four or five years to make a pearl the size of a
pea. In the Persian Gulf the finest pearls are
found. The oysters are not good to eat, but are
gathered for the pearls that are to be found in
them. Men dive for the oysters, staying under
the water long
enough to go down
to the bottom,
gather a basket of
oysters and come
up to the top—as
long as they can
hold their breath.
You can probably
hold your breath
only half a minute,
but a pearl-diver
can hold his for a
minute or longer,
and it is said that
some have been
able to do so for
an hour—but that
is a fairy-tale. A

A PEARL DIVER

He can hold his breath twice as long
as you can

little boy wrote this composition telling how it

is done: "They clamp clothes-pins on their noses and stuff wax in their earses to keep out the waterses. Then they fasten heavy stones to their feetses and jump overboard from small boatses." Many pearl-divers lose their lives each year. They burst a blood vessel or are drowned or stung to death by a poisonous fish called the ray. But millions of dollars' worth of pearls are gathered each year to ornament the necks and fingers of queens and ladies all over the World.

55

Opposite-Feet

THERE is a shop downtown with a department in the basement, underneath the sidewalk. The sidewalk is made of thick glass, and as you look up you can see the feet of the crowds of people as they pass overhead. If the World were made of glass and you could look down through it in the same way, you could see the bottoms of the feet of the crowds passing by on the other side of the World. It is the "Opposite-feet" Land. That sounds awkward, so grown-ups call it "The Antipodes," which means exactly the same thing—"opposite-feet." The Opposite-feet Land on the other side of the World is a pie-shaped country called India. It is the half-way country—half-way round the World. You go away from home till you reach India, then, though you keep on going, you are coming back. I went west around the World and a friend of mine went east. We both started at the same time and met in India. When I landed at a place called Calcutta, there he was on the dock waiting to greet me. From Calcutta we used to get a kind of cloth which we called, from the name of the place, calico.

When I say "Indians" you probably think of

tommyhawks, colored feathers, and war-paint.
But you are thinking of American Indians—the
kind that were in our country before the white
man came. There are only a few of these Indians
left. They belong to the red race.

There is another kind of Indian that belongs
to the white race, the same
as we do, and there are
more than twice as many
of them as there are peo-
ple in our whole country.
They get the name "In-
dians" from the name of
the country where they
live—India. India is the
country that Columbus
was trying to reach by go-

CALICO
COMES
FROM
CALCUTTA

ing the other way around the World. When he
bumped into America he thought he had reached
India, so he called the people he found here Indians. He did not find out until later that America was not India at all, but a new and unknown
land, and that the people were really not Indians
at all, but Red Men.

India is shut off from the rest of Asia on the
north by the highest wall of mountains in the
World; they are called the Himalayas, Him-al-
ay-as. The highest mountain on the face of the
globe is in this range; it is called Mount Everest,
after an English engineer named Everest, who
measured its height. No one has ever been to the

top, yet we know exactly how high it is. An engineer can find out such things. He can tell exactly how high a tree, a church-steeple, or a mountain is without leaving the ground. This mountain is twenty-nine thousand and two feet

It's the highest mountain in the World

high—more than five miles high. The top and sides of Mount Everest are covered with snow and ice which never melts away and will always be there until the crack of doom.

Men have tried and tried again to climb to the top and many have lost their lives in attempting the climb, but no one has ever been able to get there. The top reaches so high up into the sky that there is very little air up there, and men have to take along canned air to breathe. If they attempt to climb without canned air, they are able to take but a single step and then must stop to breathe many times, like a dog panting for breath, and every few steps they must rest awhile before going on. Two Englishmen, after weeks of struggling up the sides of the giant mountain, got nearer than any other human being ever had before—within a few hundred feet of the top. A companion whom they left at their last stop watched them as they plunged upward in their last desperate struggle, and then—whish!—an icy blast of snow and sleet swept them from sight—forever. The native people think a goddess lives at the top and that she will let no one climb to her, and that it brings bad luck and even death to try to reach such a holy place.

At the other end of the Himalaya Mountains is a high valley which is so beautiful that poets call it a vale instead of a valley. It is the Vale of Kashmir. "Who has not heard of the Vale of Kashmir," says one poet, "with its roses, the brightest the earth ever gave?" Beautiful lakes with snow-topped mountains, and roses, roses everywhere. It seems as if this should have been the Garden of Eden instead of that sun-baked mud bank between the Tigris and Euphrates.

If you will look at your map of Asia carefully

you will see something strange about two of the countries that touch India. The country next to India on the west and the country next to India on the east have the same name, Pakistan. How can two separate countries have the same name? The answer is that Pakistan is one country in two parts. Until after World War II these two parts called Pakistan were both a part of India and all India belonged to England. The people of India, like people almost everywhere, wanted to rule themselves. So finally the English said they would give up India and turn the country completely over to the Indians. This pleased the people of India but there was one trouble with the plan. Most of the people of India believed in a religion called the Hindu religion but a great many others were Mohammedans. These two religions didn't mix very well. The Hindus wanted India to remain one big country when it became independent. The Mohammedans didn't want one big country for they knew then the Hindus would do most of the ruling as there were more Hindus in India than Mohammedans. The Mohammedans wanted the country split into separate Mohammedan and Hindu countries. Then the Mohammedans could have a country of their own and not have to be part of a Hindu country. They almost went to war about it but finally both sides agreed to make two countries out of India, a Mohammedan country to be called Pakistan and a Hindu country to keep the name of India.

Now the Mohammedans lived mostly on the western and on the eastern sides of India and the Hindus lived mostly in the middle. So Pakistan became a new country with two separate parts, an eastern part and a western part with the new country of India in between. For Pakistan it must be something like living in a house with the kitchen on one side of the street and the living room on the other side. But it seems to work.

Both India and Pakistan are members of the British Commonwealth of Nations.

56

Opposite-Feet
(*continued*)

INDIA is divided into states like the United States and many of these states have separate rulers called rajahs. Many of the rajahs, however, are more interested in showing off and in having a good time than they are in ruling. They love jewels, such as diamonds and pearls, and they collect them as you might collect marbles, though one of their diamonds may be worth a million times what one of your precious marbles is worth. They own some of the largest and finest jewels that have ever been found. We think of diamond and pearl necklaces as something that only women wear, but when the rajahs appear before their subjects or ride in processions, as they love to do, they dress themselves up with their wonderful gems, some of them as big as walnuts, and wear collars of pearls, rubies, sapphires, and emeralds. In such processions a rajah rides on an elephant, which is dressed up too. The rajah sits on top of the elephant under a canopy that is so high in the air he has to use a stepladder to climb up.

Elephants are considered sacred in India, and

even though there are many wild ones, it is against the law to shoot one. So men hunt them, catch them, and tame them without shooting

A Rajah rides on an elephant which is all dressed up too

them. Hundreds of men form a long line around the place where there are elephants and beat drums and blow horns to frighten them. The elephants move away from the noise and, unknowingly, toward a pen that is left open to catch them. In this way they are driven by the terrible racket into the pen, which is then closed. After they are caught they must be tamed. This is not an easy job, for some elephants are very dangerous and can easily stamp a man to death. Once tamed, however, an elephant can be used like a camel in Arabia, a horse in Europe, or an automobile, a tractor, or a piece of machinery in our country. An elephant will wind his trunk around a log and load it on a train or ship, much as a machine called a derrick would do.

One of the things a rajah likes best to do is to hunt tigers. The tiger—a huge, orange-colored cat with black stripes—is a fearful creature. He lives in the jungles of India, and when he is hungry he raids villages and kills domestic animals and people. A rajah going forth to a tiger hunt takes good care that he is in no danger. He and a party of friends, with hundreds of servants, go out into the jungle and climb to a safe place in a tree where a platform has been built. The servants then go through the jungle beating pans and drums and anything that will make a noise, keeping up a terrific din to scare the tiger along toward the rajah and his party of friends. When he comes within range they fire upon him from above. They then take his skin home to cover the floors or walls of the rajah's palace.

There are over a hundred different religions in India but, as I told you in the last chapter, most of the people are Hindus. A Hindu believes his spirit comes back into this World in the shape of an animal or of another person. That is one reason why useful or good animals are treated well. A Hindu thinks that if he is good he will, when he dies, suddenly, in a twinkling, be born again—rich or in the shape of a good animal; if he has been bad, he will, when he returns, be poor or in the shape of a bad animal. When I look into the kindly eyes of my dog who wags his tail, puts out his paw, and whines *"m-m-m,"* I can almost believe as the Hindu does that some human being, perhaps a rajah, is in his dog body.

On the west side of India is a big city called Bombay, but Bombay does not look much different from any other large city in Europe. The buildings look much like the buildings in London or New York.

But if you travel north from Bombay for about two days you will come to a town with two buildings like none other in the World. This town is called Agra. One building is a tomb, the other is a mosque. The tomb was built by a Mohammedan prince for one of his four wives who was his favorite. It is called the Taj Mahal, and some think it the most beautiful building in the World. I had come half-way round the World to see this sight and had traveled days in such terrific heat that a sunstroke was as much to be feared as a stroke of lightning. I saw the Taj by the full moon and was so busy looking that I stepped into a pool of water up to my knees, and I had hardly clambered out when I stepped off a platform and sprained my ankle. But it was worth it. And yet to me the most beautiful building in the World is not the Taj. It is the Pearl Mosque, which is also at Agra. I don't know what the buildings in Heaven look like, but I don't believe they could be more beautiful than the Pearl Mosque.

On the east side of the country is the sacred river of India; it is called the Ganges. It has several mouths and at one of these mouths is Calcutta. Calcutta is in India but most of the mouths of the Ganges are in Pakistan.

Farther up the sacred river is the sacred city of the Hindus. It is called Benares. No one but a Mohammedan may go to the sacred city of Mecca, but any one may go to Benares. Benares is built on the banks of the river, and covering the banks are long stone steps leading down into the river. Hindus come from all over India to

I went half-way round the World to see the Taj Mahal

bathe in the Ganges at Benares, not to wash away dirt but to wash away sins. They go in about waist-deep and, filling a bowl with the sacred water, pour it over their heads. Especially do they come to the Ganges when they think they are about to die. Good Hindus are not afraid to die. In fact, if they are miserably poor and unhappy they are glad to die, for if their sins are washed away they expect, by dying, they will immediately be changed into the body of a happier creature.

The Hindus do not bury those who die; they burn their bodies on bonfires. Those who die in Benares are burned on the steps that lead down to the river, and so many are burned there that men make a regular business of selling wood for these funeral fires. The richer a man is, the bigger fire he can have when he dies; but often a man is so poor he has not left even enough money to pay for the few sticks of wood necessary to burn his body.

There are so many people in India that often there is not enough food to go around, and though the poor people live on little but a few handfuls of rice a day, thousands upon thousands starve to death for lack of even this little food. The rajahs and well-to-do people look fat and well-fed, but the poor people are usually as thin as skeletons, and as they often wear hardly any clothes, you can see every bone in their lean bodies.

From rajahs with their millions' worth of jewels to the poor wretch who dies without two sticks of wood to burn his body, that is the "opposite-feet" land.

South of India is an island called Ceylon, where men wear skirts and combs in their hair. Much of our tea comes from there. Near Ceylon are the greatest pearl fisheries i.t.w.W.—greater even than those of the Persian Gulf. Many of the rajahs' famous pearls have been found there, and even I have a black pearl that came from there. It is supposed to bring good luck whether you wear it or whether you don't. I don't.

The Indians are famous magicians, and at Colombo in Ceylon I saw some of their tricks. An Indian placed his wife in a basket, covered it with a shawl, stabbed through it in every direction, and then uncovered her alive and smiling. I saw him put a seed in a flower-pot and while you watched it it grew to a plant. How do they do such things? You can only guess just as every one else does.

57

The White Elephant

THERE was once an Indian prince named Gautama. Gautama was rich and had everything in the World he wanted, so he grew up gay and light-hearted. He had never seen any poor people, nor known any misery in his life, so he thought every one in the World was just as well off and just as happy as he. Then one day when he was grown up he went on a trip and, to his amazement, saw for the first time in his life people who were sick, poor, and unhappy. The sights he saw filled him with such pity that he gave up all he had and spent the rest of his life helping the needy. As Gautama went about from place to place he preached that certain things were right and certain things wrong. People began to call him Buddha, which meant "the one who knows," and to worship him, and thus started a religion called Buddhism. This was about five hundred years before Christ.

After Buddha died, Buddhists sent missionaries to other countries to teach the people Buddhism too, just as Christians now send missionaries to other lands to teach Christianity. After a long while most of the people in India got tired of Buddhism and took up other newer religions. Many became Mohammedans, but in the countries east of India they still held to Buddhism, although now this worship has become chiefly a worship of idols.

The two countries next door to India are Burma and Thailand. A Mohammedan church is called a mosque, a Buddhist church is called a pagoda. In the capital of Burma —a city called Rangoon—is one of the largest and most wonderful of these pagodas. This pagoda is called the Shwe Dagon Pagoda. It looks like a giant ice cream cone turned upside down and is nearly as high as the Washington Monument. It is built of brick, but the outside is covered with sheets of solid gold—a glorious, dazzling sight in the sunlight. Around the bottom of the pagoda are little cell-like rooms in each of which is an idol, and underneath the center of the pagoda is a box in which, it is said, there are eight hairs from the head of Buddha. On the tip top of the pagoda is—what

THE APPROACH TO THE SHWE DAGON PAGODA

It looks like a giant ice cream cone turned upside down

do you suppose? A church would have a cross, a mosque a crescent, but the pagoda has an umbrella!—with little tinkling bells hanging to it.

Rice is the chief and almost the only food of most of the people in Asia. They eat boiled rice just so, without sugar or cream, and they eat it for breakfast, luncheon, and dinner. Rangoon is the chief rice market of the World.

The people in Burma and Thailand are more like the Chinese than like the people in India. Burma is a republic but Thailand is a kingdom. Until after World War II, Thailand was named Siam. Then the people changed the name of this country of Siam to Thailand. If a man suddenly changed his name from Mr. Jones to Mr. Baker some people would still think of him as Mr. Jones and call him Mr. Jones instead of Mr. Baker. Many people still call Thailand, Siam.

Once, the King of Siam could do anything he wanted with his people. That is what is called an absolute monarchy. When-I-was-a-boy, if any one acted very "bossy" or ordered others around, we used to say, "Who do you think you are? The King of Siam?"

But now the King of Thailand has to rule

according to the laws of the country and cannot do just as he pleases the way his ancestors used to do.

The Buddhists believe that when they die their souls go into the bodies of animals. The kings' souls they think go into the bodies of white elephants, so in Thailand the White Elephant is sacred. The white elephants are, however, more gray than white. Once any white elephant found in a herd had to be presented to the King to bring good luck to him and to the kingdom. Because these royal white elephants did no work, we have come to call something we may have that is of no use, and yet we must keep and take care of, "a white elephant." A friend of mine has an old worn-out automobile that will not run, that he can neither sell nor give away, and as it takes up space in his garage he calls it his "white elephant."

In Burma the ordinary gray elephant is used as we use an automobile, truck, or tractor and costs about the same as an automobile does. An elephant carries people, he carries loads, he lifts logs, he plows. A driver sits on the elephant's head and taps him on one side or the other to let him know just what he is to do and he does it. He works regular hours and knows when it's time to start work and when it's time to quit. It is as if he belonged to a labor union, and he will not work at all unless he has had one or more baths each day!

We always say wood will float, but there is a kind of wood in Burma that is so heavy it will not float. It is called "Teak." They use teak instead of other woods in making furniture, for white ants eat up and destroy anything made out of softer woods. One of the jobs that elephants are used for is hauling, lifting, and loading the heavy logs of teak. I thought I should like to have an elephant myself, so I bought a nice one and brought it all the way home. There it is on my table now. It's made of bronze.

Stretching down from Thailand like an elephant's trunk is a long peninsula known as the Malay Peninsula. Just about half a mile offshore from the top of this "trunk" is a bit of an island called Singapore. It was at one time nothing but a jungle in which poisonous snakes and terrible tigers lurked. The owner tried to give it away to get rid of it and couldn't. Later, however, he sold it to an Englishman named Raffles for almost nothing, and England built a city there. Why do you suppose England wanted such a place at all? Because this spot was another gateway for ships going east or west. There is, as you will see, a narrow passageway between the islands, and this was the only good way for ships to go. Just as in the case of Gibraltar, Suez, and Aden, England wanted to control it. In World War II the Japanese captured Singapore, not with ships from the sea, but with soldiers from the land side of the city. When the Japanese were finally beaten in the war, England again took control of Singapore. Singapore is now one of the most important stopping-places for ships, and in the lobby of the great hotel called "Raffles" you may now see people from all nations of the earth.

Singapore is almost on the Equator—it is almost half-way between the North and South Poles. Sailors call the Equator "The Line." When you cross "The Line" for the first time you are supposed to be baptized by Father Neptune, the god of the sea. So I was baptized when I crossed it and this was the way it was done. As I stepped out on deck a sailor suddenly appeared on each side of me. One caught me by my arms and the other by my legs and, lifting me in the air, they threw me, with all my clothes on, into a big pool of water that had been made out of canvas on the deck of the ship. Then when I clambered out of the pool, sputtering for my breath, they shoved me into the end of a long canvas pipe, through which I had to crawl. When I came out at the other end they gave me a whack on the back with a paddle. Then I was taken before Father Neptune, a man seated on a throne and dressed up in a bath-robe with a pasteboard crown set on the side of his head, a pitchfork in his hand. He handed me a diploma, as if I were graduating from college, saying that I had been duly baptized and initiated and was now "a regular fellow" in the society of those who had crossed "The Line."

Near the Malay Peninsula are the East Indies and the Spice Islands, which Columbus tried to reach. Sumatra, which is shaped something like a fat cigar, is where the tobacco is grown for making the covers for cigars. Java, another one of the East Indies, was once famous for its coffee. I had looked forward to getting a good cup here, but I tried in a number of places and finally got a cup, but the coffee had come from Brazil!

In Java I saw bats as big as eagles and butterflies as big as your two hands.

KING NEPTUNE
AWARDING DIPLOMAS

Neptune handed me a diploma saying I had been duly baptized

58

The Land of Devils

How often do you say your prayers?

Once a day—before you go to bed?

What would you think of a boy who said a thousand prayers a day?

"He should be very good indeed."

Well, I know of a country where every one— men, women, and children—say thousands of prayers each day and yet no one is any better than you are. This country, where they say so many prayers, is high up in the Himalaya Mountains on the opposite side from India. It is called Tibet.

If the people of Tibet say so many prayers, you may wonder how they can have time to do anything else. They can, because this is the way they say their prayers. A prayer is written on a strip of paper for them and this is put in a little contraption like a baby's rattle, called a prayer- wheel. Then they swing this prayer-wheel round and round and every time it turns they think they are saying a prayer. They can turn it very fast, even while they are doing other things, as you might twiddle your fingers, so in a day they can

say countless prayers without actually saying
a word. The reason they say so many prayers is
not to be good but because they believe that the
air is full of evil spirits or devils, always trying
to do them harm, so they keep saying prayers
to keep the devils away. If a man hits his thumb
with a hammer, sprains his ankle, or cuts his
finger, he doesn't think it's an accident—he
thinks a devil did it. If he stumbles, he says a
devil tripped him up. So he wears a charm,
usually a turquoise, to keep the devils away and
says his prayers. More prayers are "said" in
Tibet than in all the rest of the World, and yet
their prayers do not mean a thing; they are just
magic words with no more sense than "hocus
pocus" or "eenie, meenie, minee, mo." One
prayer that they are continually "saying" is
"Om-mani-padme-hum," which is said to mean
"O jewel in the lotus," which doesn't mean anything either.

As you might guess from what I have said,
the people of Tibet have ways of doing things
that seem very strange to us. If a visitor came to
call at your house and you stuck out your tongue
and hissed at him instead of shaking hands, he
would think you very rude. But a man from Tibet
would be pleased to see you had such good manners; for in Tibet the polite way to greet someone
is to stick out your tongue at him. And it is extra
special polite to hiss.

The Tibetans believe in so many devils or evil

spirits that they need a great many priests, or ministers, or clergymen as we should call them, but they call them "lamas."

A lama has an easy time of it—he has nothing to do but say prayers and the rest of the people take care of him and support him. For that reason, every one who is smart enough to make others believe he is holy becomes a lama, and almost every third person is a lama. The head lama of all is called the Grand Lama, and he is not only the head of all the lamas, but he is the head of all the people; he is the ruler of Tibet.

The people of Tibet believe that when the Grand Lama dies his spirit goes into the body of a little boy. The priests then choose this boy to be the new Grand Lama and he becomes the ruler of Tibet. The priests take care of him and teach him and tell him what to do until he is grown up. They really rule for him until he is old enough to rule for himself.

In most countries of the World there are more women than men. That is one reason why in some countries, especially where the people are Mohammedans, a man may have several wives, but in Tibet there are more men than women, so in Tibet one woman may have several husbands. The woman is the head of the family, the men are the ones who "promise to obey," and one wife and her husbands live together happy and contented.

The Tibetans are so hemmed in by high mountains that they know very little of the World or of other people. For many years the Tibetans would not let any outsider into Tibet. Even now very few visitors ever go there because the journey is so hard and long and dangerous over such high and rugged mountains.

Here is a riddle for you. What is it that has a head like an ox, a body like a sheep, gives milk like a cow, and grunts like a pig? It's an animal that is found in Tibet, and in alphabet rimes. It is called the Yak.

He is found in Tibet and in alphabet rimes

59

DRAGON LAND

Cups and saucers, plates and dishes we call "china," because China made them. China is a funny little land, but the people there do many things opposite from the way

we do. Their first name comes after their last name. Instead of saying John Smith, they would say Smith John. Instead of reading from the front of the book to the back, they start at the back and read to the front. Instead of writing across the page, they write down the page, beginning at the right. Instead of a sharp-pointed pen to write with, they use a soft brush. Instead of soft pillows, theirs are hard. Instead of wearing pajamas at night, they wear them in the day.

We should call China old-fashioned. They would call us newfangled. Our latest fashions are a few months old. Their latest fashions are a thousand years old. "Thousands of years ago," the Chinese say, "when your ignorant ancestors were dressing in skins, living in huts, and eating with their fingers, our educated ancestors were wearing silk garments, living in palaces, and eating from dishes of fine porcelain." That's not very polite, but it's true.

It's true, too, that we have been "copy-cats," for we have copied many things from the Chinese and are using many things to-day that came first from China. China, silk, tea, printing, the compass, gunpowder are all supposed to have first come from China, and also playing-cards—the cards your mother plays Bridge with—and goldfish, firecrackers, and varnish—to mention only a few things. But the trouble with the Chinese was that they had been satisfied to leave well enough alone, and they kept doing things in the same way they did two thousand or more years ago—they stood still, so the white man caught up and went ahead.

China, however, has been slowly changing and taking up newfangled things like electric lights, railways, automobiles, and airplanes, and is copying some of the ways on our side of the World.

China used to be ruled by an Emperor. Then it became a republic with a president. But many Chinese became Communists and fought the republican Chinese. After years of fighting the Communists won and China became a Communist country.

A Chinaman used to wear his hair in a long braid, which reached to the waist or knees, or even to the ground. We call it a pigtail, but why a pigtail I don't know, for a pig's tail is short and curly and a Chinaman's queue is long and straight. When China became a republic, however, many of the Chinese in the cities cut off their queues; but in the towns and country they still wear them.

A Chinese gentleman used to let his finger-nails grow like long claws four or five inches long. He never cut his nails, and to prevent them from breaking off he put gold cases on them. Such long finger-nails were a sign that he did no work, that he was a gentleman. The longer a man's finger-nails, the finer the gentleman he was, for laborers who worked with their hands could not have long finger-nails.

Most of the Chinese worship Buddha, but some worship devils. All worship their ancestors, and some worship all three. The Chinese make their streets crooked on purpose to keep away the devils, for a devil, they say, walks straight ahead, and if the street is crooked he will bump his nose into the turn and hurt himself, so they discourage him in this way from walking their streets.

Many missionaries have gone to China to try to make the Chinese Christians. They have started schools for the children and grown-ups too and have tried to teach them our religion. The missionaries built hospitals for the sick and trained Chinese to become doctors and nurses in the hospitals. But when the Communists took over

A CHINESE GENTLEMAN WITH LONG FINGER-NAILS

The longer his finger-nails the finer gentleman he is

China the missionaries had to stop their work and give up their hospitals and schools which the Communists seized.

The well-to-do Chinese have other things to eat besides rice, but the poor people—and most of the people in China are very poor—have nothing much but rice to eat. A soup made out of birds'-nests is considered very delicious, and rat stew is not as bad as it sounds—I have eaten it myself. It tastes something like terrapin, which in Maryland is a great delicacy.

The Chinese eat everything, whether rice or stew, with two sticks, called chop-sticks. They hold the dish close to their mouths so as not to spill anything and with the chop-sticks in the fingers of one hand they partly push and partly whip the food down their throats. They have very little meat except of small animals, but they have plenty of fish. Fish they catch sometimes as we do, but often they use a bird to catch their fish

A NINE STORY CHINESE PAGODA

for them—a bird called a cormorant. This bird is very greedy and very fond of fish. The fisherman goes out in a boat, puts a ring around the cormorant's throat and lets him out on a string. When the bird sees a fish he dives for it and catches it in his beak, but he can't swallow it because of the ring round his neck. The fisherman then pulls him in, takes the fish away, and lets the bird out again. When the cormorant has caught a sufficient number of fish, the fisherman takes the ring off his neck and lets him catch a fish for himself.

China is the most crowded country in the World. It is about the same size as our country, but it has four times as many people—there are too many men, too many women, and too many children, so there is not enough food, not enough work, and not enough room for all. So all the people have to work all the time to make a living, and a very poor living at that. They work harder than any other people in the World and have very little fun, yet they make on the average only a few cents a day, so they have to be very saving and economical. They live on what we might put in the garbage-can, and they patch their clothes until they are all patches.

Beggars and thieves are plentiful; begging is a regular business. The beggars have a union which makes rules that tell from whom, how often, and how much the beggars may beg.

A CHINESE BOY EATING WITH CHOP STICKS

He wouldn't think of using a knife and fork because his father and grandfather never used a knife and fork

About the only play the Chinese have is flying kites, and men do this even more than children. They fly kites instead of playing golf. They make wonderful kites in the shapes of birds and dragons, and hold kite-flying contests.

60

Dragon Land
(*continued*)

FOR thousands of years China locked itself in
and the rest of the World out. Those outside of
China the Chinese called barbarians or "foreign
devils." They thought them ignorant and common and would have nothing to do with them.
White faces, light hair, and eyes in a straight
line like ours they thought ugly. Yellow faces,
black hair, and eyes on a slant like their own
they thought beautiful.

About a hundred years ago a city in the south
of China, called Canton, opened its gates and let
outsiders in and its own people out. Canton is on
the Pearl River. When we say "on" we usually
mean "by the side of," but in Canton nearly a
third of a million Chinese actually live *on* the
Pearl River—in boats. Boats are lifetime homes
of these people, and many of them are born, grow
up, and die on the boats without ever having been
ashore. Babies learn to swim before they learn
to walk. The main part of Canton is, of course,
on the land, but the houses are packed so closely
together there is no room for regular streets.
There are crooked alleys winding and twisting in

and out and back and forth, so that a white man entering the city without a guide would quickly lose his way and be quite unable to get out of the city again. When Canton opened its gates, many of its poor people came to the United States to earn a living.

A CHINESE HOUSE-BOAT

Thousands live their whole lives on these boats which never sail from shore

When-I-was-a-boy there were Chinese from Canton in almost every city and town in the United States making a living by washing and ironing collars, cuffs, and shirts. Nowadays, our own laundries do most of this work, and most of the Chinamen who are here now run restaurants where they serve chicken, rice, and other foods cooked in Chinese style, or shops where they sell goods made in China. But *we* have now done the locking out, for we let no more Chinese into the United States than we can help. White people in our country and other countries of Europe, however, forced China to open all her gates and

many nations soon owned places in China where
they lived and worked as they would at home.
Most of the white people who came to live in
China were there to buy things the Chinese made,
or to sell them things that their own countries
made, or else they were missionaries trying to
make the Chinese Christians or to teach them
Christian ways.

The chief of these cities where people of other
countries lived was Shanghai. Shanghai was
sometimes called the New York of China. When
the Communists took over China they made it
so hard for white people to live in Shanghai that
most of them had to leave. Shanghai is near the
mouth of the Great River which in Chinese is
called Yangtze. It is such a long river that if it
were in the United States it would stretch all the
way across our country from the Atlantic to
the Pacific.

Like a great snake winding and twisting its
way to the sea is another river farther north on
the map. It is called the Hwang Ho. It is one
of the few rivers in the World which has to be
drawn differently every time a map is made, for
like a live snake it changes, it twists and turns
from time to time, and each time it does so it
drowns people and washes away houses and
fields. It has drowned so many people and done
so much damage that it is called "China's
Sorrow."

The Hwang Ho is also called the Yellow

River, for it is so yellow with mud that where it flows into the blue ocean it makes the water yellow for miles, and a ship before it sights land knows by the color of the water that it is near the mouth of the Hwang Ho. The Chinese, however, speak of its golden sands, which is a poetic name for mud color.

A CHINESE WHEEL-BARROW

A Taxi in China is a wheelbarrow

Connecting the Hwang Ho and the Yangtze Rivers is a long canal called the Grand Canal. It is one of the longest canals in the World. Everywhere in China there are canals, for canals have been the railroads of China, and only recently has China had any real railroads. Instead of trains they use boats called junks, with tall sails, and eyes painted on the front so that the boat can see its way!

Many of the roads in China are too narrow for an automobile truck—they are little wider than paths; a regular size road would take up too much land that could better be used for farming. So, instead of wagons and trucks, the usual carriage in China is a wheelbarrow, pushed or pulled by men. Chinese wheelbarrows have a large wheel in the center, and passengers or loads are carried on either side of the wheel. Near the big cities, however, they have now built broad roads, for there they have brought in automobiles. In parts of China they also use camels but they are the two-humped kind.

Most maps show only God-made things such as mountains and rivers, for man-made things are too small to show—even cities are only dots on a map; but on the map of China two man-made things are shown. One is the Grand Canal I have spoken of. The other is a Great Wall across the north of China. It has been called the Eighth Wonder of the World. The Great Wall was built before Christ was born, when men used bows and arrows to keep out wild tribes from the north. The wall starts at a big rock in the sea and goes up hill and down dale across the land for nearly two thousand miles. It is nearly thirty feet high and wide as a road on top. Every few hundred feet is a watch tower, twenty thousand of them in all. A third of a million men worked a dozen years to build it, but now much of the wall is in ruins.

61

Where the Thermometer Freezes Up

MOST thermometers have numbers down to forty degrees (40°) below zero. There the numbers stop, for when the mercury gets *down* to that point it freezes *up*. But there are few places in the World where it ever gets as cold as that. The coldest place in the World is not at the North Pole; the coldest place in the World, where the thermometer does go below 40° and freezes up, is in the country called Siberia.

Siberia is a huge country north of China. In the north of Siberia the sun never rises all winter long. It is night, as it is in Norway and Sweden. But there is no Gulf Stream to warm the land, so it gets much colder than 40° below zero, and they have to use a different kind of thermometer to measure how cold it is. In one place it goes to 90° below zero, which is the coldest place i.t.w.W. People can't grow fur on their skins to keep themselves warm as animals can, so when they go outside they must cover themselves from top to toe with animal skins or they would freeze to death in a few moments.

But all of Siberia is not like this. There is a top, a middle, and a bottom part. Few people live in the northern part, however. It is so cold that no trees grow there and the ground is frozen solid many feet down. In the summer it gets very warm, and the thermometer sometimes goes just as high above zero as it goes below in the winter; that is, to 90°. The ground then thaws out cn top and moss and a few other things grow for a short while, though the ground underneath still stays frozen. Siberia is larger than the United States. It belongs to Russia, but there are people from other countries living there too.

The middle part of Siberia is not nearly so cold, and there great forests have grown, and in the forests live wild animals such as foxes, wolves, sable, and ermine, which have beautiful thick coats of fur to keep themselves warm. Trappers hunt these animals just for their furs, to be made into coats to keep people warm. One small animal, called the ermine, has a snow-white coat and a tail with a black tip. The ermine hates dirt or anything that will soil his white fur, so he keeps himself spotless. It is for this reason that the official robes of judges and kings are made of the fur of the ermine, as a sign that they too must be pure and clean in heart and mind. The skins of many such animals are sewn together to make a single cape or coat, which then looks white with little black tails spotted regularly over it.

The longest railway in the World is built through the bottom part of Siberia. It is so long it takes two weeks to go from one end of it to the other. One end of it on the Pacific Ocean is called Vladivostok and the other end in Russia is Moscow. It is called the Trans-Siberian Railway, which means the Across Siberia Railway.

A KING IN HIS ROYAL ERMINE

The little animal called the "ermine" is different from most boys—he hates dirt

Most of the people in Siberia live along this railway, and yet one may travel for hundreds of miles without seeing a town or even a house. Often the towns are far from the railroad, so that there is a long drive from the station to the town. The engines that draw the trains are fired by wood instead of coal, and along the railroad there are piles of wood at which the train stops to get fuel, as a car would stop to get gasoline. The chief Siberian cities end in "sk." They are Omsk, Tomsk, and Irkutsk.

A stranger once asked a man on the street how far it was to the railway station. The man replied, "If you keep on going the way you are headed it is twenty-five thousand miles, but if you turn round it's two blocks."

How far do you suppose it is to Siberia from our country?—how many miles away would you say?—eight thousand?—ten thousand miles? As a matter of fact, it is only about fifty miles—yes, that's right, fifty miles—for the short way is across to Alaska. Between Siberia and Alaska is a narrow strip of water called Bering Strait, and when this is frozen over, one could walk across from Asia to America. On the map there is also a long string of islands that look like stepping-stones, but one would have to be a giant to walk across that way. Some say that the Indians and Eskimos in Alaska and the United States may have come across Bering Strait from Asia long, long ago, and that they look something like the Chinese because they once came from that country.

Before World War I, when Russia had a czar, people who hated the czar or were supposed to hate the czar, or who had said anything against the czar, or even thought anything against the czar, were made prisoners, torn away from their families and friends, and sent to far-off Siberia to work in the mines. Many of them perished before reaching there. Most of them never returned.

After World War I there was a revolution. The people rose up and threw out the Czar's government. The new government was taken over by a group of Russians called Communists. These

Communists killed the czar and his family and most of the well-to-do people of Russia. The Communists made many changes. They started schools. They killed all farmers who owned large farms and gave their land to many poor people to farm. They started factories and opened stores and built railroads and airlines. They made large dams across the rivers so they could use waterpower to send electric current to the factories.

In spite of all these changes, however, the Communists didn't make the change that was needed most. In Communist Russia people who hate the Communists, or are supposed to hate the Communists, or who say anything against the Communists, or even think anything against the Communists, are made prisoners, torn away from their families and friends, and sent to far-off Siberia to work in the mines. Many of them perish before reaching there. Most of them never return.

62

A Giant Sea-Serpent

WHEN the World was young and people believed in sea-serpents they used to say there was a huge sea-serpent a thousand miles long in the sea near China. Wherever the humps on the sea-serpent's back stuck out of the water they looked like islands, and whenever the sea-serpent twisted or turned in his age-long sleep the islands would shake. Yet, long ago people from China went to these islands on the sea-serpent's back and made their homes there, in spite of the fact that he was squirming in his sleep. We now know that these islands are simply old volcanoes in the water, most of which have burned out, and when they shake, as they still do almost every day, we know that the shakes are just earthquakes. We call these islands on the sea-serpent "Japan" and the people "Japanese." The Japanese, however, don't call their island Japan; they call their country of islands "Nippon," which means the Land of the Rising Sun. Of course, the sun rises in other lands too, but when the Japanese went to Japan it was, for them, the land where the sun rose. So their white flag has on it the picture of a red sun with rays.

The Chinese and the Japanese both belong to the yellow race. But the Japanese are as different from the Chinese in most ways as the white people of our country are different from the white people of India. The Japanese are quick to learn and quick to copy. The Japanese used to copy the Chinese writing, the Chinese Buddha, the Chinese way of eating with chop-sticks, for they knew no other people and no other country but China and, like the Chinese, they kept all others out of their country. It was as if they had put up a sign, "No Admittance."

Now, for some reason or other, most people whenever they see a sign "Keep Out" want to "Go in"—like Mary, Mary quite contrary, they want to do what they are told they musn't. They are curious or inquisitive and they want to know and see why there is "No Admittance." So, over a hundred years ago, an American naval officer named Commodore Perry went to Japan and tried to get in. He took with him a shipload of presents from our country for the Japanese Emperor, presents such as the Emperor had never seen or known of before. The Emperor was so pleased with the presents that he wanted to buy more and to know more about countries that could make such things. So Commodore Perry said to the Emperor, "Let the American people come in to your country and we will sell you these things and buy other things from you." The Emperor agreed, and so the country was opened for trade and the eyes of the Japanese were opened too, for until then they had had no idea of what was going on in other countries except China. They were amazed to hear about railroad trains, the telegraph, and the marvelous machines that we had. Then Japan sent thousands of her brightest young men to our country and to the countries of Europe to learn about such things, and they returned and taught their own people, who were extraordinarily quick to learn. It was not long before they had copies of everything that we had. They made their country an up-to-date country and in a hundred years they jumped ahead of the Chinese a thousand years. But if some one sets out to copy some one else he is apt to copy the bad things as well as the good. And that's what the Japanese did. They not only copied trolley-cars, electric lights, and automobiles. They copied battleships and airplanes and tanks and guns. They built a great big up-to-date army. Then they started a great big up-to-date war by dropping bombs on American ships in Hawaii. After the Japanese were beaten in the war they were not allowed to have a big army nor to build war machines like battleships, tanks, and guns.

One of the first things the Japanese copied was a baby carriage to carry grown-up people. In Japan they have very few horses, because horses eat too much. So an American sailor, living in Japan, made for his wife a large baby carriage that could be pulled by a man, for in Japan a man was cheaper than a horse. The Japanese called it a Jinrikisha, which means a "man pull car," or a Pullman car. It seems strange that the parlor cars on our trains are also called Pullman cars. This "rickshaw," as it is called for short, seemed such a good idea that the Japanese made thousands of them, and they are now used instead of taxis or private cars, not only in Japan but in China and other countries of the East. The men who pull them are called coolies, and a coolie will dog-trot almost all day long, pulling a rickshaw behind him, without getting tired. As you see a rickshaw going away from you down the street, the coolie is hidden all but his legs, so that it looks as if the rickshaw itself were trotting along with a pair of legs of its own.

In the cities many of the men wear clothes like ours, but most of the people, both men and women, still wear kimonos like those our mothers and sisters often wear in their own homes.

There are two important holidays for Japanese boys and girls. The one for girls comes on the third day of the third month, that is March third. It is called Doll Day and the girls get out all their dolls, arrange them nicely, and play with them. The one for the boys is on the fifth day of the fifth month, that is May fifth. It is called Flag Day or Kite Day. Big paper kites in the form of a fish called the carp are hung out on poles in front of the houses where there are boys.

The carp is a fish that swims upstream against the current, which is a hard thing to do, instead of downstream, which is easy. So the carp is a model for boys—to do the hardest thing, not the easiest.

The Japanese love flowers perhaps more than any people i.t.w.W. and they have holidays when the flowers are in bloom. One holiday comes when the cherry-trees, plum-trees, and peach-trees bloom in the spring, and another when the chrysanthemums bloom in the fall. Every house in Japan has a garden, no matter how small it may be—a tiny imitation of the country-side, with tiny lakes and tiny mountains, and tiny rivers with tiny bridges over them—all so perfectly made that a photograph of such a garden looks like a picture of real mountains and lakes and rivers—like a doll garden. The Japanese grow dwarf trees—oaks and maples—which look in a picture as if they were a hundred feet tall and a hundred years old, but which are actually only a foot or so tall, but may be a hundred years old.

The Japanese school-boys seem to "hunger and thirst" after knowledge. I was looking into a shop window where beautiful Japanese umbrellas were displayed, when a school-boy came up to me and asked me in English if he couldn't act as my guide for a day without charge.

"Why," said I, "do you want to show me around?"

"Just to practise speaking English," he replied.

I visited a Japanese school, and a dozen boys gave me their calling cards and asked me to write them when I reached home, promising to reply in English if I did so.

63

Picture Post-Cards

WHEN I came home from Japan I sent picture post-cards to all the Japanese school-boys who had given me their names. I had chosen cards that I thought would give them some idea of the size and importance of our country. One card had a picture of the Capitol at Washington, another Niagara Falls, another sky-scrapers in New York. In reply each boy wrote me a letter on thin rice paper and drew or painted or inclosed a picture of some scene or common sight in Japan.

Three of the pictures were of the same thing—a beautiful mountain with a snow-white top. It is the sacred mountain of Japan, called Fujiyama or just Fuji. It is really not a mountain at all but a burnt-out volcano, the top of which is covered with snow. You can see it from afar, and the Japanese love it so they put pictures of it on every conceivable thing they want to ornament—on fans, boxes, trays, umbrellas, lanterns, screens. No movie queen or famous beauty has ever had as many pictures made of her as have been made of Fuji.

There were two pictures of a huge bronze statue of Buddha seated out-of-doors in a grove of trees. It is so large that half a dozen people can sit on its thumbs. The eyes are of solid gold

FUJIYAMA, THE SACRED VOLCANO OF JAPAN

and more than a yard long, and in its forehead is a large ball of solid silver. They call it the Diabutsu. We might call it an idol, but the Japanese make statues of Buddha as we put up monuments to famous men and saints, and their statues of Buddha are to remind them that he was wise and good. His life was an example which even Christians might imitate.

Here are some of the other pictures which the Japanese boys sent me:

A street scene in Tokyo:

Tokyo is the capital and largest city of Japan and one of the largest cities i.t.w.W. The old capital has exactly the same letters as Tokyo but arranged this way: Kyoto. If you say Tokyo

twice you say Kyoto too—TO/KYOTO/KYO.
Both Tokyo and Kyoto and all other Japanese
cities look quite different from our large cities.
There are no sky-scrapers, few buildings are

A DIABUTSU

It is to remind them that Buddha was wise and good

more than two stories high, and most of them are
built of bamboo. The reason for this is because
the sea-serpent is still shaking himself almost
every day, and they have so many earthquakes in
these islands that tall houses would be shaken
down. When an earthquake does come—and
slight ones come almost every day and terrific
ones every once in a while—the houses can easily
be built up again. The chief damage done by the
earthquakes, however, is the result of fires started

when lights and stoves are upset. Then thousands of houses may be destroyed.

There are a few big buildings that are built to withstand earthquakes. They are built on underground platforms of concrete instead of on the solid rock of the earth. This keeps them from being torn from their foundations when an earthquake shakes the ground; just as a big loose rock lying on the ground might be shaken but would not be broken apart.

A picture of a Japanese house:

Japanese houses make fine bonfires, for they are not only made entirely of wood, but the windows are made of paper and the floors are covered with straw mats. The mats are not made to fit the floor, but the floors are made to fit the mats, which are all of the same size. The rooms are built to fit six mats, ten mats, and so on. In order to keep the mats clean, the Japanese take off their shoes whenever they enter their houses, and walk about the house in their stocking feet. Their stockings are like mittens with a place for the toe, and they would no more think of stepping on the mats with their shoes on than you would of getting into bed with your shoes on.

There are no chairs in a Japanese house, for the Japanese sit on the floor. For us it is very uncomfortable to sit on the floor for any length of time, but the Japanese prefer it, and I have seen them squatting on the floor in railway stations, although there were benches to sit on right along-

side. I don't know why, but I've often seen
American girls sit on chairs with their feet up under them as if they were sitting on the floor. But
I've never seen boys do it. Perhaps girls are part
Japanese. The tables in a Japanese house have
legs only a few inches high; they are really only
trays like the bed trays we use when one is sick,
and meals are served by placing such a tray in
front of each person as he squats on his heels on
the floor. There are no beds either; they sleep
on the mats and cover themselves with a padded
kimono for a comforter and use a hard wooden
block for a pillow.

The Japanese are like elephants. In what way?
I'll give you three guesses. They bathe frequently. The Chinese, who seldom bathe, say the
Japanese must be very dirty to need so many
baths. But what seems to us peculiar, all the
family, one after another, bathe in the same tub
without changing the water. The tub is shaped
like a sawed-off barrel in which there is room to
sit but not to lie down. The water is piping hot "to
open the pores." After the bather has parboiled
himself, he then climbs out and scrubs himself.

*A picture of two Japanese carrying a big
bucket on a pole which rests on their shoulders:*

In the tub—I couldn't see them but I knew—
there are live fish. The Japanese eat little meat,
because they have few animals such as cows,
sheep, or pigs from which meat is made, and because good Buddhists do not believe in eating

meat anyway. But fish they do not call meat, and they catch and eat more fish than any other people in the World, even more than the people in Norway. As Japan is all islands, no one lives far from the sea, and fresh fish may be had all the time.

A TORII OR JAPANESE GATE

Peddlers carry them alive in tubs of water so that the fish will be absolutely fresh.

A picture of fields covered with water in which is growing rice:

Rice is the chief and almost the only vegetable in Japan, and tea is the chief drink. Tea the Japanese drink without either sugar or cream. There are tea-houses and tea-gardens where waitresses called Geisha girls serve tea to customers and then entertain them by dancing and playing on long-necked musical instruments something like a banjo.

Another letter was ornamented with high wooden gateways called Torii, which you see everywhere in Japan, standing sometimes alone, sometimes in line. Torii means a bird rest. They are sacred gateways under which one passes to a temple or shrine.

Still another letter was illustrated with pictures of large stone lanterns such as you often see around Japanese temples and in their gardens. These lanterns give very little light, but they are much more ornamental than our lan-

terns, and the Japanese think more of beauty than they do of use. They even have a festival of lanterns —the paper kind that we use at garden parties.

Another letter contained a picture of three monkeys carved in wood in the greatest of all Japanese temples at Nikko. One monkey had his paws over his ears, the next over his mouth, and the third over his eyes, meaning: "Hear no evil, speak no evil, see no evil."

A picture of two very fat men squatting on the ground and facing each other in the center of a huge building around which are sitting thousands of people watching:

The two fat men are wrestlers. Wrestling is

a national sport in Japan, as bull-fighting is a national sport in Spain and football is a national sport in the United States. There are two kinds of wrestling. One kind is done by giants weighing several hundred pounds, who wrestle before crowds such as gather to watch baseball or football games in this country. The wrestlers squat, facing each other like huge bullfrogs, and spend most of their time in this position, each watching for a chance to get a grip on the other. The game seems to an American simply one of watching and waiting, for once one gets "a hold" on the other the battle is usually over. Another kind of wrestling is called Jiu-jitsu. It is a trick wrestling, and a little chap, if he knows how, can throw a much larger and stronger person by catching his arm, hand, or leg and twisting it with a quick movement into certain positions that make it impossible for him to resist. I have seen in Japan whole schools lined up two and two, practising the various "throws" with lightning-like movements.

Wrestling is an old Japanese sport. The Japanese, however, copied new sports from other countries along with all the other things they copied. They copied baseball, and crowds at baseball games in Japan are as big as baseball crowds in the United States.

The last letter inclosed a photograph of the Emperor. Many countries have now changed from emperors to presidents but Japan, which

has been quick to change in most things, I don't
believe ever will change to a president. The same
family has been ruling in Japan for two thousand years. Even after being beaten in World
War II, the Japanese were allowed by the other
countries to keep their Emperor. Before this war
the Japanese believed the Emperor was sacred as
if he were a god. They still treat him with great
respect but are no longer supposed to worship
him.

64

Man-Made Mountains

ALL the continents begin with an "A" except one.

Asia is the largest continent.

Africa is the next largest.

But Africa was an "In-the-Way" continent. It was in the way of those who wanted to get to Asia. Every one wanted to get *around* Africa. No one wanted to get *to* it. Sailors had been shipwrecked on its shores, but few lived to tell the tale of jungles of wild animals and wild black men. Africa was called the Dark Continent because no one knew much about it or wanted to know about it. Like children afraid of the dark, people were afraid of the Dark Continent. On one edge—along the Mediterranean Sea—white men lived, but south of that edge was a great desert that men feared to cross, and south of that wild black men and wild animals. But in one corner of Africa, the corner near Asia and along the Red Sea, white people had been living and mighty kings had been ruling for thousands of years. This corner country is called Egypt.

Have you ever seen a man one hundred years old? I have seen a man five thousands years old—

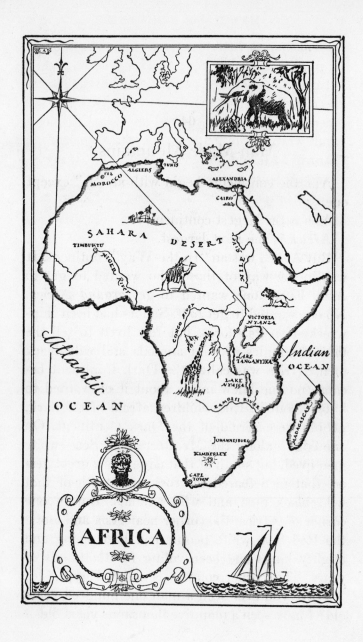

a real man, a little dried up man who was once a mighty ruler of Egypt. He did not want to "turn to dust" when he died, for how then could he rise again from the dead at the Day of Judgment? So he left orders that he should be pickled and wrapped in bandages and a mountain of stone placed over his body to make sure it would not be touched or moved away. In fact, he built the mountain of stone before he died, to make sure of that part of it. But you

Once a king of Egypt now in a Museum and the janitor moves him out of the way to clean the floor

can never tell what will happen to you after you are dead, so in spite of the mountain of stone, here he is, a ruler of Egypt whom millions obeyed, now in a case in a museum where any one can stare at him, and the janitor dusts his face and moves him out of the way to sweep the floor. A pickled man is called a mummy, and the mummies of many such rulers of Egypt are now in museums.

One of the Seven Wonders of the World was these mountains of stone called pyramids, which the kings built when they were alive, to be tombs for themselves when dead. Each king tried to build a bigger and better pyramid than the king before him. The largest pyramid was built by a king called Cheops, who died nearly three thousand years before Christ was born. It is said that it took one hundred thousand people ten years to build his tomb.

The outsides of the pyramids used to be smooth slanting walls, but people have taken out stone from the sides to build other buildings, so that now the outsides of the pyramids are as rough as piled-up heaps of stones and you can climb from stone to stone on up to the top. Cheops's tomb and most of the other tombs or pyramids are of solid rock, with just a small room in the center, which was left for the body of the king and the things he had used when he was alive. The old Egyptians thought they must keep their furniture and other things around them, so that on the Judgment Day, when they should be awakened from their long sleep, they would be all ready to go on housekeeping. After Cheops's body was put into the tomb the passageway leading to it was filled up tight with stone, and all traces of the opening were hidden so that no one could find it and steal his body away. But, nevertheless, some one did find it out, stole his mummy and all the things that had been left there for his use in the next World, and if his soul ever returns it will find no body.

The ancient Egyptians worshiped fairy-tale gods and even animals. Bulls and beetles were sacred and they made mummies of them. Now, however, nine out of every ten people in Egypt are Mohammedans and, instead of building pyramids, they build beautiful mosques.

Close by these big pyramids is the Sphinx, a huge stone figure with the body of a lion and the

THE SPHINX AND THE PYRAMIDS OF EGYPT

They were called one of the Seven Wonders of the World

head of one of the Egyptian kings. In Greece a sphinx was supposed to be an animal with a woman's head that sat by the road and asked passers-by this riddle: "What is it that goes on four feet in the morning, two at midday, and three at night?" If the traveler couldn't tell the answer the sphinx devoured him. At last some one answered, "Man, because he crawls on all fours in the morning of his life, then walks on two feet, and finally on two feet and a cane." The Greek sphinx was a "she." But the Egyptian sphinx is a "he." He has a man's head and he asked no riddles. He was a god of the sun.

The Sphinx and pyramids are on the bank of the one and only great river of Egypt, called the Nile. Have you ever heard of crocodile tears? The crocodile is a big alligator-like animal that lives in the Nile, and people used to say that he would catch little Egyptian boys and while he was eating them he would weep as if his heart would break. That's why when you cry, though you don't really mean it, we say you are shedding "crocodile tears"! The Nile splits into several branches before it empties into the Mediterranean Sea, and the land between the branches is called a delta, because it is shaped like the Greek letter "D," which was called delta and shaped like a triangle. You see, people of long ago also called places after common things which they thought had the same shape.

Hardly any rain falls in northern Egypt, but in southern Egypt there are heavy rains in the summer. Then the Nile overflows its banks and floods the country and leaves great quantities of mud. This mud is very rich soil in which the Egyptians grow wheat and a very fine kind of cotton. In the olden times the Nile used to overflow the banks only once a year, and the rest of the year the land would be dry and the people would have to climb down the banks to get water. Not so long ago a huge dam was built far up the Nile at a place called Assuan. This dam holds the water back and forms a deep lake. So now the Nile does not flood lower Egypt all at once;

the water is let out by doors in the bottom of the dam as needed. One of the most beautiful of the old temples in Egypt was right in the way when the Assuan Dam was built, but it could not be moved from there, so now the water almost covers it up.

There was once a boy named Aleck. You may know a boy named Aleck too, but this Aleck lived two thousand years ago. He was a great Greek king whose full name was Alexander. He built a city where the Nile flows into the sea and called the city after himself, Alexandria. Alexander has been dead more than two thousand years, but his city still lives and is the chief seaport of Egypt.

Near the beginning of the delta, up the river from Alexandria, is a city called Cairo. It is the largest city in Egypt and also the largest city in the whole of Africa. Even if you were flying over Cairo in an airplane you would know that most of the people there were not Christians but Mohammedans. Can you guess how? In a Christian city you would see church steeples, but in Cairo you see saucer-shaped domes and candle-shaped minarets, for some of the most beautiful mosques in the World are there.

65

Robber Lands and Desert Sands

It is only a few miles across the Strait from Gibraltar to Morocco, which is the land of the Moors. It's only a few miles in distance but thousands of miles in difference. One morning, after breakfast, I boarded a small boat at Gibraltar, where every one was Christian, wearing "regular clothes" and speaking English, and by luncheon time I was in Morocco across the Strait, where every one was Mohammedan, wearing sheets, and speaking Arabic. It was as if I had walked into a side-show at the circus.

A friend had told me to get a guide named Mohammed, saying he would probably be on the dock. The dock was swarming with white-robed Moors as my boat came alongside, so as I stepped out on shore I shouted:

"Mohammed! Is there any guide here named Mohammed?"

Instantly it seemed to me every one on the dock was crowding around me, waving his hands, and crying out, "I am Mohammed." My friend hadn't told me that Mohammedans often named their children after their prophet and that the name

"Mohammed" was about as common in Morocco as the name "John" in New York.

The Moors all looked like pirates and bandits to me, so I took no one for a guide and made my way along the narrow streets alone, jostled and rubbed against by dirty, sore-eyed people and even by lepers, from whom I struggled to get as far away as I could. It seemed impossible that these Moors were related to the same Moors who had ruled in Spain before the time of Columbus, and who had built the beautiful Alhambra at Granada.

I had intended to go down to Fez, a city of Morocco, but as there was no railroad I had to have donkeys and a guide and servants. So I went to the American Consul to help me get them. A consul is a man living in each country to take care of the business and the people of his own country.

"You can't go to Fez," said he. "The United States will not let you. There is an Arab bandit lying in wait to capture any American who starts off for Fez."

"But I'd take no money with me for him to steal," said I.

"He doesn't want your *money*," said he, "he wants *you*. Then he'll send the United States a letter saying he's got you and will murder you unless they pay a good price to get you back. You're not worth it, but the United States must look out for its people, so you can't go." That's why I didn't go to Fez, and the only Fez I know is the little red monkey cap, shaped like a flower-pot turned upside down, which the Turks used to wear.

Have you ever heard the song "Home, Sweet Home"? It was written by an American Consul who was homesick for home. He was the American Consul at Tunis—another one of the once pirate countries along the Mediterranean. I don't wonder that he wrote "Home, Sweet Home."

AN
ARAB BANDIT
"There is an Arab bandit," said he, "lying in wait to capture any American"

Every continent has deserts, some big, some small, but the biggest desert i.t.w.W. is in Africa, just south of these pirate lands. It is called the Sahara. It is bigger than the whole of the United States. It stretches across Africa from one side to the other, where it touches Egypt. The Sahara is not like the seashore; it is sometimes rocky, sometimes just dry dirt, but it is a place where nothing grows, "deserted" by every living thing. In spots, however, there is water, and in these water spots there are date palms and a few people. These spots are the oases, and some of the oases are many miles broad and long. Men travel from one oasis to another on camels, but there are no roads for them to follow, no guideposts to show the way, and they must follow the compass or the stars as if they were at sea, for like the sea the desert is moving and changing all the time. Strong winds blowing pile up the sand to make a hill here and a valley there, and then the wind changes and what was valley becomes a hill and what was hill becomes a valley. Sandstorms in the desert may be terrible things if the wind blows hard and long, as it often does. Those caught out in a sand-storm may be entirely covered and buried alive as in a terrific hail-storm —only the sand does not melt. Years after their dry bones may be uncovered by the shifting wind and others passing by may see what may happen to them, too, at any time.

66

Afraid of the Dark

It takes about two months to cross the Sahara Desert by camel from top to bottom, and there is no other way to go than by camel or airplane—no railroads, no auto roads, no roads of any kind. On the southern edge of the desert is a place called Timbuktu. When people want to describe a very long distance they often say, "from Kalamazoo to Timbuktu." Kalamazoo is in Michigan in the United States and Timbuktu is in Africa. Timbuktu is the starting point for caravans going north across the Sahara to the countries along the Mediterranean and it is the ending point for caravans coming from those countries.

The Sahara has no rain, but south of the Sahara is a part of Africa called the Sudan, which has plenty of rain. The Sudan means "the land of the Black People."

When-I-was-a-boy we used to say that God made white people in the day and black people at night. Some say black people are simply white people tanned by the sun, which is so hot where they live that the tan never wears off.

The Sudan has one great river called the Niger. Like the Nile, that other great river in Africa beginning with an "N," the Niger fertilizes the land through which it runs. The Niger empties into the great Gulf of Guinea, a name which even intelligent people sometimes mix with Guiana in South America. Along the edge of the Gulf of Guinea are little countries, all of which except one belong to countries in Europe.

This one country, at the corner of the Gulf of Guinea, is called Liberia. It is like a tiny United States; in fact, it was copied after the United States, but the president and all the people are colored, and the way it came to be so is this:

When our country was first started, the white men wanted some one to do farming and other work for them. So pirates captured black people from the shores of Africa, brought them to the United States, and sold them as slaves, just as the pirates on the Mediterranean captured white people from ships on the sea and made slaves of them. All the colored people in the United States to-day are descended from these black slaves who were brought from Africa. Many people in our country thought these poor slaves, whose fathers and grandfathers had been stolen away from their homes in Africa, should be sent back to their own land. So when Monroe was President of the United States some of our colored people who had been set free and wanted to go "home" were put on a ship and sent back. Home was Home— even if it was a jungle. There they started this little country called Liberia, which means "Land of Liberty." They named their capital Monrovia after President Monroe and named some of their villages after great cities here. Two of their villages they called New York and Philadelphia, although there are but a few hundred people in them. Instead of trying to forget the land where they had been enslaved they imitated it.

As you go farther south in Africa you reach the Equator. This is half-way land between the North and South Poles, and the second greatest river in Africa, called the Congo, runs through it. In this part of Africa it is hot and rainy every month in the year. Things grow and keep on growing. Grass grows as high as a room. Vines and trees and everything else grow so thick, so close together, and in such a tangle that one can hardly get through them. It is something like that other Equator land—in South America—the Selvas.

A hundred years ago people knew little or nothing about this part of Africa. It was an unhealthful and a dangerous country for the white man. Many of the black people were cannibals who would kill and eat any white man they caught. The marshes and jungles gave white men fever, and there was a little fly called the tsetse which gave men a disease called sleeping sickness, from which they never awoke. Besides all these terrible things there were fierce wild animals that killed those who escaped other things.

And then there was born in Scotland a boy

named David Livingstone. He was just like you or me until he was ten years old. But when he was ten years old he left school and went to work in a cotton mill. There he worked all day from six in the morning until eight at night. If you count this up you will find that it was fourteen hours a day he worked—and he was only ten years old. Every day in the week he worked this way, but when he went home at night he wasn't through working. After his supper he would study until he fell asleep over his books. Livingstone's one idea in life was to be of some good in the world and to help people who were sick and miserable. So he studied to be a doctor, and he decided he would go to China, for he thought the Chinese needed help more than any people. He thought also they should be made Christians. So he learned to be a minister as well as a doctor. But he didn't go to China at all. He was sent to Africa instead.

Every one said he would die, he would be stung by the deadly tsetse fly, or he would drink water that would give him a fever, or he would be devoured by some wild animal. "If I'm going to die," said he, "it doesn't matter which way. I'll have to die some day, but I want to do some good before that day." So he went to Africa.

Thirty years passed and though he went back home several times he always returned to Africa and at last he disappeared. He was given up for lost, and his countrymen thought him dead. But some people in our country got the idea that he might still be alive, so they sent a newspaper reporter named Stanley to look for him. They thought a reporter could find him if anybody could. Stanley landed on the west coast of Africa and asked the black men by signs if any one had seen a white man. Most of the black men said "no"—thirty years was too long a time to remember—in fact, most that were alive then were dead. But some black men said they had heard their fathers say that a white man had once passed through that way, and they pointed toward the east. So Stanley kept on going east and still east. After a long, long while he came to a long, long lake that has a long, long name —Tanganyika. When he reached this lake an old white man came to meet him. Stanley said, "Dr. Livingstone, I presume?" just as if he were greeting a stranger whom he had been sent to meet at the railroad station. Of course, it was Livingstone, and Stanley tried to get him to go back with him.

But Livingstone said, "No, my work is here, teaching the black people about God and curing their bodily diseases. I'll not go back until I'm dead. When I *am* dead, then I want to go home to be buried in England." So Stanley had to return without him.

Two years after that, with no one around him but black men, Livingstone died. He was on his knees at prayer when his black servant boy found him dead. All the black men loved him, and knowing that he wanted to be buried in England, they prepared his body by the sort of embalming they knew and bore it on their shoulders for eight hundred miles—it took two months—until they

They thought Livingstone was dead

reached the coast. There they signaled a passing ship and asked that his body be taken to England. In England he was buried in Westminster Abbey, where the famous and great men of the World are buried.

Livingstone was so beloved by the black men that anything he told them to do they would do. His was a magic name. He made black people

Christians. He also kept them from eating each other.

There was an Arab chief with the funny name Tippoo Tib who used to catch black men as if they were wild animals, chain them, and ship them to other countries to be made slaves. Livingstone with his black men fought Tippoo Tib year after year, until at last he put an end to Tippoo Tib's slave business. This is one of the big things Livingstone did.

Another thing Livingstone did was to make maps of the parts of Africa that no one knew about. He found the greatest waterfall in the World. These falls are twice as high and twice as broad as our Niagara Falls. The falls can be heard twenty miles away. He heard them sounding and resounding long before he reached them and asked the natives what the sound was. They said they are the falls of "sounding mist." He named them Victoria after the Queen of England, who was then living. The Victoria Falls are in the River Zambezi. Far north of Victoria Falls is a lake which is also called Victoria. Victoria Lake is where the Nile begins. The Egyptians had known the Nile River, of course, some three or four thousand years before Christ, but none knew where the Nile began. It might have started in Heaven for all they knew.

67

Zoo Land

HAVE you ever been to the zoo or the circus? How would you like to live in a zoo where the animals were not in cages? The land in Africa on each side of the Equator is like that. A great many of the animals are dangerous, yet some are not.

A lion is a huge cat, but he is the wildest kind of a wildcat. He is the most terrifying of all wild animals—his roar is enough to "freeze the marrow in your bones," even if he happens to be behind bars in the zoo. No wonder he is feared by all animals and fears none. Other animals have always to be on the watch against enemies, but the lion can lie down and go to sleep without watching or worrying or caring about enemies.

My father used to say if you wanted to catch a bird alive the thing to do is to put a little salt on his tail. But you can't catch lions that way and you can't catch birds that way either. If a hunter wishes to catch a lion *alive* for the zoo or circus, he must catch him in a trap called a snare, which is a pit dug in the ground and covered over with branches and twigs. The lion falls

413

into it and then must be caught with a very strong net. If, however, a hunter wishes to kill the lion, he hides near a water-hole and waits until

the lion comes for a drink, or else the hunter kills some harmless animal as you might dig worms for bait to catch fish and places him in the lion's

path. One of the animals used for bait is a zebra
—a poor, harmless animal that looks like a little
pony with stripes. Nature has given the zebra
stripes that look like the shadows of tall grass
so that he cannot easily be seen. Other animals
looking for food will come along too and must
be scared away from the bait or killed. The
first animal to come along is usually the hyena.
The hyena is an animal with a peculiar screech
that sounds like a laugh. But he laughs when he
is mad, not when he is glad. He is too much of
a coward to kill live animals, so he waits until
he can find one dead. He is the most cowardly
animal in the jungle.

In the jungle every animal must either fight,
run away, or be killed; there are no policemen to
look out for him.

The bravest animal in the jungle, strange to
say, is not the lion—he doesn't have to be; the
monkey is the bravest.

When a lion's roar shakes the jungle all the
animals start on the runaway from him, but the
last to run away are the monkeys. When a hunter
who is hiding and waiting for a lion to come along
sees the hyena pass by, he knows the lion is far
behind, for the hyena is the first to run away;
but when at last, after all the other animals have
passed by fleeing, the monkeys come along, the
hunter knows the lion is close behind. A hunter
will not shoot a monkey if he can help it—he
looks so much like a child. He will cry like a child

when hurt, and if shot try to pull the bullet out with his hands, and that's more than even hunters can stand.

Some animals will not eat meat—only growing things. The giraffe, the animal with a long neck and still longer legs, doesn't eat meat. He eats only what he can reach with his long neck —usually leaves and twigs of trees. When he wants to drink or to eat anything on the ground he must spread his legs apart like a letter "A" so that he can reach the water.

Almost every animal makes some kind of sound. It may be his language. He barks, moos, clucks, bleats, mews, whinnies, croaks, roars, grunts, cries, snarls, chirps, screeches, crows, hisses, whines, laughs, squeals, cackles, squawks, snorts, bellows, or sings. But the giraffe is said to be the only jungle animal that makes no sound.

In the rivers of the jungle lives a huge fat animal called a hippopotamus. Hippopotamus means a river horse, but he is really more like a huge fat pig. Like a pig, he loves to wallow in mud and water. When he lies asleep with perhaps only his back showing above the water he looks like a large rock or a submarine partly under the water. A magician once sold a secret for turning lead into gold. I will tell you the secret and won't charge you anything for it. This is it. "Put the lead in a pot on the fire and stir it for half an hour while you do *not* once think of the word Hippopotamus." If you can do that the lead will turn to gold. Do you think you could do that? Then you don't know how hard it is to try *not* to think of Hippopotamus. Here's another good rule if you want to learn any hard name in geography: try *not* to think of it for half an hour.

Another big clumsy animal is the Rhinoceros. He would take a prize in any Ugly Show. He has very short legs and one or two horns on his nose, and his skin is so thick that a hunter can't shoot him except in the stomach, and he can't shoot him there because his legs are so short his stomach is almost on the ground. When a person is so dumb that nothing we say seems to have any effect on him or trouble him, we say he has a hide like a rhinoceros. I have a peculiar stick and I often ask people to guess what it is made of. They usually say "horn" or "hard rubber," for it will bend. It is really made out of rhinoceros hide. The rhino has very poor eyesight. His little eyes can hardly see at all. He needs glasses. Instead of glasses he has a friend that does his seeing for him. This friend is a little bird called a rhino bird that rides on his back, does his seeing for him, and warns him of any danger.

The L. F. Ant is another animal with bad eyesight. The elephants in Africa are bigger than those in India.

In India they hunt elephants to catch them alive.

In Africa they hunt elephants to kill them.

In India they catch elephants to tame them and put them to work.

In Africa they catch elephants for their tusks, which are teeth sometimes ten feet long. Just suppose you had two front teeth as long as that. These tusks are ivory and they make fine piano keys.

The ivory business is not, however, as good as it used to be—or as bad as it used to be for the elephants—for men have learned to make a kind of ivory out of cotton and other materials. This takes the place of ivory and comes in many forms called plastics. Plastics are much cheaper than ivory and in many cases much better. Ivory turns yellow and cracks as it gets old, but plastics do not.

But the most curious animals in Africa are the human animals—the Black People. They have very funny ideas about beauty, so we think. We have funny ideas, so they think. A white person is all faded out, pale, unhealthy, sickly looking. A black man is a rich, black, coal color. Our ladies wear rings in their ears. Their ladies wear rings in their noses, where they show better. Some hunters had a box of safety-pins. The Blacks begged for the pins, and when they were given to them they pinned them through their noses. An ear-ring isn't big enough for them. They make holes in their ears and holes in their lips and gradually work the holes large enough to put their whole hand through the hole. Then they put blocks of wood or something like that in the holes. Our ladies bob their hair. Their ladies arrange their hair in huge topknots and gum it up with blood.

Some white men were building a telegraph line in Africa, but as fast as they built it the Blacks stole the wire to make bracelets, and they would completely cover their arms and legs with the wire. That showed how stylish they were and how smart and how wealthy.

You've probably heard of the little boy who was so sad that he went out into the garden and ate worms. Well, in some parts of Africa the people eat ants and grasshoppers, both raw and toasted, and they

AN AFRICAN BLACK

He thinks himself very stylish

are not sad but glad. But there is one thing that both white and black people like—that is watermelon. Our watermelons first came from Africa.

The music the black people love best is that made by beating on a kind of drum called a tom-tom. They beat it with their hands and fists and will keep it up for hours without stopping; the *thump, thump, thump* and *boom, boom, boom* seems to charm them. The sound can often be heard for miles, and they can send a sort of wireless message in this way across country to their neighbors. A little girl writing a composition on this subject said, "You can hear them beating on their *tum-tums* for miles!"

68

The End of the Rainbow

Gold!

It used to be said there was a pot of gold at the end of the rainbow, though no one has ever found it. Yet men have left their business and their families and homes and gone to the ends of the earth in search of gold and to find a short cut to riches, for gold is used for money all over the

There was supposed to be a pot of gold at the end of the rainbow

World, though small coins are not made of it because they would have to be too small and would easily be lost.

The largest gold mines in the World are in South Africa, and more than half of the gold in the World comes from gold mines near a city there called Johannesburg.

Gold is called the king of metals, for though platinum is more valuable, gold can be used for money and for ornament and for other things, and most people think it more beautiful. Pure gold is stamped 24 karat, but pure gold is so soft it wears away too easily and some other metal is usually mixed with it to make it harder. The finest rings and jewelry are usually 18 karat, which means that eighteen parts are of pure gold and six parts are of another metal. Look on a ring or watch and see if you can find the figures 18 K or 14 K stamped there.

Sometimes gold is found in little lumps which are called nuggets, but usually it is mixed through the rock and doesn't show at all. The rock has to be ground to powder and then the gold separated from the powder.

Almost every family has at least one thing that has come from South Africa—a very small thing but a very valuable one. Can you guess what it is? The diamond in your mother's ring. Nearly all the diamonds in the World come from a place called Kimberley in South Africa. They are found in a kind of blue clay in what used to be volcanoes.

Most of the diamonds used to be sent to Amsterdam in Holland to be cut and polished. The reason they are sent there rather than to some other country is because the diamond mines were

first discovered by Dutch people living in South
Africa. Now, however, many of the diamonds are
cut in Kimberley and are all finished there before
being shipped to other countries.

Diamonds are made out of the same stuff as
coal, and if they were put in the fire would turn
to coal. Sometimes people speak of coal as
"Black Diamonds." When a diamond is held to
the light it may look pure white or it may be
bluish or yellowish. The pure white diamonds are
the most valuable.

The biggest diamond ever found was about the
size of my fist. It was called the Cullinan diamond. It was too large and too valuable to be
used as a single jewel, so it was broken into two
pieces and each piece was cut and polished. The
next largest diamond ever found was called the
Great Mogul. But the Great Mogul was stolen.
Of course, the thief could not sell such a large
diamond, for, as there was only one such diamond
in the World, every one would know he was the
thief. It was something like stealing the picture
of Mona Lisa. But the Great Mogul has never
been seen since, so the thief must have broken it
up into smaller diamonds and sold the pieces.

The owners of the diamond mines take extraordinary care to prevent the black people who dig
the diamonds from stealing at least some of those
they find. The mines are closed in with a high
fence which is closely guarded, and the laborers
are not allowed to go home at night but must live

inside of the fence for three or four months. When they do leave, the guards, for they are guarded as if in prison, strip them and search their hair and ears and mouths to see that they have not hidden any diamonds away, for even a single diamond would be worth a fortune to one of the black people. They have found so many diamonds at Kimberley that, if they sold them all, diamonds would be too common and too cheap. In order to keep up the price, therefore, the owners of the diamond mines lock up millions of dollars' worth and only sell them when people are willing to pay a good price.

An Englishman named Cecil Rhodes went out to South Africa for his health. He happened to be there when diamonds were discovered and fortunes were being made, and he found his health and found wealth too. A part of South Africa was named after him: Rhodesia. When Rhodes died he left a great deal of money, part of which was to be used to send some of the best young men chosen from our country and other countries to the great university of Oxford in England. These boys are called Rhodes Scholars.

Cecil Rhodes wanted to build a railroad from the top of Africa to the bottom of Africa, from Cairo in Egypt to Cape Town at the southern point. Most of the railroad has been built since he died. It is called the "Cape to Cairo" Railroad, but more is still to be built. Rhodes was one of the few Englishmen who didn't ask to be sent home when he died. He chose a place in Africa on the top of a mountain to be buried. It was such a high point he called it "The World View."

The capital of South Africa, Pretoria, is like an English city. The chief city is Cape Town, and it too is just like an English city. Only about a hundred years ago these cities were jungle in which only savage black men lived.

If you collect stamps you may have heard of a famous stamp called "A Mauritius" that a collector paid $20,000 for, enough money to buy a good house and lot, yet the only thing he can do with it is put it in a stamp album. Why should he pay so much money for it? Just to show others something he has that no one else has. Mauritius is a little island off the east coast of Africa. There are other islands near Africa. Madagascar is the biggest. Mauritius is one of the smaller ones. Zanzibar is another small one. Pictures of their stamps you will have in your album, if not the stamps themselves. From Zanzibar come the cloves your mother uses to spice baked apples, pickles, and hams. Cloves look like little burnt match heads, and I don't believe you would ever guess what they really are. They are tiny flower blossoms that grow on the clove-tree!

69

Fortune Island

HAVE you ever been homesick? If you haven't, then you have never been far away from home for any length of time, or you never had a home. Just suppose you lived on the other side of the World from your father and mother, from your sisters, brothers, and friends, and were only able to get home once in five or ten years, or maybe never. The English people probably love their homes more and get more homesick than any other people in the World, and yet they go farthest away from home and live there.

There is a big island, so big that it is usually called a continent and so far off from England that it used to take five or six months, a half year, to get to it from England, and even now it takes a month or more by ship. On it lived only wild black men, yet the English people went there, built great cities and now rule over the island. This island is Australia, which means "South Land," for it is far, far south—south of the Equator, where it is summer when it is winter here and night when it is day here. The island was so far away the English thought it would be a good place to send prisoners, to get rid of them, because once there they could not get away and they could not harm anybody but themselves. Many prisoners were sent there and few of them ever came back. Some even died of homesickness, for even a criminal is human and gets homesick.

It was not very long, however, before the English found that this island was too good just for prisoners. The central part of Australia was a desert, but there were gold mines in the desert, and neither a desert nor danger will keep men away when gold, magic gold, is to be found. So a great many young Englishmen went out to Australia in search of gold and to make their fortunes, expecting to return home as soon as they had done so. But they found that it cost more to get the gold than it was worth—it didn't pay. They didn't give up, however. They were bound to make their fortunes in one way or another, so they tried another. In the southeastern part of this island was grass land. Grass was good for raising sheep and cattle, but there were no sheep and no cattle. So the Englishmen sent to England for sheep and cattle. But when the sheep and cattle came it was found that they would not eat the grass—it was not the right kind. And still the Englishmen were not discouraged. "If at first you don't succeed, try, try again." So they sent back again to England and got good grass seed and planted that. And then at last they did succeed, for the grass grew exceedingly well and before long the sheep and

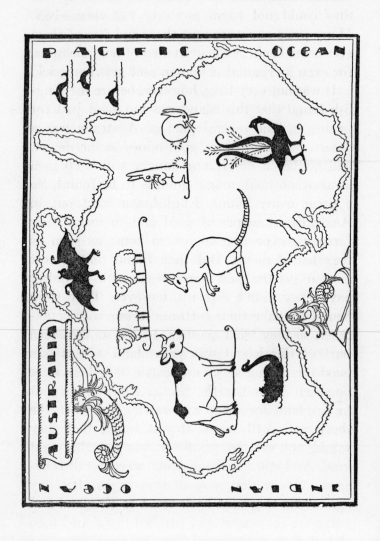

cattle turned out to be a "gold mine," better even than the gold mines they had expected to find. From the sheep that they raised they got the finest wool in the World—very long and silky. It was shipped to England and other places to make woolen clothing, and Australia is now the greatest wool-raising country i.t.w.W. And the cattle grew and prospered, and now frozen beef and mutton are sent back to England, which hasn't nearly enough beef of its own.

But not long after the sheep and cattle had gotten a good start a peculiar thing happened. An Englishman carried a pair of pet rabbits out to Australia. The pair of rabbits got loose and started to raise families. Now rabbits as well as sheep like grass. But rabbits raise families very, very fast, much faster than sheep or cattle, so before very long there were more rabbits in the country than there were sheep, and there were so many *millions* of rabbits eating up the grass and running wild over everything that there was not enough grass for the sheep. More rabbits and more rabbits and more rabbits—the people could not get rid of them. Men poisoned millions of them and trapped millions more, but for every million killed, millions more were born. It was like some of the plagues that visited Egypt in Bible times. The people built a wire fence all the way across the country to try to pen the rabbits in. But some of them escaped through the fence, so another fence was built. Men are still killing them off by the millions. They pack some of the rabbit meat in cans and send it to England, and they send the skins back also—"a rabbit skin to wrap up Baby Bunting in." But they cannot get rid of the little creatures altogether and probably never will.

The native animals in Australia are very peculiar. One curious animal is the kangaroo, an animal as big as a man. He stands on his two hind legs like a dog begging for food. He uses his tail as if it were a third leg, sitting upon his two legs and tail as if on a three-legged stool. His two front legs are very small and almost useless. He doesn't run along on all fours; he jumps over the ground on his hind legs, making long hops. The mother kangaroo carries her babies in a pocket made of the skin of her stomach; it is a nest and a cradle.

Sailors used to return from long voyages and say they had seen living in the sea beautiful girls —from the waist up—with bodies like fish from the waist down. They called them mermaids. You have heard of them in fairy-tales, of course. Well, there are real mermaids on the west coast of Australia. They do live in the sea, and they do hold their babies in their arms. From a distance a sailor might imagine them beautiful; but close up they do not look like the beautiful girls with fish tails you read about, for they are really ugly animals called sea-cows. How disappointing!

The natives of Australia are black people called

"Bushmen." They can't count even up to ten nor write their names nor read a single word. About the only thing they know is how to get food. They wear very little clothing. Instead of clothing they paint their bodies, and they raise bumps on their skin by scratching it with the edge of a shell and rubbing clay into the scratches. The more bumps they have on their bodies, the more beautiful they think they are.

The Bushmen have a peculiar plaything called a boomerang. It is made of a piece of wood shaped like a new moon. They throw it into the air away from themselves, and it turns round and round like a wheel and, if properly thrown, will come back to the thrower. I have several boomerangs which I have learned to throw. A friend of mine once said, "I hear you know how to throw a kangaroo." "To throw a kangaroo!" said I. "No, not even a Bushman can do that."

The capital of Australia used to be a city called Melbourne. But a new city called Canberra has been built for the capital. It is a made-to-order city. The city was laid out, streets made, a capitol built, and houses put up, and then people moved in. The chief city is Sydney.

The healthiest country in the World is southeast of Australia. It is called New Zealand. You will remember that Zealand is a part of Denmark and you may remember that it is the healthiest country in Europe. New Zealand is made of two big islands that look something like Italy or a boot turned upside down. They do not seem to be far away from Australia on the map, but it takes four or five days to get to them by ship from Australia. In the northern part of New Zealand are natives called Maoris, but they are quite different from the Bushmen in Australia. They used to be cannibals, but they have brains, and they learned so much from the white men that now some of them are as well educated as their teachers, and are even members of the New Zealand Parliament.

70

Cannibal Islands

I SUPPOSE you know what cannibals are—savages who kill and eat each other. They used to live on little islands in the Pacific Ocean, which is the biggest, broadest, deepest ocean of all. The Atlantic Ocean has very few islands in it—you could cross the Atlantic without seeing a single island, but in the Southern Pacific Ocean there are thousands of islands, and if you were shipwrecked there you would probably be in sight of one. Many of these islands are so tiny that they are only specks on the map, and some of them are not on the map at all.

If you could drain all the water out of the Pacific Ocean as you drain water out of a bathtub, you would not see a level bottom but thousands of mountains all over the bottom. These mountains were once volcanoes, but they are now drowned by the ocean. Where their tops are high enough to reach above the water you see islands. In the warm water around these islands live the tiny little sea animals called polyps, which I told you made Florida. Their tiny little bones pile up until they reach the top of the water and form rings round these mountain tops. These we call coral islands.

On some of these coral islands live brown-skinned people who once were cannibals; on other

islands no one lives. On all these islands grows a tree from which the native gets his food, drink, clothing, house, and furniture. This tree is the *cocoanut*-palm. I have told you before of that other palm on which dates grow. The cocoanut-palm has a tall trunk with all the leaves at the top, and in the center of the cluster of leaves grows a bunch of cocoanuts.

Cocoanuts are about the size of a baby's head. There is a shuck around the outside, and when this is taken off, the *nut* is inside. Strange to say, the cocoanut has what looks like two eyes, a mouth and a sort of coarse brownish hair. Inside the shell of the cocoanut is white meat, and inside of that is a kind of milk. The natives eat the meat of the nut as we would bread, and drink the milk, so the cocoanut is like bread and milk. From the hair on the nut they make rope and string and cloth and everything that we would make with cotton or silk or wool. From the cocoanut shells they make the cups, saucers, and all other dishes they use. From the leaves of the tree they make short skirts, which are all the clothing they wear. From the leaves they also make the roofs to their houses. Their houses often have no sides—they have roofs of leaves held up by poles made of the cocoanut-tree, and a floor which is raised a few feet off the ground.

When the native tribes had fights with other native tribes they would eat those whom they killed. Missionaries went out to teach them to be Christians, and at first the cannibals ate the missionaries, but many of the natives became Christians and almost all have stopped eating people. The missionaries thought the women were not dressed properly, so they made them wear long dresses called "Mother Hubbards," because they looked like the dress that Mother Hubbard in the nursery book wore. When the native women go to town they wear these dresses, but when they are in the country or want to climb a tree for food, they wrap the dresses around their necks. When the white people went to these islands they took their diseases with them, and the natives, who had never had such diseases before, caught them and many died. They did not seem able to get well even from measles.

The natives live an easy life. They have no money, but they want none, for they have nothing to buy. They do no work, and if they want anything to eat, all they have to do is to climb a tree and get a cocoanut. This is easy, for the trees usually slant, and I have seen boys start at the ground and run up a tree as you might run up a sliding-board.

An Englishman named Captain Cook was the first person to explore these islands and write about them, so one group of islands is named after him.

White men became interested in these islands because they found that the cocoanut meat could be sold in their countries for good prices, so they put the natives to work gathering cocoanuts. It was not necessary to pay them with money, because money meant nothing to them. They wouldn't work for a thousand dollars a day, but they would work for a ten-cent string of beads. They were very fond of jewelry, so the white men paid them with glass beads or with victrolas to amuse them. Shredded cocoanut is called copra and is used in various ways. The cocoanut oil is used for making soap and a sort of butter.

Ships and steamers seldom pass many of these islands, and only at a few of the largest do they ever stop. Many stories have been told of men who were shipwrecked on coral reefs where no one lived, and where they lived alone and waited for years before they saw a sail and were picked up.

Many of these islands are so small that they have no names. Some of the groups, however, are named. There are the Solomon Islands, named so because the discoverers expected to find the wealth of Solomon there; there are the Cook Islands, named after Captain Cook; there are the Fiji Islands, and there are the Samoan Islands, some of which belong to the United States.

One of the largest groups, called the Philippines, once belonged to the United States, but now is a free nation. The Philippines, however, are nearer China, and the natives are more nearly like the Chinese. Near the middle of the Pacific are the Hawaiian Islands, which still belong to the United States. In Hawaii are raised most of the pineapples we eat. Honolulu is the capital of Hawaii, and from Honolulu come some of the greatest swimmers. They spend much of their time in the water, and young boys and girls are able not only to swim like fish but to ride the waves standing on a board. The ukulele, which you probably have heard and seen, is a musical instrument with a Hawaiian name. When a visitor comes to Honolulu the Hawaiians throw garlands of flowers called lei over his head, and when the visitor leaves he throws the lei into the water so that he will return some day. There is one word the Hawaiians use very often; it is "Aloha." It means "Hello, Welcome, Good-by, God bless you."

Aloha!

71

Journey's End

AND so back home once more after a trip Around the World in 440 pages! Home, Sweet Home! " 'Mid pleasures and palaces though we may roam, be it ever so humble, there is no place like home." Every one feels the same way, whether he is an Eskimo or a Tibetan. Home is where we were born and brought up—whether it is on a block of ice or under a cocoanut-tree.

I once knew an old sea captain. He had been sailing the seas for fifty years. He had been round the World a score of times. He had been in every port from Punta Arenas to Archangel. He could speak a dozen languages. He had been in every land and on every sea; he had been everywhere and had seen everything. For a dozen years he had looked forward to the day when he could at last "settle down" and go home. At last that day came. I never saw any one happier as he headed toward home—the place where he was born—a little village in southern Maryland, near the sea.

A year later I met him again in New York. I never saw any one happier. He was all dressed up, with a flower in his buttonhole as if he were going to be married. "Where are you going?" said I. "I'm sailing, sailing at 12 o'clock," said he, "for a trip round the World!" and I thought he was going to dance a sailor's hornpipe right there on the street.

"Au revoir," said I. "I thought you were going to settle down at home." "Home," said he, "is a place to come back to," and he waved a jubilant farewell.

PRONOUNCING INDEX

This is a list of the most important names in the book. It tells you on what page you may find each name and respells the way they sound those words you may not know how to pronounce. The sound of some foreign words cannot be given exactly with English letters.

Sound		as in hat
"	air	" " hair
"	aw	" " saw
"	ah	" " ah!
"	ay	" " say
"	ee	" " see
"	e or eh	" " get
"	er	" " her
"	i or ih	" " hit
"	igh	" " right
"	o	" " hot
"	oh	" " oh!
"	oo	" " boot
"	ow	" " how
"	u or uh	" " up
"	ew	" " few
"	you	" " you

Happy Birthday
to Teddy
from his
God mother Marie

Oct. 19, 1956